BOW

VIE

ALBUM BY ALBUM

PAOLO HEWITT

INTRODUCTION BY ROBERT ELMS

CARLTON
BOOKS

This edition first published in 2016 by

Carlton Books Ltd
20 Mortimer Street
London W1T 3JW

Created and produced by:

PALAZZO EDITIONS LTD
15 Church Road
London SW13 9HE
United Kingdom

www.palazzoeditions.com

Publisher: Colin Webb
Art Director: Simon Halfon
Design Manager: Ben Hamilton
Editorial Consultant: Kevin Cann
Managing Editor: Robby Elson
Photo Editors: Phil King and Emma O'Neill

A CIP catalogue record for this book is available from the British Library.

ISBN: 978-1-78097-834-5

10 9 8 7 6 5 4 3 2 1

Printed and bound in China.

Opening Page: Portrait of Ziggy Stardust and The Spiders From Mars – guitarist Mick Ronson, drummer Mick 'Woody' Woodmansey, bassist Trevor Bolder and David Bowie. Mick Rock, San Francisco, October 1972.

SOURCES

Pages 12, 27b, 63, 98, 109, 150–151 In *Q*, May 1993; **15** In *Any Day Now: David Bowie The London Years* by Kevin Cann, Adelita, 2010; **16, 69** Interview with Mark Stuart in *Music Scene*, June 1973; **22, 25, 27c, 30a** Interviewed by Chris Welch in *Melody Maker*, October 1969; **27a, 30c, 54, 63** In *Moonage Daydream: The Life And Times Of Ziggy Stardust*, by David Bowie and Mick Rock, 2nd ed. Cassell Illustrated, 2005, p70, ibid, p72, pp11&12, p14; **30b** Lindsay Kemp interview with Mick Brown in *Crawdaddy*, September 1974; **32** Interview with John Mendelsohn in *Rolling Stone*, April 1971; **37** Interview with Raymond Telford in *Melody Maker*, March 1970; **38a&b** Interview with BBC Radio, 1976; **40** In 'Turn and Face the Strange: David Bowie and the Making of *Hunky Dory*', *Uncut*, April 2011; **43** Interview with Steve Turner in *Beat Instrumental*, August 1972; **44, 239** Interview with Bill DeMain, *Performing Songwriter*, September 2003; **50** Interview with Cameron Crowe in *Rolling Stone,* February 1976; **58** In *BowieStyle* by Mark Paytress, Omnibus Press, 2000; **59** Interview with Paul Du Noyer in *Q*, April 1990; **60, 70** Interview with Charles Shaar Murray, *NME*, June 1973; **64a** Interview with Clark Collis, *Blender*, August 2002; **64b** Interview with Charles Shaar Murray, *NME*, January 1973; 73a From www.5years.com; **73b, 101, 105, 115** Interview with Robert Hilburn, *Melody Maker*, February 1976; **74** Interview with Charles Shaar Murray, *NME*, August 1973; **80** Interview with Richard Cromelin, *Rolling Stone*, October 1974; **85** From *The David Bowie Story*, BBC Radio, 1993; **88, 94** Interview with Anthony O'Grady, *RAM*, July 1975; **91** Interview with Robert Hilburn, *Melody Maker*, September 1974; **91–93, 108** Geoff MacCormack in *From Station To Station: Travels With Bowie, 1973–1976*, by Geoff MacCormack, Genesis Publications, 2007, p143, ibid, p183; 96 Interview with Timothy White, *Musician*, May 1983; **112, 228, 232b, 234b** Interview with Chris Roberts, *Uncut*, October 1999; **118, 124** Interview with Allan Jones, *Melody Maker*, October 1977; **121a&b** Interview with Tim Lott, *Record Mirror*, September 1977; **127** Interview with Charles Shaar Murray, *NME*, November 1977; **128, 130, 141a&b** Interview with *Uncut*, February 2001; **136** Interview with Cynthia Rose, *City Limits*, June 1983; **139, 160** Interview with John Tobler, *Zigzag*, January 1978; **140** Tony Visconti interview with *Uncut*, February 2001; **144** Interview with *Musician*, July 1990; **149, 150a** From *Scary Monsters Promo Interview*, RCA DJL1-3840, 1980; **150b** Interview with Andy Peebles, BBC Radio One, 1980; **156, 159, 161, 162a&b** Interview with Chris Bohn, *NME*, April 1983; **164, 167, 170a&c, 177, 232** Interview with Charles Shaar Murray, *NME*, September 1984; **170b, 184b, 186, 189, 190c** Interview with Adrian Deevoy in *Q*, June 1989; **172** Interview with Stephen Dalton, *NME*, February 1997; **175, 176** Interview with *Movieline*, June 1986; **180, 217** Interview with Chris Roberts, *Ikon*, October 1995; **184a** From 'Stardust Memories' by Kurt Loder, *Rolling Stone*, April 1987; **184c** Interview in *Interview*, September 1995; **190a&b** Interview with Charles Shaar Murray, *Q*, October 1991; **192** Interview with Mat Snow, *Mojo*, October 1994; **195** Interview with Glenn O'Brien, *Interview*, May 1990; **196, 198, 203b** Interview with *New Zealand Herald*, 1993; **201, 205** Interview with *Record Collector*, May 1993; **202, 203a** From 'Black Tie White Noise Video EP', 1993; **206, 210, 211** Album liner notes to *The Buddha Of Suburbia*, 1993; **212, 216a, 218** Interview with Steven P. Wheeler, *Music Connection*, September 1995; **215** Interview with Dominic Wells, *Time Out*, August 1995; **216b** From *1.Outside* EPK, 1995; **216c** Interview with Paul Gorman in *Musicweek*, 1995; **220, 227b** Interview with David Cavanagh, *Q*, February 1997; **223** Interview with Linda Laban, *Mr Showbiz*, 1997; **227a&c** Interview with Andy Gill, *Mojo*, March 1997; **231** Interview with Robert Phoenix, *Dirt*, October 1999; **232a** From the *'hours...'* EPK, 1999; **234a** Interview with William Harms, www.GameCenter.com, October 1999; **235** Interview with Steffen Jungerson, *B.T.*, December 1999; **236, 242a&b, 243** Interview with www.concertlivewire.com, June 2002; **243** Interview with Paul Du Noyer, *Word*, October 2003; **244, 249b** Interview with Dylan Jones, *GQ*, October 2002; **247** Live MSN chat, June 2002; **249a** Interview with Anthony DeCurtis from www.beliefnet.com, 2003; **249c** Interview with Ingrid Sischy, *Interview*, October 2003; **249d** Interview with Richard Buskin, *Sound On Sound*, October 2003; **250** From official press release, 2004; **252** Tony Visconti interview with *Rolling Stone*, January 2013; **256** Tony Visconti Facebook message, 11 January 2016; **260** Kate Bush tribute, *Observer*, 17 January 2016; **262, back cover** From speech to Berklee College of Music's Class of 1999, 8 May 1999.

CONTENTS

INTRODUCTION: 'EVERYBODY WAS BOWIE'

BY ROBERT ELMS

From the moment he appeared on *Top Of The Pops* performing 'Starman' on that fateful Thursday evening in July, 1972 – skinny and skin-tight, pale and pretty, hair vivid orange and teased to the heavens, acoustic guitar slung over his back, arm draped around Mick Ronson in a gesture which took your teenage breath away – everything and everybody was Bowie.

It didn't matter where you came from, if you were a skinhead or suedehead, a rocker or reggae boy, a small-town teen, surly suburban oik or an in-your-face inner-city dude, from that life-changing, epoch-making Thursday onwards you had been touched by the Starman and you stayed touched. What Elvis and his pelvis were to a generation of Americans before – a catalyst and a cause célèbre, a reason to rebel, perform and create – so Bowie, with those alien eyes, was to kids growing up in crappy, strife-torn, early closing, corrugated-iron clad seventies Britain.

It was of no importance that David Bowie/Jones had spent the previous decade desperately trying to find his persona and his voice. Who knew or cared that this new leper messiah had a slew of former lives? Suddenly he'd hit perfect pitch and for the next dozen or so years he stayed at the vanguard of just about everything good and wild that came out of Britain. There was barely a band or an artist, designer or writer, photographer or hairdresser who didn't trace their creative lineage back to Bowie and, in particular, Ziggy Stardust and The Spiders From Mars.

To understand the full potency of Bowie back then, you have to realise just how grey and broken Britain was in the early seventies. If the sixties had been a massive party this was the hangover: dreary, depressed and dominated by a suffocating corporatism that saw the country lurch from crisis to crisis while listening to leaden, long-haired rock bands in flapping flared jeans. Backward-looking, culturally conservative, prone to random violence and still fighting former wars, Britain was seen as the sick man of Europe and the prospects for a teenager growing up here were pretty bleak.

Previously, lurking beneath this grim monotone façade, there was a vibrant youth culture born of the streets – vast reserves of teenage desire and creativity manifested as teddy boys and beatniks, mods and rockers, hippies and skinheads, a litany of trouser tribes with glorious soundtracks to match. But by 1972 it seemed to have run out of steam. The new decade had no real cult to call its own. What was needed was a figurehead, a charismatic leader who could rally the troops with a song and a style. That's when the man fell to earth.

Glam rock was not a youth cult as such. Burly navvies wrapped in BacoFoil, like Sweet or Slade, were never going to provoke a generational shift and a unified movement, but the gorgeous pair of cockney chameleons – Bowie and Bolan, the glitter twins, the best of buddies and the most intense of rivals – hit a riff that made plenty swoon. And it was Bowie, only Bowie, who by his very presence, his elegant artifice and otherworldly air, opened the eyes of thousands of slack-jawed urban urchins to another world.

Bowie, with his coiffure and his couture, his arts labs and mime acts, bisexual hints and louche lyrics, his kabuki and Nietzsche, was like a portal to a glamorous, forbidden planet none of us even knew existed. Before David stepped out as Ziggy Stardust, fellating Mick Ronson's Les Paul while wearing Kansai Yamamoto, the average British teenager was furtively reading *Razzle* and wearing a donkey jacket. Afterwards the Bowie boys, as they became known, could be seen groovily strolling down the streets, in the coolest clubs and boutiques. These maverick manqués, council-estate exotics with fabulous hair, exaggerated cheekbones and attitude to spare, styled on David and high on style, were the hippest kids in any town. There were Bowie girls too – plenty pretty, sexy and aloof and besides it was hard to tell which was which in this androgynous new scene where being seen was the aim.

Almost everything that was to follow – the slick soul boys with their wedges and their pegs, the original punks in Westwood's radical attire, the new romantics posing and preening to glory – can be dated back to the seismic shock of Ziggy as generations of British kids found a way to emulate their idol. And of course, Bowie didn't stop there. For the Brixton boy, 1972 was an amazing year. First Ziggy made him a star; then, with 'All The Young Dudes', he made Mott The Hoople stars; he made Lou Reed a made man by co-producing the magnificent *Transformer*; then he even made Iggy Pop (who inspired Ziggy) a name to drop.

Like a musical equivalent of Andy Warhol with his New York Factory, Bowie in London was at the centre of a creative maelstrom, a centrifuge of talent that spun out like a spider's web from his outrageous stage persona to reach thousands of kids, most of them still dreaming and scheming in suburban bedrooms. Armed with a bottle of peroxide and a talent to provoke, the likes of Siouxsie Sioux and Steven Morrissey, Boy George and Phil Oakey, were all little Ziggy acolytes in the making. And then he stopped.

Of course, we know now that killing off Ziggy Stardust was just the start of a journey that saw David Bowie shape-shift his way though a dazzling array of musical and stylistic incarnations, each one somehow just right for the turbulent times. The joyous stomp of 'The Jean Genie' was the perfect soundtrack to football terraces and youth-club discos – all camp aggression, Ziggy on steroids. While 'John, I'm Only Dancing', a sublimely ambiguous song, which itself underwent numerous personality changes, was the next great hit and a harbinger of amazing things to come.

Out on the streets, and deep in the night, the new big thing was jazz-funk imported from Philly and beyond: a crisp, swish sound designed for dancers and picked up by the coolest youths who wove an entire new nocturnal craze around those insistent, horn-laden sides. Recorded in 1974 (though not released until 1979), 'John, I'm Only Dancing (Again)', with its searing sax break, was an early sign that Bowie was veering in a funky direction, but his next volte-face was one of the most dramatic and timely of the lot.

As well as the throbbing soul clubs of the mid-seventies, there were always Bowie Nights, where the most arch and arty kids gathered to cast shapes to Bowie tunes and a smattering of his fellow travellers', Roxy Music. Then, one night in 1975, it all came together. I can still recall the shock. I was dressed in the epitome of soul-boy style – pink pegs, plastic sandals (same as Bowie wore in *The Man Who Fell To Earth*), floppy wedge haircut falling over one eye – shuffling across a West End dance floor when a strange, beguiling new tune hit me. This was soul, but not as we knew it: arch, crystalline, fake but perfect. And as the opening chords of 'Young Americans' swirled around the room, so a tiny group of kids emerged from the shadows dressed like I'd never seen before: decadent, art-full, hair dyed pillar-box red and gun-metal blue, plastic strides, exposed bras, t-shirts ripped and held together with safety pins, make-up applied with startling effect. I was watching the future dancing to David Bowie and it was not yet called punk.

That cabal of scarily hip kids who first paraded their sartorial radicalism to Bowie's brilliant new plastic soul became known as the Bromley Contingent. They were the shock troops of the punk vanguard, and it's no coincidence that they came from the same south London suburb Bowie had grown up in when his family moved from Brixton. Siouxsie Sioux, Billy Idol, Steve Severin, Adam Ant, Catwoman et al. were hardcore Bowie-ites who would shape the coming punk revolution in his image.

And that image had morphed again to meet the times, Bowie sporting the best-ever red-wedge hair and suave suits to go with his slick new sound. For a while the Bowie crowd and the proto-punk scene were intrinsically interwoven and almost all the prime players in punk's early, highly fashionable phase were really Bowie boys and girls with guitars. This was also the peak of his live powers, a time of great theatrical extravaganzas where the cracked actor dominated the stage. These were indeed Golden Years.

Punk was a glorious conflagration set alight by a gang of Bowie-obsessed art students, hairdressers and anarcho-waifs gathered around a bizarre Kings Road boutique called Sex. And although it was undoubtedly inspired by the Thin White Duke and his ilk – Iggy Pop in particular – the man himself was never going to sit easily within punk's harsh musical confines. So he left town and lay low, taking his wedge and his duffel coat to Berlin to plot the next twist in the tale.

Low and *"Heroes"* – electronic, Teutonic, epic and angular – were distinctly at odds with the prevailing three-chord zeitgeist, but soon became part of the template for the next great creative outpouring. Punk was beautifully brief in its original explosive outburst and by 1978 a post-punk depression had descended. Then word filtered out of a new scene gathering in the subterranean places, where peacock kids gathered to parade their elaborate finery to electronic tunes.

The Blitz, and all the other impossibly trendy clubs which emblazoned the early eighties, were basically born-again Bowie nights, fuelled by another younger generation of kids who'd been wowed by Ziggy back in '72, and who now believed they could be heroes, for more than just one day. Boy George, Steve Strange, Gary Kemp, Toyah Wilcox, Pete Burns, Gary Numan, Ultravox, the Duran gang… The list of musicians who emerged from that scene is almost endless, and you can throw in a host of designers, artists, scribes, dancers and filmmakers, many of whom would go on to huge success, all of whom were influenced and inspired by the returning Thin White Duke. Yet again, he'd managed to be at the very forefront of the coming cultural wave.

The boys kept swinging and the albums kept coming, culminating in *Scary Monsters* and the epochal 'Ashes To Ashes' – which came out in 1980 and yet has somehow become one of the defining songs and videos of the entire decade that followed. Referencing his own illustrious past while creating the future, Bowie, with a coterie of his camp followers, a Pierrot and a pied piper, led the way as he always did.

Bowie's immense cultural impact is still reverberating every time a new artist emerges to combine art and pop, the avant-garde and the mainstream, pushing the boundaries of theatricality and musicality to reach out to kids everywhere. It would be impossible to imagine the pop firmament, particularly here in Britain, without the enduring influence of the man who became Ziggy Stardust all those decades ago, and showered stardust over generations to come.

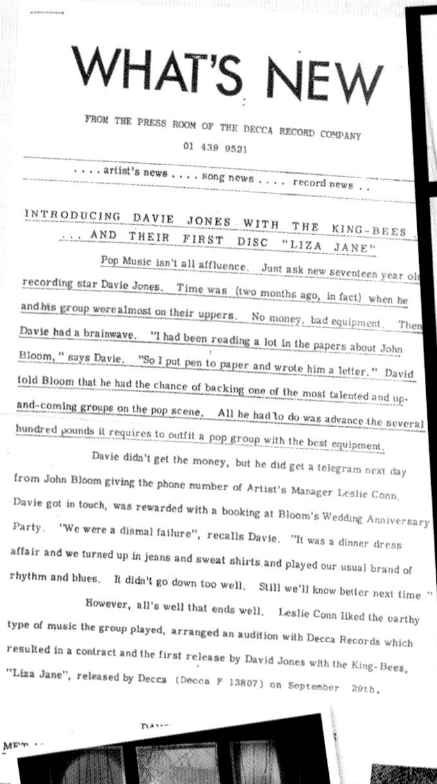

WHAT'S NEW

FROM THE PRESS ROOM OF THE DECCA RECORD COMPANY

01 439 9521

. . . . artist's news . . . . song news . . . . record news . .

INTRODUCING DAVIE JONES WITH THE KING-BEES . . . AND THEIR FIRST DISC "LIZA JANE"

Pop Music isn't all affluence. Just ask new seventeen year ol recording star Davie Jones. Time was (two months ago, in fact) when he and his group were almost on their uppers. No money, bad equipment. Then Davie had a brainwave. "I had been reading a lot in the papers about John Bloom," says Davie. "So I put pen to paper and wrote him a letter." David told Bloom that he had the chance of backing one of the most talented and up-and-coming groups on the pop scene. All he had to do was advance the several hundred pounds it requires to outfit a pop group with the best equipment.

Davie didn't get the money, but he did get a telegram next day from John Bloom giving the phone number of Artist's Manager Leslie Conn. Davie got in touch, was rewarded with a booking at Bloom's Wedding Anniversary Party. "We were a dismal failure", recalls Davie. "It was a dinner dress affair and we turned up in jeans and sweat shirts and played our usual brand of rhythm and blues. It didn't go down too well. Still we'll know better next time."

However, all's well that ends well. Leslie Conn liked the earthy type of music the group played, arranged an audition with Decca Records which resulted in a contract and the first release by David Jones with the King-Bees, "Liza Jane", released by Decca (Decca F 13807) on September 29th.

Who can I be now? Bowie changed his look – and his bandmates – with dazzling frequency. May 1963, aged just sixteen, playing saxophone at a youth club in Biggin Hill (opposite, bottom). By 1964, he was fronting The King Bees in Robin Hood-style jerkin and boots, performing his first single 'Liza Jane' (above, left). In The Lower Third he became a sharp-suited mod (photo strip, above). In April 1966 he played the first of a two-month series of Sunday-afternoon concerts called the 'Bowie Showboat' at Soho's Marquee Club with yet another group, The Buzz (opposite, top).

marquee club

GERRARD 8923 | 90, WARDOUR STREET, LONDON W.1.

JUN 196 Program

Wed. 1st	ALEX CAMPBELL plus his Special Guests
Thur. 2nd	THE MOVE The Triad
Fri. 3rd	GARY FARR and the T-BONES The Objects
Sat. 4th	Modern Jazz TONY KINSEY QUINTET RAY WARLEIGH QUINTET
Mon. 6th	GRAHAM BOND ORGAN-ISATION The Soul Agents
Tue. 7th	MANFRED MANN The Alan Bown Set (Members' tickets 7/- in advance from May 31st)
Wed. 8th	GERRY LOCKRAN Johnny Silvo Martin Winsor
Thur. 9th	Let's go Surfin' TONY RIVERS and the CASTAWAYS SUMMER SET
Fri. 10th	GARY FARR and the T-BONES The Soul System
Sat. 11th	Modern Jazz DICK MORRISSEY QUARTET RONNIE ROSS QUINTET
Mon. 13th	JIMMY JAMES and the VAGABONDS Felder's Orioles
Tue. 14th	SPENCER DAVIS GROUP Jimmy Cliff Sound (Members' tickets 7/- in advance from June 7th)
Wed. 15th	THE SPINNERS THE FRUGAL SOUND and Guests
Thur. 16th	JOHN MAYALL'S BLUES BREAKERS featuring Eric Clapton Amboy Dukes
Fri. 17th	GARY FARR and the T-BONES Graham Bell Trend
Sat. 18th	Modern Jazz DICK MORRISSEY QUARTE GORDON BECK QUARTET fe the voice of NORMA WINSTO
Sun. 19th	Sunday Special JIMMY WITHERSPOON with TUBBY HAYES BIG BAND Robert Stuckey Trio (Members: 7/6 Non-members: 10/- (Tickets available in advance from
Mon. 20th	SHOTGUN EXPRESS Peter B'S, Beryl Marsden, Ro Sands
Tue. 21st	THE YARDBIRDS James Royal Set (Members' tickets 7/- in advance fr
Wed. 22nd	RAM HOLDER BROS. NEW HARVESTERS Mike Rogers
Thur. 23rd	THE MOVE The Rift
Fri. 24th	GARY FARR and the T-BON and supporting group
Sat. 25th	Modern Jazz DICK MORRISSEY QUART and A. N. Other
Sun. 26th	Sunday Folk Special ALEX CAMPBELL and Gue (Members: 6/- Non-members: 8
Mon. 27th	THE STEAM PACKET Long John Baldry, Julie Dri Brian Auger Trinity The Herd
Tue. 28th	THE SMALL FACES Sands (Members' tickets 7/6 in advance
Wed. 29th	THE CHRIS BARBER BA featuring Kenneth Washin RAM HOLDER BROS. (Members: 5/- Non-members:
Thur. 30th	THE ACTION The Alan Bown Set

(All Programmes are subject to alteration and cannot be held responsible for non-appearance

Every Saturday afternoon, 2.30–5.30 p.m.

"THE SATURDAY SHOW"

Top of the Pops both Live and on Discs
Introduced by Guest D.J.s,
featuring Star Personalities

Members: 3/6 Non-members: 4/6

Every Sunday afternoon, 3.00–6.00 p.m.

"THE BOWIE SHOWBOAT"

DAVID BOWIE and the BUZZ

Top Ten Discs
Guests

Members: 3/- Guests: 5/-

COMING IN JUL

Mon. 4th	GRAHAM BON
Tue. 5th	ALAN PRICE
Tue. 12th	MANFRED MA
Tue. 19th	SPENCER DA

1947
8 January
David Robert Jones born,
40 Stansfield Road, Brixton, London

1953
The Jones family moves to the south London suburb of Bromley

1957
David becomes chorister at St Mary's Church, Bromley, alongside lifelong friends and sometime collaborators George Underwood and Geoffrey MacCormack

1958
August
First known performance of popular music, at 18th Bromley Cub Scouts summer camp, Isle of Wight, with George Underwood
September
Joins Bromley Technical High School

1959
25 December
Receives his first musical instrument, a plastic alto saxophone

1962
David has a fight with George Underwood, suffering an injury that leaves the pupil of his left eye permanently dilated
June
David joins The Konrads

1963
David's half-brother, Terry Burns, shows first signs of schizophrenia
Summer
Leaves school with one O-Level qualification – in art – then starts work as a trainee commercial artist at Nevin D. Hirst Advertising, New Bond Street, London
29 August
First recording, with The Konrads, 'I Never Dreamed'
December
Leaves The Konrads

1964
April
Forms The King Bees, a five-piece R&B group also including George Underwood
Spring
Signs with his first manager, Leslie Conn
***c.* May**
With The King Bees, David signs his first recording contract – with Vocalion Records (part of Decca)
June
Leaves Nevin D. Hirst Advertising
5 June
UK release of Davie Jones and The King Bees' 'Liza Jane'/'Louie Louie Go Home' (Did Not Chart)
6 June
First TV appearance promoting 'Liza Jane' on BBC TV's *Juke Box Jury* (the song was voted a 'miss')
July
Leaves The King Bees and joins The Manish Boys

1965
March
UK release of The Manish Boys' 'I Pity The Fool'/'Take My Tip' (DNC)
April
Leaves The Manish Boys
May
Joins The Lower Third
August
Ralph Horton becomes Bowie's first full-time manager
UK release of Davy Jones' 'You've Got A Habit Of Leaving'/'Baby Loves That Way' (DNC)
16 September
Changes his official stage name to David Bowie, to avoid confusion with Davy Jones (later of The Monkees)
November
The Lower Third signs a recording contract with Pye

1966
January
UK release of David Bowie with The Lower Third's 'Can't Help Thinking About Me'/'And I Say To Myself' (DNC)
Leaves The Lower Third
February
Forms The Buzz
April
UK release, as David Bowie, of 'Do Anything You Say'/'Good Morning Girl' (DNC)
10 April–12 June & 21 August–13 November
Performs the 'Bowie Showboat' concerts at the Marquee, London
August
UK release of 'I Dig Everything'/'I'm Not Losing Sleep' (DNC)
October
Signs a recording contract with Deram
December
The Buzz break up
UK release of 'Rubber Band'/'The London Boys' (DNC)

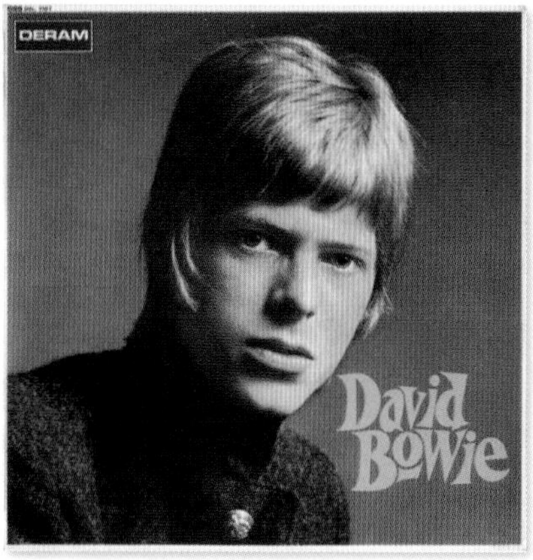

‘OUR RECORD PLAYER ONLY PLAYED AT 78RPM... SO I GOT THIS VERY WEIRD PERCEPTION OF WHAT ROCK 'N' ROLL SOUNDED LIKE AT A VERY EARLY AGE. THAT COULD EXPLAIN A LOT.’

DAVID BOWIE, 1993

1967
February
US release of 'Rubber Band'/
'There Is A Happy Land' (DNC)
March
David joins The Riot Squad
April
Kenneth Pitt becomes Bowie's sole manager
UK release of 'The Laughing Gnome'/
'The Gospel According To Tony Day' (DNC)
May
David leaves The Riot Squad
1 June
UK release of *David Bowie* (DNC)
July
UK release of 'Love You Till Tuesday'/
'Did You Ever Have A Dream' (DNC)
August
US release of *David Bowie* (DNC)

Previous page: Portrait by Dezo Hoffmann, 1967.

Opposite: 'The weekend starts here!' Rehearsing 'Can't Help Thinking About Me' for cult Friday-evening music show *Ready Steady Go!*, 3 March 1966.

It was a different age, a time when record companies allowed their artists the freedom to fail, betting that soon they would hit the style and sound that would bring the world to them.

In this now-forgotten spirit, Deram Records signed David Bowie and allowed him free rein in the studio. As a result, he did not make an album in 1967. Instead he made a musical and committed it to vinyl. He dreamt up a succession of characters and set their lives to brass, strings, penny whistles, every instrument it would seem except electric guitar. And this in the year of Jimi Hendrix...

Bowie wrote songs about children, bitter retired soldiers, and an 'Uncle Arthur'; he wrote about the 'Maid Of Bond Street', the 'Little Bombardier' and 'Silly Boy Blue'. Then he cast his characters against a backdrop of theatrical riffs and melodies inspired by traditional British music hall.

The result is an album out of time, out of place, but simultaneously startling. It is the kind of album a major musician might make once they've earned an audience and been allowed one album – and one album only – to indulge themselves. It is not, usually, the record of a young man on the make in the year of 1967, a year that saw massive album releases by Pink Floyd, Traffic, Captain Beefheart, Procol Harum, Jimi Hendrix, Tim Buckley, The Byrds, The Small Faces, Mothers Of Invention, and The Doors; the year, in other words, of LSD, psychedelic fashions and freak-outs.

Intriguingly, Bowie had no interest in taking the easy road. Rather, he was expressing a unique style and he chose to do so in the year of *Sgt. Pepper*. Later, he said:

'I got some airplay, as we say in the biz. But I didn't get people buying me and I wasn't asked to perform, so I suppose in that respect it was a bit of a failure. But the idea of writing short stories was quite novel at the time – excuse the pun.'

DB, 1976

So who exactly is this character, who goes swimming so bravely against the tide in his mohair suit and bouffant hair? David Bowie was born David Robert Jones on 8 January 1947 in Brixton, London. He is born in tough times. The war has ended and necessities are scarce. When he is three years old he enters the tenant's bedroom and smears his face in her make-up and lipstick. His mother tells him boys do not wear make-up. 'You do, mummy,' he replies.

His parents are of their time – distant, not tactile. In later years Bowie struggles hard to recall a compliment from his mother, a hug from his father. But there are compensations. His father is 'a great humanitarian' and encourages David to explore different religions, other cultures. It is encouragement that will stand him in good stead.

At age five he dresses up again for the school nativity play, puts on a robe and holds a shepherd's crook. The die is cast for already the boy has something about him. His mother, Margaret 'Peggy' Jones said, 'He absolutely loved it. It was then that we realised that there was something in David. If there was anything [on the radio] that caught his ear he would tell everyone to be quiet and listen, and then fling himself about to the music. In those days we thought he might become a ballet dancer.'

Mrs Jones is near the mark with her ballet observation. At his junior school, a progressive headmaster divides pupils into groups of four, hands them percussive instruments and tells them to dance to the sounds of the rhythms they make. Such experiences sink deep into David; he is shy but can perform in public. A valuable lesson.

'Inchworm', sung by Danny Kaye in the film *Hans Christian Andersen*, catches his ear. He later describes it as a vitally important song for him and its influence – its use of counterpoint melodies – is heard best on his debut album in the gorgeous 'Sell Me A Coat'.

He starts sounding out the world. A school friend recalls him enthusing about America and Japan at age eight. At thirteen, as the other kids play football, David dons an American footballer's outfit (given to him by the American embassy – after he wrote to them asking for more information about the sport he was hearing on US Forces radio) and walks around school in a helmet with a ball under his arm. 'Quite bizarre,' says his schoolmate but it is the perfect image of that which is to come: Bowie separated from the mainstream by a striking uniform.

In 1961 Bowie saw Anthony Newley in the stage musical *Stop The World – I Want To Get Off*. The show had a massive impact on him; he adored Newley's voice, his clever use of the stage and the fact that he sang 'ordinary words that I could understand and weren't all gooey... That's when I started formulating my own style.' He would recall:

'In the early days when I was in a rhythm and blues band I didn't like singing about America. I wanted to sing about the things that directly influenced me at the time. Anthony Newley... was the only singer who didn't put on a false American accent.'
DB, 1973

His half-brother Terry gives him Jack Kerouac's *On The Road* and Bowie becomes obsessed with beatniks and jazz music; he learns the saxophone. He learns how to sing, play guitar, how to perform.

Above: Released in the summer of psychedelia and LSD, Bowie's debut album owed far more to music hall and the musicals of Danny Kaye and Anthony Newley.

Opposite: Bowie had performed his first overseas concert, in Paris, as early as New Year's Eve, 1965. Here he is recording an appearance on Germany's *4-3-2-1 Musik Für Junge Leute*, broadcast 16 March 1968.

1
4
d
y

At school he meets George Underwood. If anyone is going to be a star, it is George, with his striking good looks and charisma. George joins a band called The Konrads. At the same time he and David both fall in lust with a girl. Bowie makes a sneaky move and robs George of a date; George punches Bowie and renders his friend's eye permanently dilated. Not long after, a guilt-ridden George invites Bowie to join The Konrads. Bowie sings and plays saxophone.

Later they form The Hooker Brothers – named after blues legend John Lee Hooker – then Davie Jones and The King Bees.

Between gigs, Bowie cheekily writes a letter to a pop impresario. We are the next Beatles he tells him, and you could be the next Epstein. The impresario, John Bloom, smiles and recommends a manager called Leslie Conn. Conn takes on the band and books them for Bloom's wedding. Guests include Adam Faith and Lance Percival.

Conn's next move is to secure the band an audition with Decca. In June 1964 The King Bees release their debut single, 'Liza Jane'/'Louie Louie Go Home'. Both songs are blues and R&B influenced. Conn somehow receives writing credits. The single got some attention – the popular TV show *Juke Box Jury* reviewed it, though only comic Charlie Drake liked it, and the influential *Ready Steady Go!* invited the band to perform. But sales were poor and the band fell apart.

The Manish Boys were next. Again R&B was the template, although Bowie's look – long hair and Robin Hood attire – was (shall we say) rather unexpected for an R&B singer. The band's debut single, 'I Pity the Fool'/'Take My Tip', produced by Who-man, Shel Talmy, again sold poorly.

His next band was named The Lower Third. Bowie dumped manager Conn and asked Ralph Horton to guide his career. Horton pushed him into mod clothing. The band's debut single, 'You've Got A Habit Of Leaving', was fast, frenetic and did what it set out to do by gaining them a modish audience in London.

Their next single (produced by Tony Hatch), 'Can't Help Thinking About Me'/'And I Say To Myself', was Bowie's best effort to date – a resounding pop record with self-examining lyrics.

Another band follows: The Buzz. The London pop sound – that of The Who, The Yardbirds – is not the template.

This page and overleaf: When I live my dream… In 1967, Bowie was yet to enjoy commercial success, but he was building a reputation as a talented singer-songwriter with a distinctive style – and amassing press photographs to match.

The band cuts a single, but the record is credited to David Bowie. 'Do Anything You Say'/'Good Morning Girl' has striking guitar shapes, backing vocals and a rushed breathy Bowie vocal foreshadowing what will become a trademark. In other words, Bowie is finding his own vocal style and, although chart success is again elusive, the musical steps he is making will prove more valuable in the long term.

Another single, 'I Dig Everything'/'I'm Not Losing Sleep', was released the same year. For this session, producer Tony Hatch dumped the band and brought in seasoned session musicians. But yet another slice of Bowie's London-style pop missed the charts by a mile. Bowie didn't mind. He simply changed tack, again.

His next release, 'Rubber Band'/'The London Boys', had a Newleyesque vocal and, for the A-side, a brass band backing. Again it sold nothing. Undeterred Bowie released 'The Laughing Gnome'/'The Gospel According To Tony Day'. When Bowie-mania hit the world in 1973, millions

of teenagers eagerly backtracked through Bowie's career, delighted to discover albums such as *Hunky Dory* and songs such as 'The Man Who Sold The World', until they hit 'The Laughing Gnome' and just didn't know what to make of it. It can be viewed either as a great children's composition or one of those moments in a musician's career when he simply isn't thinking straight.

For his debut album Bowie further pursues his Newley obsession, adopting a particularly English voice mixed right to the forefront of each track. He isn't Newley on every song – traces of Pink Floyd's Syd Barrett and The Kinks' Ray Davies can be detected on 'There Is A Happy Land', his paean to innocence and childhood, and there are echoes of Burt Bacharach elsewhere – but Newley is certainly prominent.

There is a great wistfulness in his vocals – David's has been a childhood spent apart. He does have close friends, George Underwood in particular, but much of his time has been spent in his lonely, lonely room, the room all songwriters sit in as children and dream and shape the life ahead.

For sure, rock 'n' roll music, and Little Richard in particular, speaks to him just as it does all the other kids in Britain. But Bowie also seeks out other sources of inspiration, looks in places others don't.

What did Deram see in this thin young man? Musical talent, for sure; the album carries some stunning melodies, some lovely songs – 'Silly Boy Blue', 'Sell Me A Coat', are prime examples. And in places the album does manage to chime with the London of 1967. 'Little Bombardier' and 'She's Got Medals', for instance, tap into that year's Edwardian fashions. But most of this record stands alone. Pop culture at the time demanded music that broke boundaries. Bowie took them at their word and gave them an album with no guitars, full of waltzes and show tunes, that ends with him delivering a poem called 'Please Mr Gravedigger' during which he sneezes and delivers the rest of the words as if with a heavy cold.

Of course, the album sold poorly on its release. No one knew what to make of it. No one knew who to sell it to. It is only now we can see the brilliance of the work and begin to make sense of Bowie, age twenty, and his strange and wonderful fascinations.

DAVID BOWIE/SPACE ODDITY 1969

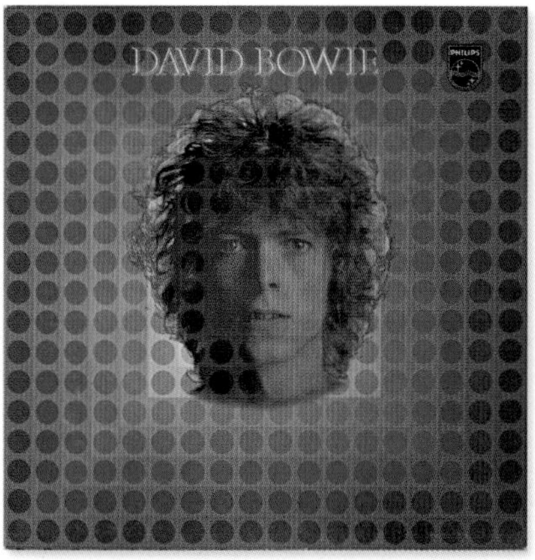

'THE RECORD IS BASED A LOT ON THE FILM *2001*. IT'S A MIXTURE OF SALVADOR DALÍ, *2001* AND THE BEE GEES. REALLY IT'S JUST A RECORD WHICH AMUSES PEOPLE.'

DAVID BOWIE, 1969

1967

18 December
Records first BBC radio session, for John Peel's *Top Gear*
28 December
First performance of Lindsay Kemp's *Pierrot In Turquoise,* in which Bowie appears as 'Cloud'

1968

30 March
Final performance of *Pierrot In Turquoise*
September
Forms mixed-media trio Turquoise (later Feathers) with girlfriend Hermione Farthingale and Tony Hill

1969

January–February
Records promotional film *Love You Till Tuesday*
February
Feathers breaks up
Summer
Makes numerous appearances at Beckenham Arts Lab
June
UK release of 'Space Oddity'/ 'Wild Eyed Boy From Freecloud' (5)
July
US release of 'Space Oddity'/ 'Wild Eyed Boy From Freecloud' (DNC)
5 August
Death of father, Haywood Stenton 'John' Jones, aged 56
9 October
First appearance on BBC TV's *Top Of The Pops,* performing 'Space Oddity'
14 November
Release of *David Bowie* (later retitled *Space Oddity*) (DNC)

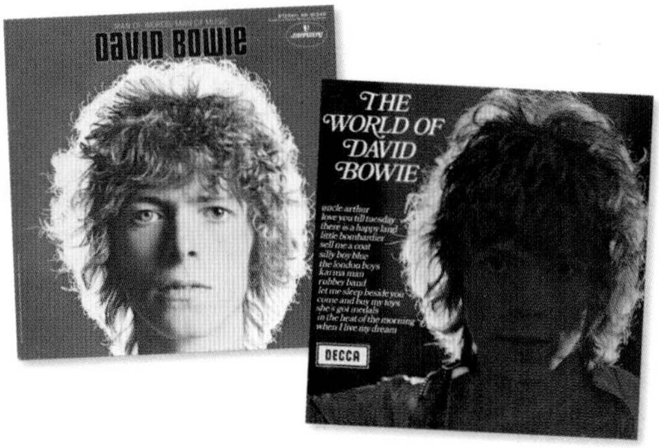

Previous page and opposite: Like his new look, Bowie's new album was a mixture of the space-age and the pastoral.

Bowie in 1969, already so different from the Bowie of 1967. Gone are the suits, the mod haircut, and the Newley-driven songs about London. Now he wears long hair and flares, plays acoustic guitar and writes very wordy songs à la Bob Dylan. Times have changed and so has David Bowie, who seems to have developed a very non-chalant approach towards his music. He tells *Melody Maker* after the release of his second album:

'I haven't really wanted to make any records for ages but people have been on at me to record again, so I went to the studios. I have been doing mime for a year and a half so this is my comeback! The first album I did in fifteen minutes for five shillings and sixpence. You could say I was rushed. I got discouraged with pop by the lack of work.' DB, 1969

Don't believe the man. It is a front, a disguise. All song-writers need validation, all need to have their work alive in the world. Bowie is desperate to be taken as seriously as Dylan and knows that to do so he must cut his own cloth, go his own way.

Example: since the release of his debut album, he has immersed himself in both Buddhism and the art of mime, activities not traditionally associated with young musicians on the way up. It is a trait that will define his career, seek-ing out new experiences and art forms and then bringing them into the musical arena.

Bowie came to Buddhism through the novels of beat-generation writer Jack Kerouac. By the summer of 1967 he was deeply immersed in the religion and had already paid a visit to the UK headquarters of the Buddhist Society. Soon, he was talking about leaving behind all ambitions, turning his life around and becoming a Buddhist monk. His first biographer, George Tremlett, quotes him saying at the time, 'Material things just don't interest me. I have one good suit in case I have to go anywhere important, but I don't want a car and I live with my parents. I'm not interested in clothes at all really.'

That he should be ditching the sartorial for *satori* shows the depth of the man's commitment. David remained highly interested in Buddhism until 1970 when doubts

about his guru surfaced. David later commented, 'See, I am not the only one playing a character.'

At about the same time, a girlfriend secured tickets for a mime show called *Clown's Hour* in Covent Garden.

'A mime, what could be less interesting? Then she told me that he was using my one album as his interval music. A mime, how interesting.' DB, 2002

Bowie loved it. Afterwards, he met the show's creator, Lindsay Kemp. The two men instantly clicked and soon Bowie was attending Kemp's classes in London. In a 1974 interview Kemp said, 'I taught him to exaggerate with his body as well as his voice, and the importance of looking as well as sounding beautiful. Ever since working with me he's practised that, and in each performance he does his movements are more exquisite.'

Through Kemp's tutelage, Bowie learnt much about stagecraft, use of space and use of audience. By December 1967 they were appearing together in a production entitled *Pierrot In Turquoise* in which Bowie both mimed and performed his own songs. It was generally thought that he was a fine mime artist.

'I was desperately keen on mime at the time… the way you could transform an open space and create things by suggestion… I knew at the time that I wanted to present music in a very theatrical fashion but I wasn't sure exactly how. I used to go and see The Living Theatre and those American concept groups at the Roundhouse and think, if I could put this to a band format it would be very exciting.' DB, 1993

Through Kemp, Bowie met a young dancer called Hermione Farthingale. Hermione was beautiful and bewitching and Bowie was smitten. They performed together in an acoustic trio called Turquoise with guitarist Tony Hill. When Hill quit, John Hutchinson came on board and the three formed a multimedia outfit, Feathers, singing, dancing, reciting poetry and performing mime.

In February 1969 David and Hermione split up. David was devastated and retreated to Beckenham. By April he was seeing a young writer named Mary Finnigan. Together, they decided to open a folk club in the back room of a local pub. The club was based on the concept of an arts lab, something originally pioneered by a forward-thinking American called Jim Haynes at the Drury Lane Arts Lab.

'There isn't one pseud involved… arts labs generally have such a bad reputation as pseud places. There's a lot of talent in the green belt and there is a load of tripe in Drury Lane. I think the arts lab movement is extremely important and should take over from the youth club concept as a social service.' DB, 1969

The nights proved highly popular with Bowie miming, reading and performing for an audience that grew every week. Some who witnessed Bowie at these events say that he delivered absolutely riveting performances. And it was here that Bowie honed many of the songs that would make up his second album.

He had now dropped his London-centric material in favour of an acoustic rock sound. The new songs were lengthy, wordy and displayed his wide musical skills. Bob Dylan was a big influence, as were Simon and Garfunkel, and this major shift in his songwriting is best viewed through the story of the track by which the album – originally titled, like his debut, simply *David Bowie* – would come to be known: 'Space Oddity'.

In November 1968, Bowie had been dazzled by the Stanley Kubrick film *2001: A Space Odyssey*. From that point on, space, alien life forms, astronauts would exert a huge influence.

Inspired by Kubrick's vision, by December Bowie had written the punningly titled 'Space Oddity'. After playing it to Mercury Records (as well as performing it in the short promotional film *Love You Till Tuesday*, financed by his manager Kenneth Pitt), he secured himself a new record deal and entered the studio in June. NASA had announced that by mid-July they would land a man on the moon and Mercury wanted Bowie's song out as a single at the same time.

Rehearsing with then-girlfriend Hermione Farthingale as part of the mixed-media trio Feathers, late 1968. Although both the group and the relationship were soon to break up, Hermione's influence on Bowie's second album was to be considerable: three of its songs were written for or about her.

The man who would produce the rest of the album, Tony Visconti, whom Bowie had met and bonded with over a mutual interest in Eastern mysticism, dismissed 'Space Oddity' as a gimmick so Bowie entered the studio with producer Gus Dudgeon instead, as well as pianist Rick Wakeman, bass player Herbie Flowers, drummer Terry Cox and guitarist Mick Wayne. They emerged with a near-perfect single: a catchy musical arrangement with intriguing sound effects, and a concise story concerning the travails of an astronaut named Major Tom who winds up floating forever in space.

With 'Space Oddity' finished in December 1968, the songs that completed the album tended to be longer, full of shifts in time and texture. Many began on acoustic guitar and ended up with the full band jamming. None of them is as concisely arranged as the precise pop of 'Space Oddity', which would go on to give Bowie his first top-ten single in the UK.

Three of the songs that followed were written for or about Hermione Farthingale – 'Letter To Hermione', 'Unwashed And Somewhat Slightly Dazed' and 'An Occasional Dream'. There is a sense of hurt and confusion attached to all of them which tells us Hermione did the walking, not David.

He also wrote about a free festival he had helped to organise – 'Memory Of A Free Festival' – and added a 'Hey Jude'-like chorus at the end of it. It was re-recorded and released as a single in June 1970 but did not chart.

He wrote 'Janine' about his best friend's girlfriend and sounded like Peter Sarstedt who had dominated the UK charts that year with 'Where Do You Go To (My Lovely)'. Having read a newspaper report about a middle-aged woman who had been caught stealing, Bowie wrote a song from her point of view and called it 'God Knows I'm Good'. And it *was* good. Then he attacked the slavish nature of the hippie movement in the long and intricate 'Cygnet Committee'.

By 1969, hippies had replaced mods at the centre of youth culture but Bowie disliked their snobbishness; speaking to *Disc and Music Echo* that year he said he preferred the skinheads, a radical statement to make given that youth cult's fearsome reputation, and added, 'a cygnet is pretty to look at but is totally helpless'.

Even after 'Space Oddity' hit the charts, the album did not sell in great quantities. Bowie would have to wait for the breakthrough of *Ziggy Stardust* to see it fly. In the meantime, it now seemed like a very good idea to stop trying to be accepted as a sensitive singer-songwriter, put on a dress and make a heavy metal album.

Bowie's manager, Kenneth Pitt, approached George Martin to produce 'Space Oddity', but the legendary Beatles producer didn't rate the song. This low opinion was shared by the album's producer, Tony Visconti, who handed over production of the song to Gus Dudgeon.

BECKENHAM ARTS LAB

'I never knew there were so many sitar players in Beckenham.'
DB, 1969

The original Arts Lab was founded in 1967 by the American Jim Haynes, a leading figure of the British counter-culture and co-founder – with Barry Miles and John Hopkins – of *International Times* and, later, *Suck*.

The Drury Lane Arts Lab ran for just fifteen months but was incredibly influential, and even exhibited John Lennon and Yoko Ono's first artwork in May 1968.

Bowie founded his lab on 4 May 1969, with then-girlfriend Mary Finnigan and friends Christina Ostrom and Barrie Jackson at The Three Tuns, a pub on Beckenham High Street. Originally a folk club called 'Growth', it proved a huge success and between 1969 and 1973 a surprising amount of talent passed through its doors, including Marc Bolan, Steve Harley, Peter Frampton, Rick Wakeman and Lionel Bart.

As a fundraiser for the lab, on 16 August 1969, Bowie organised a free festival at Beckenham Recreation Ground, a low-key, almost village-fete-like affair later immortalised, through somewhat rose-tinted glasses, in 'Memory Of A Free Festival'.

THE MIME BEHIND THE MOVES

'I was singing the songs of my life with my body; he was singing the songs of his life very fabulously with his voice, and we reckoned that by putting the two together the audience couldn't help but be enthralled.'
LINDSAY KEMP, 1974

Dancer, choreographer and actor Lindsay Kemp was born in 1938 in South Shields, north-east England. As a young boy he would don make-up and dance on the kitchen table. Later in life he studied dance with Hilde Holger and mime with Marcel Marceau before forming his own dance company in the early sixties.

Kemp doesn't consider himself a mime artist, rather a conceptual dancer; he is particularly keen on the Japanese dance technique 'Butoh' – from where the 'traditional' mime's look of the white-painted face and body is derived.

Kemp's influence on Bowie cannot be overstated. Bowie's study of theatre is, arguably, the defining activity that set him apart from other sixties wannabes; grist for a mill that would produce such fine-grained theatrical creations as Ziggy Stardust and the Thin White Duke, not to mention a host of intelligently produced live shows.

'From make-up to costume, [Lindsay Kemp's] ideas of an elevated reality stuck and his commitment to breaking down the parameters between on-stage and off-stage life remained firmly in my soul.'
DB, 2002

Reciting poetry at the Beckenham Arts Lab, summer 1969 (left). Lindsay Kemp, seen in the role of Salome at London's Roundhouse (above), had a profound influence on Bowie, who performed as Cloud in Kemp's touring production *Pierrot in Turquoise* from December 1967 to March 1968.

THE MAN WHO SOLD THE WORLD 1970

‘I REFUSE TO BE THOUGHT OF AS MEDIOCRE. IF I AM MEDIOCRE, I'LL GET OUT OF THE BUSINESS.’

DAVID BOWIE, 1971

1970
February–May
Performs with backing band Hype
March
UK release of 'The Prettiest Star'/'Conversation Piece' (DNC)
***c.* March**
Tony Defries and Laurence Myers of Gem Productions take over Bowie's management
20 March
Marries Mary Angela 'Angie' Barnett
10 May
Wins Ivor Novello Award for Best Original Song for 'Space Oddity'
June
UK release of 'Memory of a Free Festival (Part 1)'/'Memory of a Free Festival (Part 2)' (DNC)
4 November
US release of *The Man Who Sold The World* (DNC)

1971
January
UK release of 'Holy Holy'/'Black Country Rock' (DNC)
February–May
Travels to the US for the first time to promote his new album
April
UK release of *The Man Who Sold The World* (DNC)

Previous page: Taking a break during a recording for Dutch TV show *Ready, Eddy, Go!*, 18 July 1970.

Opposite: On the threshold of success, Bowie sets his gaze on higher things. Haddon Hall, Beckenham, Kent, 1970.

Above: Mr and Mrs Bowie pose for wedding photographs with Bowie's mother, Peggy, outside Bromley Registry Office, 20 March 1970.

With the promise of royalties to come from his top-five hit single 'Space Oddity', in summer 1969 Bowie moved into a large gothic building named Haddon Hall in Beckenham. He took a flat on the ground floor with his new girlfriend, Angie Barnett. He had met Angie at a King Crimson gig at the Speakeasy and they had been inseparable ever since. They would marry within the year.

Haddon Hall would prove vital in changing Bowie's character. He and Angie began experimenting on many levels, not least sexually. Decadence hung over their living quarters; as well as drugs, the sexual explorations Bowie embarked upon came to be reflected in his music. On *The Man Who Sold The World* Bowie finally started to sound like a sexual creature singing in a lustful, daring manner.

Despite all this Bowie, artistically, was depressed, unsure of himself. His father had recently died and his second album had sold poorly. Tony Visconti and his girlfriend, Liz Hartley, had also taken a room at Haddon Hall. Speaking to BBC Radio in 1976, Visconti remembered, 'He really did not know what he wanted to do. At the end of the whole *Space Oddity* album we said, "This is not the direction to go in", because for such a good single the album did nothing.'

Another single, 'The Prettiest Star', recorded in early January 1970, simply added to the misery. It was a straight-forward pop song – guitar courtesy of Marc Bolan – but again the British public remained unimpressed.

Things started to move when Bowie played the Marquee in early February and met the man who would help steer him to the highest of musical heights. His name was Mick Ronson. He and Bowie hit it off within minutes.

As evidence of their compatibility, two days later the men were performing a new Bowie composition, 'Width Of A Circle', for a *John Peel Radio Show* session. Ronson's heroes were Jeff Beck and Eric Clapton and he was a huge admirer of the band Cream; this heavy rock sound and his undoubted skills as a lead guitarist were the perfect embellishment to Bowie's new material.

When Visconti told Bowie he had to change tack, the singer agreed. What they needed, Bowie argued, was a band. With Ronson in place on guitar and Visconti on bass, Bowie brought in drummer John Cambridge. They called

themselves David Bowie and Hype and a gig was arranged at London's Roundhouse for 22 February. Visconti now states that the gig was the precursor to the phenomenon of glam rock which would soon sweep the UK. If so, it was because of David and Angie's relationship.

Bowie knew the value of clothes and image. In 1967 he had worn the mod look. In his attempt to crack the singer-songwriter market with the *Space Oddity* album he had worn conventional contemporary rock-star attire – long hair, flares, tie-dyed shirts. For this new venture, he and Angie decided to drop the jeans and dress weirdly and strikingly.

'We've had these costumes made by various girlfriends which make us look like Dr Strange or the Incredible Hulk. I was a bit apprehensive about wearing them at the Roundhouse gig because I didn't know how the audience would react. If they think it's a huge put-on the whole thing will backfire but they seemed to accept it which was nice.' DB, 1970

The band was also brought into the venture and given new names and costumes. Visconti was dubbed 'Hyperman' and wore a cape and silver knickers. Ronson was 'Gangsterman' in a gold lamé suit, and Cambridge was 'Cowboyman'. The crowd were stunned and awed in equal measure, although Bowie recalls the gig as a disaster, later claiming that only Marc Bolan, standing at the front of the crowd wearing a child's plastic Roman soldier's chest plate, applauded.

In the same year Bowie rejoined Lindsay Kemp for some more performances, adding to his inner confusion. Was he singer-songwriter, rock performer or mime artist? It was at Haddon Hall that he finally glimpsed his future.

Shuffling the pack: inside Haddon Hall, Bowie strikes a pose on the chaise longue that he would adapt for the original UK cover of *The Man Who Sold The World*. Famously, he would also change into something more comfortable. The US release used a less controversial gunslinger illustration (previous page).

'I realised it was all because I wanted to be well known. I wanted to be thought of as someone who was very much a trendy person rather than a trend. I did not want to be a trend. I wanted to be the instigator of new ideas. I wanted to turn people onto new things and new perspectives... I pulled myself in and decided to use the easiest medium, which was rock 'n' roll, and then add bits and pieces to it over the years so that by the end of it I would be my own medium.' DB, 1976

As Ronson would later say, 'We knew David had something but we didn't know quite what.'

The group entered the studio in April 1970 with only one song fully written: 'Width Of A Circle'. Bowie had a few song titles and a few chord changes, but that was it. One of the titles was 'The Man Who Sold The World', inspired by a 1950 science-fiction novella by Robert Heinlein called *The Man Who Sold The Moon* about a man who wants to travel to, and take control of, the moon.

Visconti, as producer, was keen for everything to go smoothly but he later recalled recording as a hair-raising experience, mainly because Bowie was not as focused as he'd been on other projects.

The allure of his new wife, Angie, and the decadent lifestyle they were developing was proving something of a distraction. Still, Bowie wrote eight songs in the period allotted, many of them musically dense affairs. He would show the assembled band his work, record his parts, and then hand over the responsibility of producing and arranging to Visconti and Ronson.

Ronson urged Visconti to play like Jack Bruce as he matched him with his Clapton/Beck-infused guitar style. The result was a heavy-rock album, full of songs whose subject matter dealt either with Bowie's family problems channelled through science-fiction imagery – 'All The Madmen' was widely held to be about his half-brother Terry – or radical philosophical ideas taken from the books Bowie was currently reading. In 1975 he stated that he would often read a book and try to distil its essence into song; hence 'The Supermen', based on Friedrich Nietzsche's *Beyond Good And Evil*.

Even though it did not sell, there are those (Morrissey is one) who cite *The Man Who Sold The World* as their favourite Bowie album. Its creator was not so sure.

'It was a nightmare. I hated the process of making it. I had never done an album with that kind of professionalism and that scared me a lot. It felt invalid somehow. I wished we had been doing it on four-track at the time. It all ended up too glossy...'
DB, 1976

Not long after recording, Bowie, Mick Ronson, Tony Visconti and Mick 'Woody' Woodmansey (who had replaced John Cambridge as drummer in March 1970) went their separate ways. In April 1971 the album was released in the UK (having come out in the US with an alternative cover in November 1970) and all involved gulped when they saw the cover. There was Bowie, lying on a chaise longue, holding a playing card and looking nonchalantly towards the camera... wearing a dress.

The dress had come from a London tailors called Mr Fish on Clifford Street, Mayfair. An old school friend of Bowie's, Geoff MacCormack (later to be known on various Bowie recordings as Warren Peace), worked there and brought him in. Fish had designed the dress that Mick Jagger had worn at the Stones' Hyde Park gig, staged two days after the death of guitarist Brian Jones in July 1969. Bowie had absorbed the image and was running with it in a far more provocative way.

Said Visconti in 1975, 'He always wanted to be outrageous. He invited a lot of outrageous people to our flat, which was another reason why I left. I couldn't put up with this constant parade of freaks coming in and out of the house. But as soon as someone would leave, say someone with a teddy boy style, David would rush to the loo and start brushing his hair like that. He was definitely searching for an image in those days.'

The instigator of new ideas was upon us.

Opposite: In performance with his new band, Hype, at the Roundhouse, London, 11 March 1970.

This page, top: Hype's guitarist, Mick Ronson, was to make a massive contribution to Bowie's career over the next three years, through not only his masterful guitar playing but also his all-round skills as an arranger.

This page, bottom: Frock 'n' roll star – in the grounds of Haddon Hall, the gothic mansion in which Bowie rented a flat from 1969 until 1973 and launched several of his provocative new images.

HUNKY DORY 1971

‘I WASN’T AN R&B ARTIST, I WASN’T A FOLK ARTIST AND I DIDN’T SEE THE POINT IN TRYING TO BE THAT PURIST ABOUT IT... I LOVED THE IDEA OF PUTTING LITTLE RICHARD WITH JACQUES BREL AND THE VELVET UNDERGROUND BACKING THEM. WHAT WOULD THAT SOUND LIKE?’

DAVID BOWIE, 2011

DAVID BOWIE
Exclusively on RCA
RCA Records and Tapes

1971
May
UK release of Arnold Corns' 'Moonage Daydream'/ 'Hang On To Yourself' (DNC)
30 May
Birth of son, Duncan Zowie Haywood Jones
23 June
Performs at Glastonbury Fayre
September
Travels to New York to sign recording contract with RCA
Meets Andy Warhol for first time
17 December
Release of *Hunky Dory* (UK 3, US 93)

Previous page: Publicity shot for *Hunky Dory*, Bowie's first album for RCA.

Opposite and above, right: On his first visit to America, Bowie jams at a party thrown by an acquaintance of publicist Rodney Bingenheimer, Los Angeles, February 1971.

Above, left: Pictured with clothes designer Freddie Burretti on the cover of *Curious*, 'the sex education magazine for men and women'. As well as designing many of Bowie's stage costumes, Burretti was also to serve as a notional frontman in the Arnold Corns side project.

All his life America – and Japan – had entranced Bowie. For him America was a continent of promise and opportunity available at every level. England was a minnow by comparison. It was grey and tight and sent its people to bed at twelve with a cup of tea and the national anthem. America was vivid, expansive and open to determined winners, of which Bowie was certainly one. He arrives in February 1971 and is instantly taken by its energy, its sense of largeness.

He is there to sell copies of his album *The Man Who Sold The World*, but he will not be very successful. Despite a lot of attention, the album does not break into the charts. Far from it. But on another level the trip is a complete success. Bowie will absorb America and it will change his music irrevocably, placing him on the path to stardom. He will move away from the epic towards the concise. *Hunky Dory* is the first of his records to demonstrate this shift. That is why it is his first truly classic album.

'There are reasons for the change. Two big events happened… Firstly I went to the States for three months to promote The Man Who Sold The World *and when I returned I had a whole new perception on songwriting. My songs began changing immediately. Secondly, by the time I came back I had a new record label, RCA, and also a new band.'* DB, 1972

Hunky Dory is a spontaneous and confident work, a record of revelation rather than deception. Although the album's cover portrait shows David evoking the spirit of Greta Garbo, in the songs themselves he is not playing a character or attempting to hide in any way. *Hunky Dory* is Bowie the songwriter, an artist moving between several satisfying styles, establishing himself as a lyricist of great potential. Like all classic albums it exists in its own space, exerts its own sense of logic. Recorded in just two weeks, it does not sound rushed but flows with clever musical ideas and striking – if at times slightly disturbing – imagery.

Bowie entered the studio in early June 1971 in an optimistic and confident mood. He had already written the majority of the tracks that would appear on the album – and more that would later appear on *Ziggy Stardust*. His song

'Oh! You Pretty Things' was about to become a major chart hit for singer Peter Noone (UK 12, May 1971). Bowie's management company Gem – soon to be MainMan – had failed to sign Stevie Wonder so were putting their all behind him. And he had reunited with guitarist Mick Ronson ('You don't want to stay in Hull, do you?' he memorably asked him) and drummer Mick 'Woody' Woodmansey, who brought with them bassist Trevor Bolder to form a musical bedrock he knew he could rely on. The result of these changes was instant.

Hunky Dory contains two inarguable classics in 'Changes' and 'Life On Mars?'. In the album's open spirit, both demand that Bowie sing without restraint for them to function fully. What's more, 'Changes' – bursting with melody and endowed with one of Bowie's most rousing choruses – clearly states the artist's new musical position and inspiration: 'Ah, strange fascination fascinating me'.

'Life On Mars?' is epic pop with a melody and lyric uniquely Bowie. It was inspired by rejection: not, as often reported, the ending of his brief but intense affair with the actress and dancer Hermione Farthingale but more Frank Sinatra's success with an English version of a French tune, 'Comme d'Habitude', for which Bowie's own lyric, 'Even A Fool Learns To Love', had been turned down in 1968. Sinatra's chosen version, written by Paul Anka, was called 'My Way'.

Bowie's revenge – other than dedicating it to 'Frankie' on the sleeve notes – is to utilise chord changes from 'My Way' within 'Life On Mars?'. Full of spliced images of America, he later defined it as a love song, a song about a girl living a small-town life, looking for big-time dreams.

What is remarkable about *Hunky Dory*, and perhaps explains its initial chart failure (though it has subsequently become Bowie's second most successful album, after *Ziggy Stardust*, based on weeks in the chart), is that it has precious little to do with the world of music in 1971. Apart from Mick Ronson's Faces-type guitar on 'Eight Line Poem', Bowie's occasional vocal appropriation of Ray Davies singing 'Lola', and the fact that a lot of the album is piano-driven – like Carole King's multi-million-selling *Tapestry* – *Hunky Dory* exists alone.

It is an album that allows us to focus on Bowie the songwriter, to admire his effortless skill in conjuring up melody and changing moods, from the charming 'Kooks' (written about his new-born son, Zowie, later Duncan) to the warm-hearted 'Fill Your Heart' (a Biff Rose cover), to more mature excursions into singer-songwriter territory on 'Quicksand' and 'The Bewlay Brothers'.

'Quicksand' is a case in point. While the demo version – with Bowie on acoustic guitar – is already absolutely beautiful, on record the song is slower in pace with more emphasis on the words, the dramatic musical stops and flourishes highlighting Bowie's vivid imagery and the songwriter's indecision.

Mick Ronson has to take credit here. Bowie gave him free rein over the songs in terms of arrangement and the guitarist repaid him in full, devising a set of musical moves that never lean towards the obvious.

America's influence is signposted by the album's title (an American expression little known in the UK at the time), and the inclusion of 'Andy Warhol', 'Song For Bob Dylan' and 'Queen Bitch' together (and after 'Fill Your Heart', co-written by US singer and comedian Biff Rose).

Andy Warhol's pop-art approach to cultural icons chimed with Bowie's own aesthetic. He met Warhol in New York and for an hour they stood and said nothing. Then Warhol started to enthuse about Bowie's shoes.

'They were these little yellow things with a strap across them, like girls' shoes. He absolutely adored them. Then I found out that he used to do a lot of shoe designing when he was younger. He had a bit of a shoe fetishism.' DB, 2003

In later life when Bowie's song came on the radio Warhol would turn it off straight away and ask whether royalties were due for the use of his name. The answer was no.

'Don't pick fights with the bullies or the cads, 'cause I'm not much cop at punching other people's dads': out for a stroll with Angie and new-born son, Zowie, Beckenham, June 1971. Zowie later chose to be known as Joe and then as an adult reverted to his birth name, Duncan Jones. He has become a successful film director, creator of *Moon* (2009) and *Source Code* (2011).

'Song For Bob Dylan' is also crafted in pop art, Bowie's instant message to a man whose brilliance had entranced a generation. Dylan's retreat from the madness he had created in the mid-sixties had confused many. Bowie's conceit is to see Dylan as the front for Robert Zimmerman, a knowing acknowledgement that behind every star lurks the human being.

'Queen Bitch' is Bowie's tribute to The Velvet Underground. A huge fan – he owned an original acetate of their debut album, given to him by Kenneth Pitt, who had acquired it directly from Andy Warhol in November 1966 – his song is not only hewn from Lou Reed's New York of seedy hotels, drag queens, drugs and wild, illicit sex, but points the way musically to *Ziggy Stardust*.

The album's closer, 'The Bewlay Brothers', is suitably portentous, full of red herrings that Bowie later admitted to laying so as to deliberately confuse the most ardent student of his lyrics.

Hunky Dory did precious little business on its release – it sold only 5,000 copies in the first three months and wouldn't take off commercially until after Ziggy-mania had broken out. It was an album out of time, out of place. It had nothing to do with the rock or pop of its day. With no grand theme or overt purpose, it is simply a collection of timeless songs. The fact that while Bowie was writing and recording such a fabulous album he was simultaneously working on its follow-up illustrates why he would soon be such a huge star.

'... the most inventive piece of songwriting to have appeared on record for a considerable time' ***Melody Maker*, January 1972**

ANDY, IGGY AND LOU

When Bowie arrived in New York in 1971, he made a bee-line for the city's avant-garde arts scene centred on Andy Warhol's Factory and Mickey Ruskin's nightclub, Max's Kansas City. The people he met there would play important roles in his life and career.

On one level there were Max's regulars Cherry Vanilla and Leee Black Childers, who became involved with Bowie's management company, MainMan. And then there was the legendary Lou Reed and the soon-to-be legendary Iggy Pop.

Bowie helped reignite Reed's post-Velvet Underground career, covering his songs, inviting him on stage at London's Royal Festival Hall and co-producing *Transformer* at the height of Ziggy-mania. After coming to blows while dining together in 1979, they didn't speak for nearly twenty years until Reed performed at Bowie's fiftieth birthday concert in 1997. In 2003 Bowie was a guest vocalist on Reed's album *The Raven*.

In 1972 Bowie also helped produce Iggy and The Stooges' classic *Raw Power*. Three years later, when Iggy Pop checked himself into hospital to tackle his ongoing drug abuse Bowie was a regular visitor. In 1976 the two relocated to Berlin in an attempt to wean themselves off their respective addictions. After recording *Low*, Bowie helped write and record Iggy's solo debut, *The Idiot*, and toured with him as a low-key, keyboard-playing member of the band. Immediately after, in just eight days he co-wrote and co-produced the follow-up, *Lust For Life*. And in 1986 Bowie co-produced Iggy's *Blah Blah Blah*.

Bowie's relationship with Warhol was rather more distant. The two never became close but Bowie went on to portray the artist in the 1996 movie *Basquiat*.

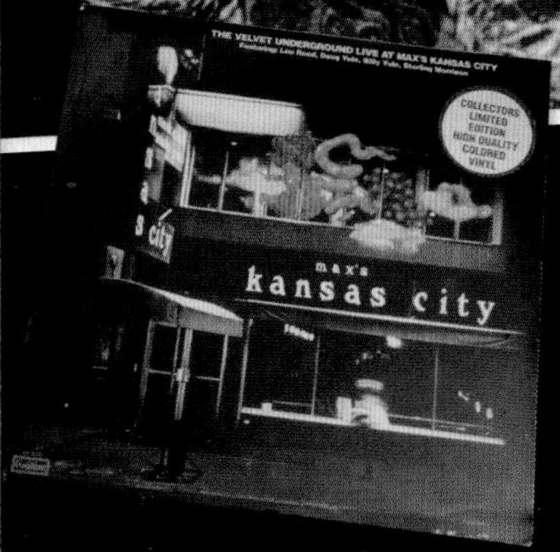

Just a perfect day? David Bowie, Iggy Pop and Lou Reed at London's Dorchester Hotel, July 1972. Bowie had first hung out with Iggy and Lou the previous year in New York clubs such as Max's Kansas City, shown here on the cover of The Velvet Underground's *Live At Max's Kansas City*. However, he didn't perform a full-scale concert in the US until 22 September 1972, at the Cleveland Music Hall (shown overleaf, with Mick Ronson).

‘I BECAME ZIGGY STARDUST. DAVID BOWIE WENT TOTALLY OUT THE WINDOW. EVERYBODY WAS CONVINCING ME THAT I WAS A MESSIAH... I GOT HOPELESSLY LOST IN THE FANTASY.’

DAVID BOWIE, 1976

1972

January
Release of 'Changes'/
'Andy Warhol' (UK DNC, US 41)

22 January
Declares himself bisexual in a *Melody Maker* interview

29 January
First performance by Ziggy Stardust and The Spiders From Mars, at the Friars in Aylesbury, Buckinghamshire

April
Release of 'Starman'/
'Suffragette City' (UK 10, US 65)

6 June
UK release of *The Rise And Fall Of Ziggy Stardust And The Spiders From Mars* (5)

17 June
Simulates fellatio on Mick Ronson's guitar for the first time, at Oxford Town Hall

30 June
Tony Defries establishes MainMan and becomes Bowie's sole manager

July
UK release of Mott The Hoople's 'All The Young Dudes'

6 July
Legendary performance of 'Starman' broadcast on BBC television's *Top Of The Pops*

8 July
Performs at the Save the Whale charity concert, Royal Festival Hall, London, duetting with Lou Reed in Reed's first UK performance

August
UK release of Arnold Corns' 'Hang On To Yourself'/
'Man In The Middle' (DNC)

19–20 August
Relaunch of the Ziggy Stardust tour with notable shows at the Rainbow Theatre, London

September
UK release of
'John, I'm Only Dancing'/
'Hang On To Yourself' (12)

1 September
US release of *The Rise And Fall Of Ziggy Stardust And The Spiders From Mars* (75)

Previous page: Jamming good (though not with Weird and Gilly on this occasion), Birmingham Town Hall, 17 March 1972. Portrait by Mick Rock, a seasoned Ziggy observer. Often referred to as 'the man who shot the seventies', Rock also directed the videos for 'John, I'm Only Dancing', 'The Jean Genie', 'Space Oddity' and 'Life On Mars?'.

Opposite: Captured mid-interview at home, April 1972. The music press had taken a keen interest in what Bowie had to say since he had announced his bisexuality in January.

On the evening of Thursday 6 July 1972, millions of British teenagers watched David Bowie walk over to guitarist Mick Ronson, sling his arm around his shoulder and sing, 'There's a starman waiting in the sky…'.

In that one act David Bowie went from being a pop star to a phenomenon. The next day at schools up and down the country thousands and thousands of boys and girls ran into playgrounds and asked each other, 'Did you see that guy last night on *Top Of The Pops* with his arm round the guitarist?'

By Friday lunchtime they had slipped out of school and were in the record shops buying an album called *The Rise And Fall Of Ziggy Stardust And The Spiders From Mars*. Bowie-mania was underway. And it *was* mania, that special moment in pop culture when the whole of the teenage nation fully embraces someone. For that to happen, several key elements have to be in place, including: great music of a singular type, a look, a style and a philosophy. Bowie had all corners covered. After years of toil, finally he had been able to put together a sound and vision that drove deep into the teenage heart. All rushed to him, boy and girl alike.

The rush of creativity that brought about this memorable moment had started on that American trip in early 1971. In Chicago Bowie was given a single made by a fellow Mercury artist, The Legendary Stardust Cowboy. Norman Carl Odom – the Cowboy's real name – was a psychobilly artist with a fascination for the moon.

Two weeks later at a radio station in San Jose, California, Bowie heard the name Iggy Pop for the very first time. This appellation struck Bowie so much that he took the name Iggy, added a Z to the front of it, and then coupled it with Stardust. Ziggy Stardust. Bowie was completely gripped. By creating an alter ego he suddenly recognised how he would be able to coalesce all his seemingly clashing interests – clothes, mime, theatre and rock 'n' roll – into one brilliant whole.

It was Bowie's eureka moment. At once, uncertainty fell away and the world opened up. He now embarked upon a run of creativity that would sustain itself throughout the whole of the seventies. His golden years were about to unfurl and they were signalled by the strength of the songs he had written for *Hunky Dory*.

Yet despite that album's studied brilliance, Ziggy remained foremost in his thoughts. Four months before the release of *Hunky Dory*, Bowie announced his intention to create *The Ziggy Stardust Stage Show*. His idea was to create a musical accompanied by an album of the same name – a rock opera in the tradition of The Who's *Tommy*. It would tell the story of an alien arriving on an earth with only five years of existence left. Bowie would play Ziggy every night and when he tired of him he would pass the job on to another actor/singer.

'The idea of a larger-than-life style rock figure struck me around the end of 1970. Rock seemed to have wandered into some kind of denim hell. In fact, all was rather dull attitudinising with none of the burning ideals of the sixties.' DB, 2002

Three months later, in November 1971, Bowie entered Trident Studios with Ken Scott as his co-producer, just as he had done for *Hunky Dory*. Before the sessions began he told Scott, 'You are not going to like this album. It's much more like Iggy Pop.' That it wasn't would remain one of Bowie's greatest artistic regrets.

Bowie had met Pop in New York in September of that year, Andy Warhol also. Warhol was distant and disdainful yet Bowie remained in awe of him. Bowie had been singing his praises since 1967. Warhol was bizarre, creative and successful. He was living proof that you could create a vision and gain the world. His presence alone gave Bowie great confidence.

Iggy Pop was a full-on powerhouse of adrenalin. He was in the middle of a three-day run without sleep and overwhelmed Bowie with his unrestrained energy, at one point smashing a beer bottle over his own head. Bowie determined to match his raw power on his next album.

He had already laid down a demo for a new song, which would not make the final cut – 'Shadow Man' – and now started work on three others, which he would not finish: 'It's Gonna Rain Again', 'Only One Paper Left' and 'Looking For A Friend'.

That he was overflowing with ideas is confirmed by the fact that he then went on to record no fewer than thirteen originals, ten of which would make it onto the *Ziggy* album, and two cover versions: Ron Davies's 'It Ain't Easy' and Jacques Brel's 'Amsterdam'. Between 8 and 15 November 1971, he and his band recorded 'Star' (originally titled 'Rock 'n' Roll Star'), 'Hang On To Yourself', 'Moonage Daydream', 'Five Years', 'Soul Love', 'Lady Stardust' (originally titled 'He Was Alright – The Band Was All Together'), 'Sweet Head', 'Velvet Goldmine' (originally titled 'He's A Goldmine'). ('Sweet Head' and 'Velvet Goldmine' would not make the final cut.) They also had time for a reworking of 'The Supermen' for the 1972 compilation album *Revelations: A Musical Anthology For Glastonbury Fayre*.

By the time of *Hunky Dory*'s release in December 1971, *Ziggy Stardust* was already two-thirds complete. The rest of the album – 'Suffragette City', 'Rock 'n' Roll Suicide' and 'Starman' – was finished in just two more short sessions between 12 and 18 January and on 4 February 1972.

In considering the Ziggy Stardust phenomenon, one has to consider Bowie's clothes. In pop culture, intellectual concepts are easier to sell when they look cool, as Bowie himself later acknowledged:

*'Both [*2001: A Space Odyssey *and* A Clockwork Orange*] provoked one major theme: there was no linear line in the lives that we lead. We were not evolving, merely surviving. Moreover, the clothes were fab:* 2001 *with its Courrèges-like leisure suits and* Clockwork*'s droogs, dressed to kill.'* DB, 2002

In America Bowie had worn dresses by Mr Fish. At Haddon Hall he had experimented with hair and make-up. He was certainly one of the first acts to apply make-up and experiment with costume but, to his great frustration, he had been beaten to the commercial punch by his friend and rival Marc Bolan.

Bolan had worn glitter on TV in 1970 (not long after Bowie's brightly costumed Roundhouse appearance) and was now being hailed as the pioneer of glam rock. Bowie could only stand by in envy as he issued a series of catchy singles and swept to success.

Space-age outfits like this one – light years away from the 'denim hell' of early-seventies rock – were at the heart of Ziggy's 'wild mutation' into a rock 'n' roll star.

Bowie knew that to trump the competition at his own game you had to take things ten steps further. Jagger wore a dress at a gig; Bowie wore a dress on an album cover. Bolan changed his appearance a little with glitter and make-up; Bowie became a different person. With a little help from designer Freddie Burretti.

Bowie and Burretti met in 1971 at a London nightclub on Kensington High Street called Sombrero. The two got on well, sharing a love of clothes and their possibilities. Soon, Burretti was a regular visitor at Haddon Hall. Bowie, in fact, formed a band called Arnold Corns with Burretti as the front man. A single featuring two songs that would later appear on *Ziggy*, 'Moonage Daydream' and 'Hang On To Yourself', was released in May 1971 but, like most Bowie releases to that point, it failed to connect meaningfully with the charts. It was Burretti – as well as Bowie's wife Angie – to whom he turned to help shape

Left: Moonage daydream – Mick Rock captures a momentary pause for reflection during perhaps the most exciting year of Bowie's life. Haddon Hall, 1972.

Above: Freddie Burretti with Suzi Fussey, the Beckenham hairdresser who helped to look after Ziggy's shock of orange hair and who would go on to marry Mick Ronson.

Ziggy's look. Their starting point was the Stanley Kubrick film, *A Clockwork Orange*. Bowie already owed the director for inspiring 'Space Oddity'. He would fall further into his debt when, in January 1972, he saw the costumes that *Clockwork*'s main characters – Malcolm McDowell and his gang of droogs – were decked out in.

'The jumpsuits in that movie I thought were just wonderful. I liked the malicious kind of malevolent viscous quality of those four guys, although the aspects of the violence did not turn me on particularly. So I wanted to put another spin on that.'

DB, 1993

The original Ziggy costumes were all one-piece suits in garish colours on top of which Bowie added inventive touches such as wrestling boots.

His timing was spot on. Glam rock was now safely anchored in the mainstream and Bowie – always far too clever to hook himself up to any one movement – had the alternative. He presented himself as an outsider, an alien in society. By doing so he tapped straight into teenage life and its own sense of alienation. The new generation finally had a saviour. He was aggressive, never camp. He threatened authority just as much in his glitter and make-up as anyone else did. By simply playing on notions of sexuality, he sent parents into a frenzy. On 22 January *Melody Maker* ran a two-page interview with David in which he told them, 'I am gay and always have been, even when I was David Jones.'

It was a master move. The next day all the papers were on the line wanting to talk to him. Yet all of this meant nothing without one crucial element – the music. And *Ziggy Stardust* is an album that brilliantly satisfies the criterion of great pop: strange enough to annoy the old, striking enough to seduce the young.

The young do not run into the arms of an uncaring individual. They run to a performer because they think he has something they need, answers usually. Many people talk of Bowie the person, at that point in time, as stand-offish, aloof, and this was probably true. Separation is the hallmark of all great artists. Yet through music the essence of a character is revealed. There's no hiding place in great music and that is what the listener responds to.

Bowie's vocals on *Ziggy* are warm and enticing, conspiratorial. On 'Starman' he sings as if letting us in on a great secret. On 'It Ain't Easy' he is otherworldly, yet strangely sexual. On 'Five Years' you can hear the tinge of distress behind the apocalyptic scenes he describes.

A lot of the songs carry sing-along choruses – 'Five Years', 'Lady Stardust' and 'Starman' – and sing-alongs are always warm-hearted invitations to the listener. Bowie might have been presenting a cold, alien persona but his music wasn't. Far from it. Furthermore, the *sound* of Ziggy is important. Crucially, no other album sounded like this in 1972; the sound was as alien as Ziggy.

'You're not alone!' he screams on 'Rock 'n' Roll Suicide', 'Gimme your hands'. Which is precisely what teenage Britain did. From now on, the young had a new idol. Bowie, meanwhile, had Ziggy Stardust to contend with.

Memorabilia begins to accrue, including, opposite, this scrawled-on photo by Mick Rock, taken at Oxford Town Hall, 17 June 1972, which appeared as a full-page ad in British music weekly *Melody Maker*.

WHO WAS ZIGGY STARDUST?

Bowie named Ziggy's prime inspiration as Vince Taylor, a leather- and make-up-clad British rocker who wrote the classic 'Brand New Cadillac'. After early success, Taylor's mind succumbed to drink and drugs until he became convinced he was the son of God.

The name was inspired by Iggy Pop and Bowie's label-mate The Legendary Stardust Cowboy, real name Norman Carl Odom – the extent of whose success was a Billboard top 200 single, 'Paralysed'. Bowie later covered his 'I Took A Trip On A Gemini Spaceship' on *Heathen* in 2002.

THE ART OF THE COVER

Brian Ward's iconic cover photograph was taken outside his studio on Heddon Street, London. Shot in black and white on a cold, wet night, it was hand-coloured by Terry Pastor, co-owner of the Main Artery design company with Bowie's childhood friend George Underwood. Much has been read into it, not least the 'K. West' sign above Bowie's head – is this 'quest'... or perhaps 'Key West'? Certainly, it's a clever piece of work. The typography puts David Bowie and Ziggy Stardust on equal terms, blurring the lines between art and artist. And Ziggy – bright-haired and blue-jumpsuited – is in stark contrast to his dreary surroundings; an alien from a new world, standing in the old.

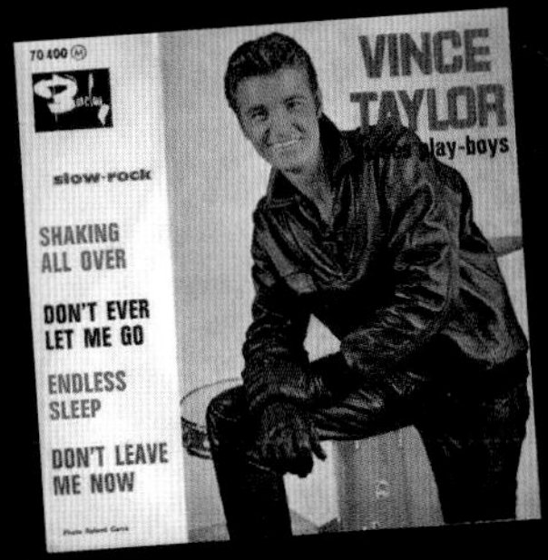

'He [The Legendary Stardust Cowboy] was a kind of Wild Man Fischer character; he was on guitar and he had a one-legged trumpet player, and in his biography he said, "Mah only regret is that mah father never lived to see me become a success." I just liked the Stardust bit because it was so silly.' DB, 1990

ALADDIN SANE 1973

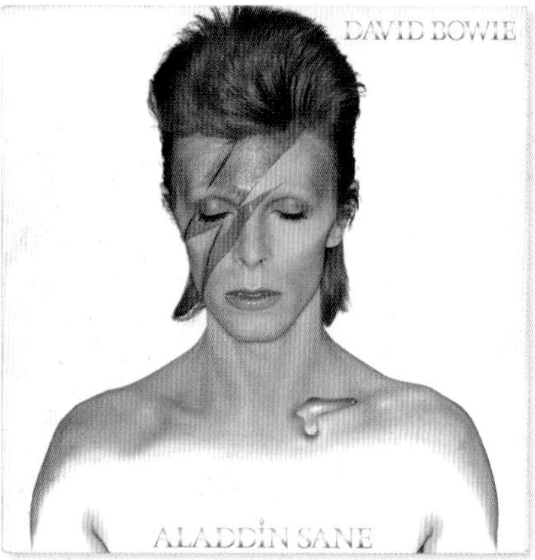

‘AT TIMES I FEEL THAT I MAY BE A VERY COLD AND UNEMOTIONAL PERSON AND AT TIMES I WISH THAT I WASN’T SO MENTALLY VULNERABLE. I DO TEND TO STAND ON THE OUTSIDE SOMETIMES.’

DAVID BOWIE, 1973

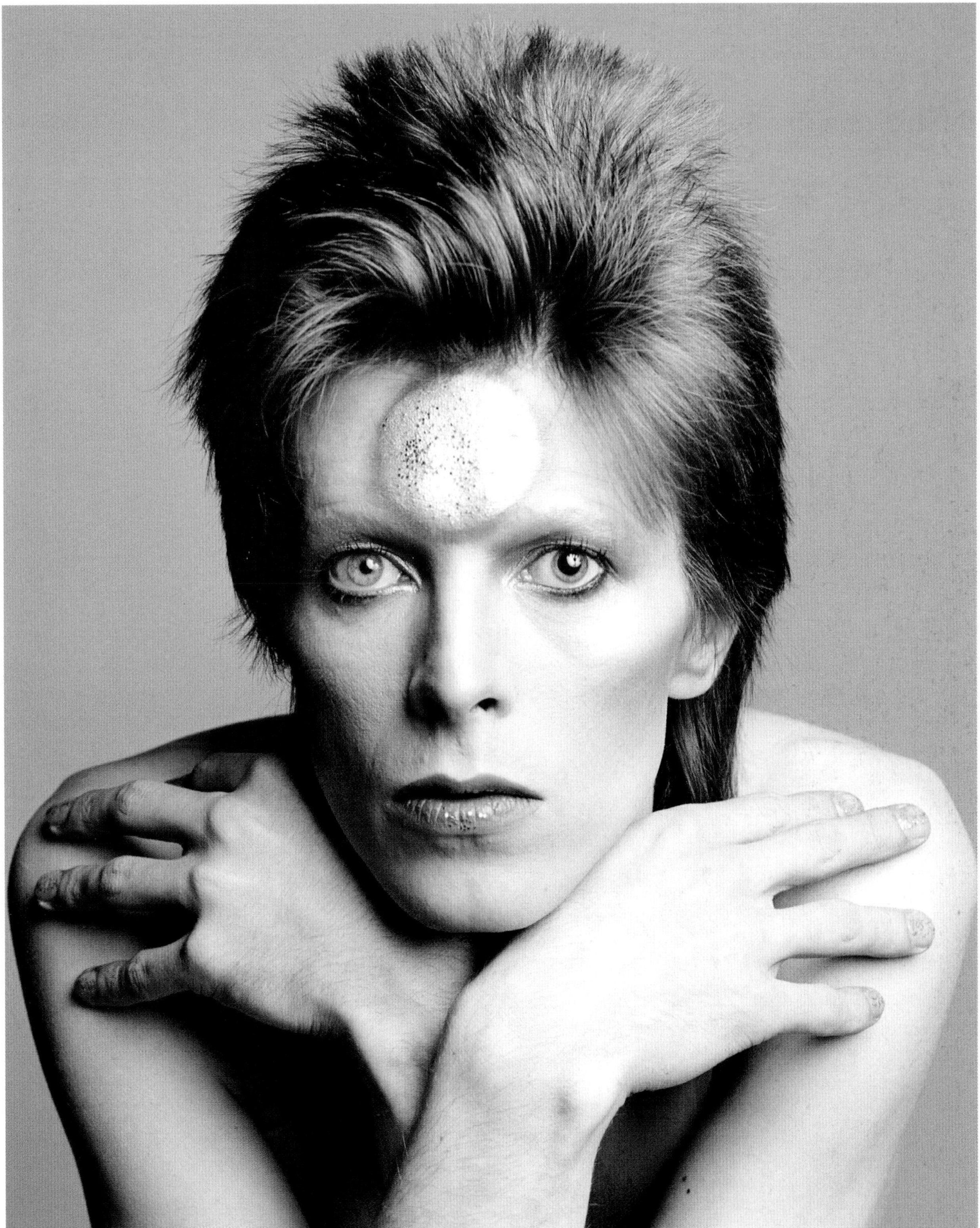

2/1258 17
2/1258 18
2/1258 19
2/1258 13
2/1258 16
2/1258 15
2/1258 14

1972

22 September

First US performance, at the Music Hall in Cleveland, Ohio

November

UK release of 'The Jean Genie'/'Ziggy Stardust' (2)

US release of 'The Jean Genie'/'Hang On To Yourself' (71)

8 November

Transformer by Lou Reed released

1973

January

US re-release of 'Space Oddity'/ 'The Man Who Sold The World' (15)

7 February

Raw Power by Iggy and the Stooges released

April

UK release of 'Drive-In Saturday'/'Round And Round' (3)

13 April

Release of *Aladdin Sane* (UK 1, US 17)

Previous page: Portrait session with Masayoshi Sukita at RCA Studios, New York, February 1973. Sukita has produced some of the most memorable photographs of Bowie throughout his career, including the front cover of *"Heroes"*.

Opposite: Contact sheet from Brian Duffy's iconic photoshoot for the *Aladdin Sane* cover, January 1973.

Everything he did had to have style, had to have impact. Control of his image was of paramount importance and never more so than on the cover of *Aladdin Sane*, the album that was released at the height of his extraordinary fame – in April 1973.

Fifteen months before Aladdin's birth, Bowie had slipped into a patterned jumpsuit, rolled up the trouser legs, pulled on some wrestling boots and posed in a gloomy London street for the cover of his breakthrough album. But one element of his look remained untouched by the alien weirdness: his hair. It was mod-like, reminiscent of the style he had worn in the mid-sixties. In March 1972, that all changed with the public appearance of the now-famous Ziggy cut.

The hairdresser responsible for tending the cut was one Suzi Fussey. Fussey worked for Evelyn Paget's Ladies' Hairdressers in Beckenham. Bowie liked her and she was soon employed on his tours. Mick Ronson liked her too, and later the two would marry.

Two months later, his hair had grown out considerably and he had started dyeing it a light red. The idea for the dye had come from Freddie Burretti's best friend, Daniella Parmar, whom Bowie recalls as 'the first girl I had seen with peroxide white hair with cartoon images cut and dyed into the back'. The colour came from pictures of Marie Helvin modelling the latest fashions from Japanese designer Kansai Yamamoto – whose designs Bowie later wore on the Ziggy tour. 'It was a men's traditional kabuki wig,' recalled Helvin in 2009. Fussey smothered Bowie's hair in red, pushed it up, cut it round the sides.

'I thought it was the most dynamic colour, so we tried to get mine as near as possible. I remember the colour was Schwarzkopf red. I got it to stand up with lots of blow-drying and this dreadful, early lacquer.' DB, 1993

It was an important, provocative move by the twenty-five-year-old singer. In 1973, hair was still the prime battleground between young and old. Authority figures – teachers, police – associated long or unruly hair with drugs and bad behaviour. Which was great news, if you were young and wanted an easy way to rebel. Thousands now poured into local hairdressers to ask for a 'Bowie' when before they'd asked for a 'Rod' (Stewart).

Bowie wore the cut on all his tours and all his photo sessions. It complemented his clothing perfectly. The band had similar cuts and, despite initial jitters, wore similarly glittery clothing.

'Woody Woodmansey was saying, "I'm not bloody wearing that!" There were certainly comments, a lot of nerves. But when they realised what it did for the birds. The girls were going crazy for them, because they looked like nobody else. So within a couple of days it was, "I'm going to wear the red ones tonight!"' DB, 2002

In January 1973, Bowie, still sporting his red Ziggy hair, visited photographer Brian Duffy's north London studio. Duffy was part of a trio of London photographers – with David Bailey and Terence Donovan – who had helped revolutionise fashion photography. He had met Tony Defries, Bowie's manager, in the sixties.

According to Duffy – who died in 2010 – the iconic lightning flash on Bowie's face was inspired by Elvis Presley, although it was also a motif used by Kansai Yamamoto in the same 1971 collection that inspired Ziggy's hair. Duffy nevertheless recalled: 'Bowie was interested in the Elvis ring which had the letters TCB [taking care of business] as well as a lightning flash. I drew on his face the design and used lipstick to fill in the rest.'

Using make-up artist Pierre La Roche, the design that appeared so prominently on Bowie's face was actually lifted from a National Panasonic rice cooker in the photographer's studio. It brilliantly evoked a mind split in two; significantly, his half-brother Terry had recently been diagnosed with schizophrenia.

To add to the provocation, on the inside of the gatefold sleeve Bowie posed as if naked, with his lower body concealed with graduated air-brushed silver by the artist Philip Castle. Bowie also listed, against the song titles, the location of where each had been written. Of the ten songs, six had been written on tour in America; hence the record came to be referred to as the 'Ziggy goes to America' album.

It was the first album Bowie had written as a major rock star, the world hanging on his every word, watching his every move. Under the twin pressures of expectation and a tour of America, he created a set of songs whose sound and substance perfectly echoed the manic excess he was then experiencing.

Although the 1972 US tour was badly planned, and some dates did not sell out, there was enough excitement generated for the entourage to swell to a massive forty-six people; Tony Defries, ever the hustler, managed to get RCA Records to pick up the bill for each and every one of them. Craziness ensued.

Bowie wrote compellingly about the experience. 'Watch That Man' was penned after a party held in his honour in a New York hotel. 'Panic In Detroit' was inspired by Iggy Pop's tales of late-sixties Detroit radicals such as John Sinclair, manager of the legendary MC5. 'Cracked Actor' was a sleazy snapshot of Hollywood: a fading star making it with a young call girl, Bowie describing the kind of loveless sex that was presumably happening all around him.

'Drive-In Saturday' was written on a train between Los Angeles and Chicago. So pleased was Bowie with the song's chorus and surreal call of images – name-checking Twiggy and Jagger, a big influence on him at the time – that he premiered it at a show in Miami on acoustic guitar, unfurling a story of a society that had forgotten how to make love and needed reminding via old porn movies.

'Time' was written in New Orleans and memorably contained references not only to a man masturbating and falling to the floor, but also to Billy Murcia, the New York Dolls drummer who had just died from an overdose; it also had a last verse that was pure poetry.

'I thought it was about time, and I wrote very heavily about time, and the way I felt about time – at times – and I played it back after we recorded it and, my God, it was a gay song! And I'd no intention of writing anything at all gay… I thought well, that's the strangest…' DB, 1973

'Crouching in his overalls': from the Sukita session at RCA. The outfit is by the renowned Japanese designer Kansai Yamamoto, whom Bowie had met through Sukita and who went on to design many of Ziggy's most flamboyant costumes.

Opposite: A notoriously reluctant air traveller, Bowie accepts assistance from a station porter at the Gare du Nord in Paris ('or maybe hell'?).

Below, left: Portrait by Brian Ward, 1972.

Below, right: Signing autographs during the British leg of the 1973 Aladdin Sane tour.

Undoubtedly the most lucrative song Bowie wrote in this period was 'The Jean Genie'. On the tour bus his entourage had taken to singing, 'We're going bus, bus, bus-ing,' in the style of The Yardbirds' 1965 cover of Bo Diddley's 'I'm A Man'. While staying at the apartment of Cyrinda Foxe – a strikingly sexy girl he had met at the party that inspired 'Watch That Man' – Bowie took the riff and set to it a lyric about Iggy Pop. (Cyrinda is 'Lorraine', the Chicago moll in the song.) The title was a pun on Jean Genet, a French writer and artist whom Bowie admired. He recorded the song in early October in New York and released it in the UK in late November. It stayed in the charts for thirteen weeks and gave him his biggest UK hit to date.

Of the other four songs, two were written in London. One was a re-visiting of 'The Prettiest Star' and the other was the album's stand-out track, 'Lady Grinning Soul'. Meanwhile the title track – yet another album highlight – was written on the boat coming back to England. (Bowie, then, famously never flew; instead he created the persona of a slightly eccentric yet classy international traveller.) The remaining song was a cover of The Rolling Stones' 'Let's Spend The Night Together'.

Joining the band for *Aladdin Sane* was Mike Garson, a jazz pianist recommended to Bowie by the musician and composer Annette Peacock. Garson's piano was allowed to roam free on tracks such as 'Aladdin Sane' and 'Lady Grinning Soul', adding a whole new dimension to Bowie's music. The extensive use of backing vocals added extra colour and hinted at the sound he would create on *Young Americans* two years later.

At the time Bowie reflected on this subtle shift in direction in an interview with *Music Scene*.

'Some of the music on my new album Aladdin Sane *is very strange. I've allowed myself to become influenced by some of the best avant-garde jazz musicians like Mike Garson the jazz pianist, and Keith Tippett. Mike is, in fact, playing with The Spiders and the music that's evolving basically takes a theme and then myself and the different musicians improvise using that theme as a nucleus to hold it together. This is the problem: the glam rock thing has everything going right for me, but still leaves me with very little direction.'* DB, 1973

Just like the tour it was written on, *Aladdin Sane* has a messy feel to it. It contains a jumble of images set to melodies hewn in light and dark with little hint of grey. Yet, despite the pressure he was under, Bowie was still able to conjure a high-quality collection of songs, some of which remain highlights of his career. And the public agreed with him. Advance orders of 100,000 copies were lodged with RCA Records and Bowie returned home from the US to reveal that the album's title was a pun alluding to his fear of madness, a fear stemming from the all-too-real troubles of his half-brother Terry. For sure, mania is written all over the record, but it was nothing compared to the mania happening in teenage bedrooms the world over.

Opposite: On stage in Santa Monica, October 1972, in an outfit partly borrowed from Cyrinda Foxe, the eye-catching inspiration for Lorraine in 'Watch That Man'.

Above: After one more album, Bowie and Ronson would be moving in different directions – on and off stage.

PIN UPS 1973

'I'M NOT AT ALL INTO GLORIFYING ROCK 'N' ROLL... AT THE TIME IT SEEMED TO BE MY CANVAS. IT REALLY IS AS BASIC AS THAT: IT'S JUST AN ARTIST'S MATERIALS.'

DAVID BOWIE, 1973

1973

June

US release of 'Time'/'The Prettiest Star' (DNC)
UK release of 'Life On Mars?'/
'The Man Who Sold The World' (3)

August

US release of 'Let's Spend The Night Together'/
'Lady Grinning Soul' (DNC)

3 July

Final performance by Ziggy Stardust and The Spiders From Mars, at Hammersmith Odeon
(filmed by DA Pennebaker and released in 1983)

September

UK re-release of 'The Laughing Gnome'/
'The Gospel According To Tony Day' (6)

October

UK release of 'Sorrow'/'Amsterdam' (3)

19 October

Release of *Pin Ups* (UK 1, US 23)

NEW MUSICAL EXPRESS
BOWIE QUITS
ZAPPA FOR WEMBLEY page 2
Ally festival album
CAROLE KING RUSH
'That's it.' page 3

Previous page: It was to be the first time a man had featured on the front cover of *Vogue* magazine. The concept and photo session were by Justin de Villeneuve, who had planned to create a special Twiggy/Bowie image for the magazine. However, when Bowie saw the result he decided that the image would instead make the perfect cover for *Pin Ups*. *Vogue* were naturally none too pleased and didn't speak to De Villeneuve for years to come.

Opposite: In this Mick Rock photoshoot for the back cover of *Pin Ups*, an album with its roots in the sixties, Bowie wields the instrument he played in his first band, The Konrads.

Above: 'Not only is it the last show of the tour, but it's the last show that we'll ever do' – Bowie's announcement shocked his fans… and some of his band members.

Success is the dream that deceives when turned to reality. In 1973 RCA Records came to David Bowie and told him he owed them an album. Bowie baulked at their request. He had been touring non-stop for two years, written and recorded *Aladdin Sane* while doing so, and now he was tired, frazzled. Plus, it wasn't as if he wasn't making his company money, a fact RCA acknowledged in their latest Bowie advert.

'Unbelievable but a fact – David Bowie takes five places in the Top Fifty album charts for ten whole weeks – a music achievement unique in our time.'

But still they wanted more. His salvation came in the guise of Bryan Ferry. News leaked out that the Roxy Music vocalist was planning a solo album of covers. Bowie seized on the idea. It was perfect. Such a project would allow him to fulfil his contract without having to call upon his depleted creativity. At the same time, he was considering losing his famous backing band, The Spiders From Mars. This he decided would be the perfect way to stage their last hurrah, go out in a blaze of glory.

'I knew the band The Spiders From Mars was over. It was a last farewell to them in a way.' DB, 1974

Ziggy Stardust had given Bowie unprecedented success, success he had dreamt of all his life. However, he was beginning to feel trapped.

'The Aladdin Sane *album was Ziggy's viewpoint about, "Oh, God, I actually have made it and it's really crazy and I'm not sure what to make of this…". The album was full of self-doubt. It was half still posing – as Ziggy Stardust – but at the back of it saying, "I don't know if I wouldn't be happier back at home."'*
DB, 1976

So, musically at least, he went home. The songs he chose to cover were all culled from the period 1964 to 1967, the time of London's transition from mod to flower power. 'Each one meant something to me at the time. It's my London of the time.' Bowie's London was either Soho or south London. As a teenager he'd come to town to witness gigs at the Scene and the Marquee. He also ventured out of town, to Eel Pie Island in Twickenham and the Ricky Tick in Windsor. Many of the songs he chose (some in conjunction with vocalist Scott Richardson) were by well-known, widely influential bands including The Who, The Yardbirds, Pink Floyd, The Pretty Things, The Kinks and The Easybeats.

What is interesting about *Pin Ups* is not the songs he covers but the ones he does not. There is no soul music or blues, for instance, yet Bowie was a big fan of both – it was the staple diet of the sixties musician. He'd left The Konrads due to their refusal to cover Marvin Gaye's 'Can I Get A Witness'.

Some explain this absence by the fact that he was already thinking ahead to the soul music of *Young Americans* two years later. Maybe, but it doesn't explain the lack of blues material, the likes of which he was playing with The King Bees and The Manish Boys.

Back then Bowie was often photographed in mod attire, as dictated by his then-manager Ralph Horton. Horton had been influenced by Brian Epstein's success in getting the unruly and scruffy Beatles into suits and was pursuing a similar policy with his client. Bowie applauded the feminisation of male fashion that modernism brought about – allowing young men to leave behind their father's suits and jump into brightly coloured shirts and trousers – but he would never have called himself a mod, for that was to define oneself and David Bowie was far too mercurial to put on a stylistic straitjacket. His sense of self was always far too large to hitch to one cause, one look. One of Bowie's great achievements in the pop arena has been to introduce the idea of constant visual change as a vital element of artistic excellence.

While recording *Pin Ups* he spoke to Charles Shaar Murray for the *NME* and redefined the concept of mod in his own image.

'I knew that being a mod meant that I had to wear clothes that no one else was wearing. The reason there were mods is because there were rock 'n' roll stars.' DB, 1973

In fact, many around Beckenham in the early sixties remember him wearing what they termed 'weird clothes', one girl squirming in embarrassment every time Bowie spotted her on a train and came and sat next to her.

Bowie's interest in fashion deepened at this point in life, 1964 being the year he became a professional musician and, more importantly, a front man. As lead vocalist it was crucial he look the part. Which explains why, having seen George Underwood wearing a pair of high-length suede boots, he briefly adopted a Robin Hood look, wearing the same boots, a jerkin and thick, curly hair.

All the bands he covered on *Pin Ups* had exerted an effect on his look and stagecraft. The Pretty Things wore their hair long, their clothes scruffy, creating an intimidating presence that Bowie absorbed. The Who's auto-destructive, guitar-smashing antics thrilled him. Syd Barrett's strange but beguiling compositions for Pink Floyd and Ray Davies's beautifully constructed vignettes of London life and its characters for The Kinks proved to be of vital importance to his development as a writer.

Some singers he did not cover also played their part – in different ways. Rod Stewart, for example, intrigued Bowie with the revelation that he wore women's underwear because it was comfortable and could not be seen through the trousers.

The album was recorded near Paris, at the Château d'Hérouville. T. Rex had made *The Slider* there the year before, and Elton John and Pink Floyd had also used the facilities. Following Ziggy's 'retirement' at London's Hammersmith Odeon on 3 July, Aynsley Dunbar replaced Mick Woodmansey on drums and Bowie wanted to work with former Cream bassist Jack Bruce. Bruce was unavailable so Bowie once again called in Trevor Bolder who, aware of his second-choice status, recorded his parts and quickly left.

Despite the potential tensions, the musicians gelled together extremely well. *Pin Ups* sounds like a garage band at full throttle. The guitars are loud, the rhythm section is tight and the vocals veer from cockney to playful, soulful and expressive. It's the rock 'n' roll sound of *Aladdin Sane* notched up another digit on the volume control.

Hard at work at the Château d'Hérouville with Mick Ronson on this covers album, the impetus for which was initially more contractual than artistic.

8
1
3
L
R
16
2
4

Surprisingly, for the most part Bowie approaches the songs with religious deference, sticking to their original formats. Only on The Who's 'I Can't Explain' does he really deviate from the blueprint, slowing it down, turning the riff into a drone and filling his vocal with yearning and confusion.

On Pink Floyd's 'See Emily Play' he cheekily adds strange, varispeed backing vocals that are uniquely 'Bowie' and provide the listener with a real clue as to the birthplace of a crucial element of his sound.

The album was recorded quickly – tours lay ahead – but proved a success none the less. It entered the charts at twenty-one, rose to number one and stayed on the charts for twenty-one weeks. David's lovely and moving version of The McCoys' 'Sorrow' also gave him a top-three single. It was proof that, for the moment at least, everything he touched turned to gold.

Previous page (main image): In full cry during recording of *The 1980 Floor Show* at the Marquee, October 1973. The show was broadcast a month later as an episode of NBC's *Midnight Special*.

Top: Meeting fans in Los Angeles, 1973. Although the red, white and blue check suit may suggest homesickness, a year later Bowie was to move to America and never returned to live in the UK.

Bottom, left: The cartoon-strip cover of *Images 1966–1967*, a compilation of early material re-released in 1973 to take advantage of Bowie-mania.

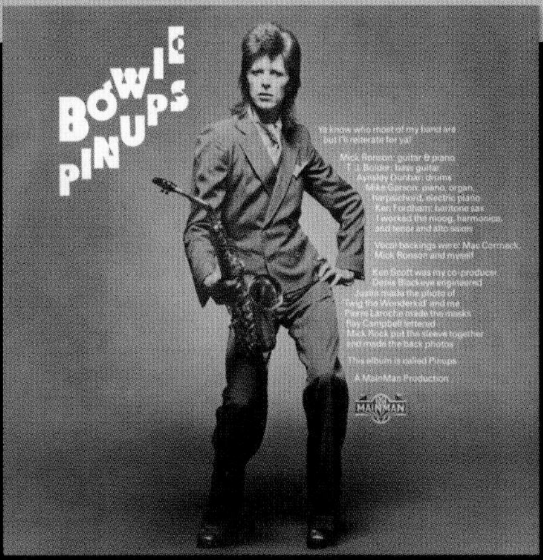

THE ART OF THE COVER

In 1973 photographer Justin de Villeneuve – real name Nigel Davies – was dating the iconic English model Twiggy (name-checked on 'Drive-In Saturday'). While she had appeared on the cover of *Vogue* many times, no man ever had and De Villeneuve convinced editor Bea Miller that Bowie should be the first.

On arrival at the shoot, Twiggy's tan clashed sharply with Bowie's white skin so make-up artist Pierre La Roche created 'masks', turning Twiggy's face the same colour as Bowie's chest, and vice versa.

The portrait suggests two souls subsumed by their images. Twiggy engages the camera, her fate, with a resigned lifelessness; Bowie wears a look of barely contained desperation.

Bowie immediately saw the photograph's cover potential. In 1999, De Villeneuve recalled: 'I asked David, "How many albums do you sell?" He said, "About a million, hopefully." *Vogue* would sell about 80,000 copies in the UK. I owned the picture, so I let him have it… I knew that I had made the right decision giving David the photograph when months later I was driving through Los Angeles and I saw a 60ft billboard of the album cover on Sunset Boulevard.'

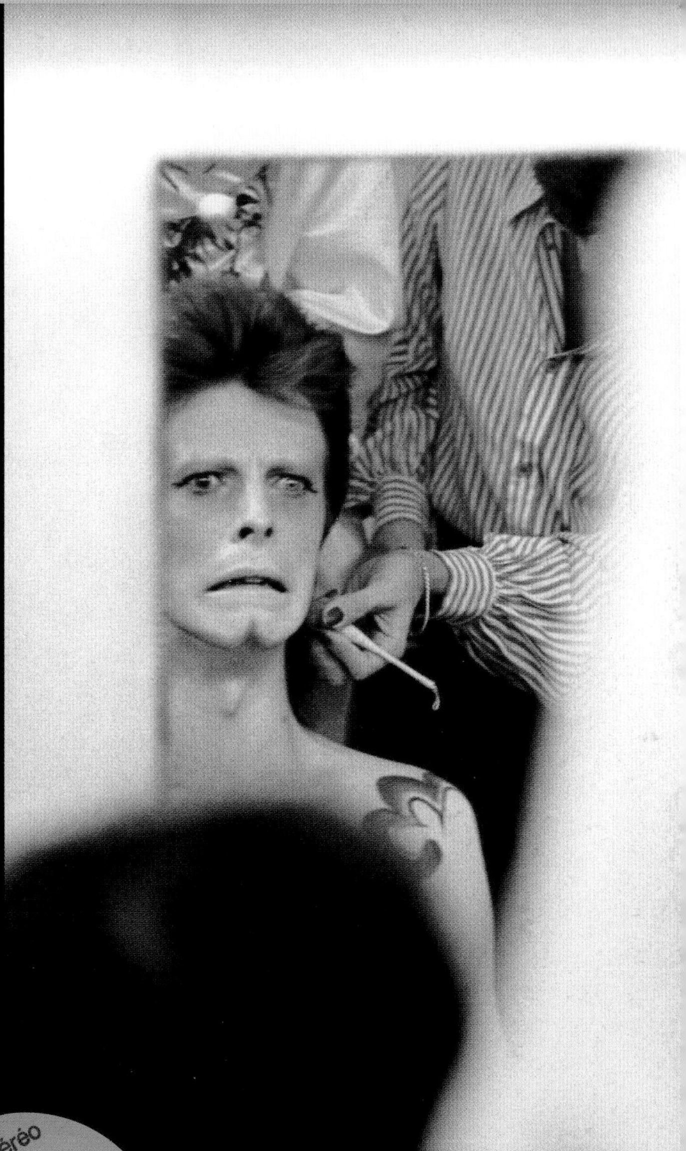

Above: The back-cover photo selected from Mick Rock's shoot.

Right: Far from being angry with his make-up artist, Bowie is actually mimicking a kabuki performer.

DIAMOND DOGS 1974

> 'A MUSICAL PARODY BASED ON THE MASS DEATH OF TENS OF THOUSANDS OF PEOPLE.'

DAVID BOWIE, 1974

1973

November

US release of 'Sorrow'/'Amsterdam' (DNC)

16 November

The 1980 Floor Show (recorded at the Marquee in October) is screened in the US by NBC

1974

February

UK release of 'Rebel Rebel'/'Queen Bitch' (5)

April

UK release of 'Rock 'n' Roll Suicide'/'Quicksand' (22)

Moves to New York

May

US release of 'Rebel Rebel'/'Lady Grinning Soul' (64)

31 May

Release of *Diamond Dogs* (UK 1, US 5)

Previous page: Wondering if we see things his way – a quizzical glance in this Terry O'Neill photoshoot for *Diamond Dogs*.

Opposite: Performing 'Rebel Rebel' on Dutch music show *Top Pop*, 13 February 1974.

In 1970 Mick Ronson and Mick 'Woody' Woodmansey find themselves crammed into a taxi, surrounded by equipment and heading for Birmingham. Their employer, Mr David Bowie, is, to their great annoyance, travelling stress free in a Rover. This is not the only source of their discontent. Since hooking up with Bowie their wages have been paid only sporadically.

As they approach Birmingham, they suddenly instruct the driver to bypass the city and head instead for Hull, their home town. Bowie is left to do the gig on his own. Although Ronson and Woodmansey are brought back into the fold nine months later, it is a slight that Bowie will never forget. And thus the seeds for the recording of *Diamond Dogs* are sown.

In January 1973 the boys in the band are on tour and up in arms again. They have discovered that new recruit, pianist Mike Garson, is receiving £300 a week more than they are. To offset this financial imbalance, Ronson, Woodmansey and bass player Trevor Bolder come up with a plan. They reason that they are now as well known as the singer they back. Wasn't it time they cashed in, got themselves a slice of the action? CBS Records have already been in contact offering big money for a Spiders From Mars album, sans Bowie.

Tony Defries, Bowie's manager, gets wind of the situation, and tells them to wait; he is sure he can talk RCA into making them an offer that will significantly trump the CBS deal. The boys leave the matter with him. Bad move.

Defries is quietly furious with the band members and intends to send them off course. First he takes Ronson aside and offers him a solo deal with RCA, a deal that will not include his band mates. He then turns on Woodmansey and Bolder, telling them, during the Japanese leg of the tour, that the members of the road crew are more important than they are. Meanwhile, Bowie, who is unaware of what is happening, has told Ronson that he intends to retire at the end of the tour. Woodmansey and Bolder are kept in the dark.

On Tuesday 3 July 1973, the band play the Hammersmith Odeon. The director D.A. Pennebaker (previously responsible for *Don't Look Back*, the famous Dylan documentary)

is present to film the gig. Mick Jagger and Rod Stewart are in the audience, as is Ringo Starr. Towards the end of the gig, Jeff Beck appears and plays on 'The Jean Genie' and 'Round And Round'. And then it happens. Bowie steps up to the microphone and announces, 'Not only is it the last show of the tour, but it's the last show that we'll ever do.'

Woodmansey and Bolder are in shock. This is the first they have heard of it. Bowie has rendered them unemployed onstage in front of thousands. They later discover that everyone else on the tour knew this was the final show. It was ruthless, thoughtless and simultaneously groundbreaking. No solo artist had ever retired on stage before. It was yet more fuel to Bowie's inferno of publicity.

Interest in him rose instantly, especially in America. Bowie would cash in on it a year later. In the interim he planned to prove that he did not need the team that had accompanied him to the top. He would show the world that he could do without them, and his producer.

For his next album, Bowie decides to assume all production duties, as well as playing lead guitar, saxophone and percussion. He brings back Aynsley Dunbar on drums, Herbie Flowers on bass and Mike Garson on keyboards.

His first idea had been to create a musical adaptation of George Orwell's dystopian novel *1984*. But Orwell's estate refused him permission so, necessarily, *Diamond Dogs* metamorphosed into a somewhat different creature. Bowie had long been fascinated with apocalyptic visions, societal breakdown, the illusion of mass happiness, and governmental control of the people. Ever since reading the Frank Edwards book *Strange People* as a youngster, he had also been intrigued by malformed characters, those whose impairments cast them to the edges of society. He now sought to tackle these images on record.

The decade he was commanding chimed with these artistic impulses. The seventies was a time of economic uncertainty, fuel shortages and recession. Crises loomed around every corner; the general public bubbled with violence, be it on town high streets or in football grounds.

Above: Lost in the music at the Tower Theater, Philadelphia, July 1974. To balance the cover's typography, this photo was reproduced the wrong way round on the front of *David Live*, which was recorded during a six-night run in the city.

Opposite: Tuning up before his appearance on *Top Pop* (see also previous page). Bowie was already in the Netherlands at the time finishing recording of *Diamond Dogs*.

Bowie painted a world where the cities were dying and the young were running amok. In a way, it was a prophetic vision of punk.

'They were all little Johnny Rottens and Sid Viciouses really. And, in my mind, there was no means of transport, so they were all rolling around on these roller-skates with huge wheels on them, and they squeaked because they hadn't been oiled properly. So there were these gangs of squeaking, roller-skating, vicious hoods, with Bowie knives and furs on, and they were all skinny because they hadn't eaten enough, and they all had funny-coloured hair.' DB, 1993

The sound was abrasive, Stones-influenced in part, but in keeping with the kind of punch that bands such as The Stooges were delivering (Bowie had co-produced their *Raw Power* album). Moreover, Bowie's ambitions were, as ever, far-reaching. From the track 'Sweet Thing' through to 'Rebel Rebel', Bowie created a piece of music that's consistently compelling, complex and creative.

It is a remarkable piece of work. Bowie's repeated refrain that music is simply a means he uses to achieve other ends is dramatically refuted by the startling moods and changes he oversees on *Diamond Dogs*. It contains moves only a great songwriter can make. This remarkable collection of music ends with 'Rebel Rebel', his next big hit single, an astute account of the havoc he had wreaked on the parents of his fans. 'You've got your mother in a whirl, she's not sure if you're a boy or a girl...' summed up the Bowie era brilliantly. He later called the object of his song 'a juvenile success'.

It is pertinent to note two other songs: '1984' with its wah-wah guitars instantly brings to mind Isaac Hayes' huge hit single 'Shaft' and suggests the direction Bowie will take a year later. The album's closer, the remarkable 'Chant Of The Ever Circling Skeletal Family', hints at the experimental direction he will take three years later.

Diamond Dogs was well received upon its release, hitting the number one spot in the UK and number five in the US. Yet its strength is that it is an album that has taken time to settle. On first hearing, many dismissed it. Not hard to see why. Not much of the music carries the immediacy of *Ziggy* or *Aladdin*. However, Bowie had wrought something deeper, music that revealed and rewarded in equal measure, music he had wrapped in a sound so foreboding that it suggested the end of glamour itself.

It was also the last time for many years that David Bowie would concern himself with 'rock' music in its traditional sense. *Ziggy Stardust*, *Aladdin Sane* and *Diamond Dogs* helped him conquer the world. Now he would use that success and turn himself into the most interesting and thrilling artist on the planet.

THE ART OF THE COVER

The strikingly iconic cover for *Diamond Dogs* was painted by Belgian artist Guy Peellaert – also responsible for The Rolling Stones' *It's Only Rock 'n' Roll* and the best-selling book *Rock Dreams* with Nik Cohn.

Early in his career Peellaert worked as a set designer at the Crazy Horse, the legendary Parisian nightclub which Bowie visited with friend Geoff MacCormack and Ronnie Wood in 1974. Later, Bowie admitted to appropriating the dotted lighting effect of his 1978 Stage tour from the Crazy Horse.

Peellaert's illustration showed the dog's genitalia but, after an initial run of covers was printed, RCA ordered an airbrushed castration. The original covers are now among the most collectible in the world.

Peellaert used as reference photographs by Terry O'Neill, one of which was used in the album's promotion. The book at Bowie's feet (right) is a novel entitled *The Immortal* by Walter Ross. It appeared in several editions, one of which (although not the one in Peellaert's painting) had a cover designed by Andy Warhol.

In 2000, Guy Peellaert designed the cover of *Bowie At The Beeb*. He died in 2008.

Angie and two-year-old Zowie accompanied Bowie to Holland for the final *Diamond Dogs* sessions. While there, Zowie joined his father for a press conference (opposite) and the family found time for a portrait session (left).

YOUNG AMERICANS 1975

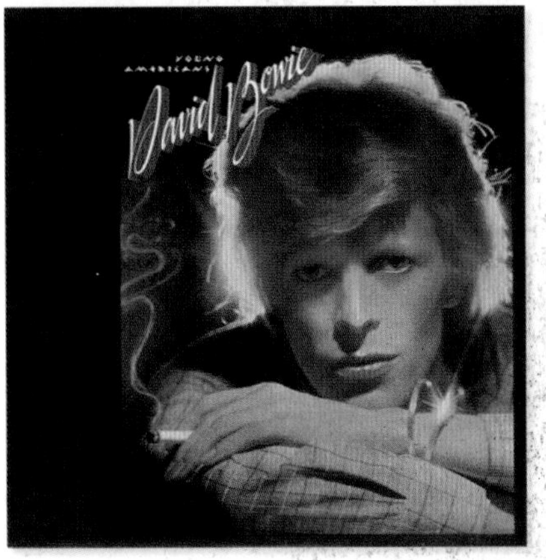

‘PEOPLE REALLY
NEEDED ROCK ’N’ ROLL...
BUT IT’S JUST BECOME
ONE MORE WHIRLING
DEITY, GOING ROUND THAT
NEVER-DECREASING CIRCLE.’

DAVID BOWIE, 1975

1974

June

Release of 'Diamond Dogs'/'Holy Holy' (UK 21, US DNC)

14 June

Diamond Dogs tour opens at the Forum, Montreal

20 July

Diamond Dogs tour closes at Madison Square Garden, New York

September

UK release of 'Knock On Wood (live)'/
'Panic In Detroit' (10)

US release of 'Rock 'n' Roll With Me (live)'/
'Panic In Detroit' (DNC)

2 September

Philly Dogs tour opens at the Universal Amphitheater, Los Angeles

29 October

Release of *David Live* (UK 2, US 8)

1 December

Philly Dogs tour closes at the Omni, Atlanta

1975

January

Ending of Bowie's management by Tony Defries
and MainMan to be replaced by Michael Lippman

26 January

Cracked Actor documentary broadcast on BBC television

February

UK release of 'Young Americans'/'Suffragette City' (18)

US release of 'Young Americans'/'Knock On Wood (live)' (28)

7 March

Release of *Young Americans* (UK 2, US 9)

Previous page and opposite: 'Never no turning back' – the young American gets used to a new life in a new country.

In 1975 David Bowie makes an announcement: 'Rock 'n' roll is just a toothless old woman.' And he might have a point. The Beatles are finished; the Stones have been hijacked by Keith's addictions and Mick's avarice; Led Zeppelin are running out of steam; The Faces have split up and all the glam rock bands are finished. There are some bands still creating vital sounds – Dr Feelgood, Thin Lizzy, Graham Parker – but not enough for the period to qualify as a golden age.

Maybe the last great rock album made by anyone was *Diamond Dogs* and so what is the creator of that work up to? David Bowie is making a soul album in Philadelphia.

The signs were already there. Bowie arrived in America in April 1974 to prepare for a huge tour promoting *Diamond Dogs*. While there he spent a lot of time in New York, travelling up to Harlem and watching concerts by The Temptations and Marvin Gaye. He loved the anonymity such shows offered him.

'That was one of the great things about this trip, I could go to any black place in America and not be recognised. And that was really fantastic. The only time, really, we got any kind of recognition on a large scale was at the Jackson 5 concert because there was a younger audience. But at most of the R&B shows, they're married couples, not kids, so it was marvellous for me to be able to go out and rave and yell. I went to the Apollo a lot, saw dozens of people.' DB, 1974

Bowie's boyhood friend and backing vocalist Geoff MacCormack was a long-standing soul fan: 'Arriving at the Apollo… was a special occasion for me,' as 'this was where the hardest-working man in show business – AKA James Brown – had recorded his live albums.'

But according to Geoff, the Bowie entourage wasn't, perhaps, as low-key as the singer himself suggests.

'I remember clearly the first time Tony [Mascia] drove us to the Apollo Theater in Harlem. The drive itself was pretty scary. Emerging from the bright lights and elegant streets of Manhattan into the drab of Harlem was, for a couple of south London boys, a bit of a shock. Travelling by limousine only

enhanced our paranoia for on every dimly lit street corner groups of bored, forlorn-looking dudes seemed to stare at us with malicious intent. Although in retrospect we were probably being wimps and they probably couldn't have given a shit about us and our ostentatious show of wealth, I still wouldn't have wanted to test the theory by rolling down the window and shouting: "What choo looking at?"'

Geoff MacCormack, 2007

In his hotel room Bowie switched on to R&B radio stations and, like John Lennon, was knocked sideways by the Ann Peebles single 'I Can't Stand The Rain'. He started talking about taking Lulu down to Memphis and cutting something similar. He announced that from now on he wanted his band to sound funky. Bowie was about to embark on a radical musical journey.

His life for the last three years had been crazy – wild, decadent, amazing and turbulent – but musically it had become predictable. The urge to recast himself in a new persona was setting in. Trouble was, Bowie could not follow his instincts. He had a six-month US tour to complete and there was no way he could back out of that. Financially, it would ruin him.

The show itself was huge. Choreographed by Toni Basil and complete with theatrical special effects, the high-budget stage production started with Bowie singing 'Space Oddity' while seated in a chair hoisted high above the audience. Its finale broke all the rules by offering no encores.

The tour's first leg finished at the end of July and Bowie headed straight into the Sigma Sound Studios in Philadelphia – the same studios used by the red-hot writing and production team of Kenny Gamble and Leon Huff responsible for such successful acts as The O'Jays, Billy Paul and Harold Melvin and The Bluenotes.

He already had a double LP in the can – *David Live*. MainMan wanted it out quickly in the hope it would boost

Opposite: 'Went to the Apollo…' – for his next album, Bowie rejected the 'toothless old woman', as he described rock 'n' roll, and took a walk on the soul side.

Left: Sharing a cigarette and an embrace with one of his most famous fans, Elizabeth Taylor, in Beverly Hills, 1975.

ticket sales for the rest of the tour. It was like 1971 again: Bowie moving between two projects, loving one and wanting to get the other out of the way as soon as possible.

On entering Sigma, Bowie's intention was to record with the rhythm section from the band MFSB, whose single 'TSOP (The Sound Of Philadelphia)' had topped the charts in March 1974 and heralded a new 'disco' sound. But confusion over arrangements meant that he could use only the band's conga player, Larry Washington.

Bowie brought in guitarist Carlos Alomar, bass player Willie Weeks, drummer Andy Newmark and saxophonist David Sanborn. All were established names in the world of soul and funk. Mike Garson remained on keyboards, as did Bowie's old friend Geoff MacCormack on backing vocals, more than ably assisted by new additions Ava Cherry – then David's latest lover – and a young Luther Vandross. Tony Visconti engineered the sessions assisted by Sigma's Carl Paruolo.

Bowie explained the concepts behind some of the tracks to an Australian journalist in 1975. The interview, during which, with hindsight, it's probably fair to say Bowie wasn't entirely coherent, was originally for *Rock Australia Magazine*. It was later reprinted in the UK's *NME*, and caused controversy for Bowie's apparent call for a new Hitler. Starting with 'Young Americans' he said:

'It's about a newly wed couple who don't know if they really like each other. Well, they do but they don't know if they do or don't. It's a bit of a predicament. The next track, 'Win', was a "get up off your backside" sort of song really – a mild, precautionary sort of morality song. It was written about an impression left on me by people who don't work very hard, or do anything much, or think very hard – like don't blame me 'cause I'm in the habit of working hard. You know, it's easy – all you got to do is win. 'Right' is putting a positive drone over. People forget what the sound of man's instinct is – it's a drone, a mantra. And people say: "Why are so many things popular that just drone on and on?" But that's the point really. It reaches a particular vibration, not necessarily a musical level. And that's what 'Right' is… and 'Somebody Up There Likes Me' is a "watch out mate, Hitler's on his way back". It's your rock 'n' roll sociological bit.'

DB, 1975

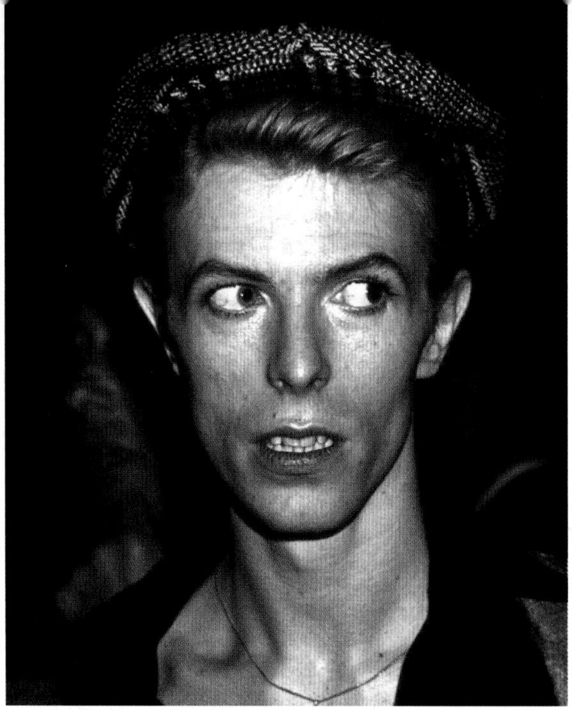

Bowie returned to the tour in September but couldn't help himself in the face of his new enthusiasm. By October he had put the Diamond Dogs name to sleep and turned the jaunt into the Philly Dogs tour, bringing in funk drummer Dennis Davis and bass player Emir Kassan as well as Carlos Alomar and Ava Cherry.

With Tony Visconti and the band he returned to Philadelphia in November to finish what they'd started in August. Then, in January 1975, Visconti – who was back in London mixing the album – was amazed to receive a phone call from New York. It was Bowie telling him he had recorded two more songs, one of which he'd written with Carlos Alomar and a certain John Lennon.

Bowie and Lennon met in a New York nightclub. They spent hours discussing the nature of fame, how both had desired it so much and, now that they had it, how it was nothing like they'd imagined. It was a subject close to Bowie's heart then. He had just discovered that his finances weren't quite as tidy as he'd imagined. What followed was a bitter break with Tony Defries and the MainMan management company.

After their meeting, Bowie headed into the studio and recorded a version of Lennon's 'Across The Universe'. Tony Visconti recalled, 'He later played the track to Lennon, who thought it was cool, then David asked him if he would like to write and record a new song together. This led to the making of 'Fame'. David apologised for not including me. There wasn't time left to send for me, because of the release-date constraints. For me, it would have been the most wonderful experience of my recording career. Oh well.'

The song sat on a great riff by Carlos Alomar, and got its title from Lennon.

'God, that session was fast. That was an evening's work! While John and Carlos Alomar were sketching out the guitar stuff in the studio, I was starting to work out the lyric in the control room. I was so excited about John, and he loved working with my band because they were playing old soul tracks and Stax things. John was so up, had so much energy; it must have been so exciting to always be around him.' DB, 1983

It was a fantastic-sounding record that would lead directly to the making of Bowie's next album. 'Fame' was funky futurism and no less a legend than the Godfather Of Funk himself, James Brown, borrowed the riff for his own song 'Hot'. Some compliment. It was also, according to Bowie, a 'nasty little song' whose cynical lyrics had been aimed in part at MainMan.

Bowie's appropriation of soul and funk music allowed him the chance to bury all the characters he had played on stage and on record, to forget about and find success beyond rock 'n' roll. *Young Americans* set him free, but more importantly it pointed him in yet another intriguing artistic direction.

While Bowie was making the album, ten or so devoted fans would often wait for him outside the studio in Philadelphia. After the second set of sessions was finished, he invited them in to listen to a playback. No one was really sure what to make of this new sound until one fan shouted: 'Play it again!' Then everybody, including Bowie, got up and danced through the night.

Previous page: Bowie's enthusiasm for the sounds of Philadelphia led to such a change in his live sound and line-up that the autumn leg of the Diamond Dogs tour became known as the Philly Dogs tour.

Opposite: At the 1975 Grammys, where he presented the award for 'Best R&B Performance by a Female Artist' to Aretha Franklin. With John Lennon and Yoko Ono (top); Art Garfunkel, Paul Simon and Roberta Flack join the photocall (bottom, left).

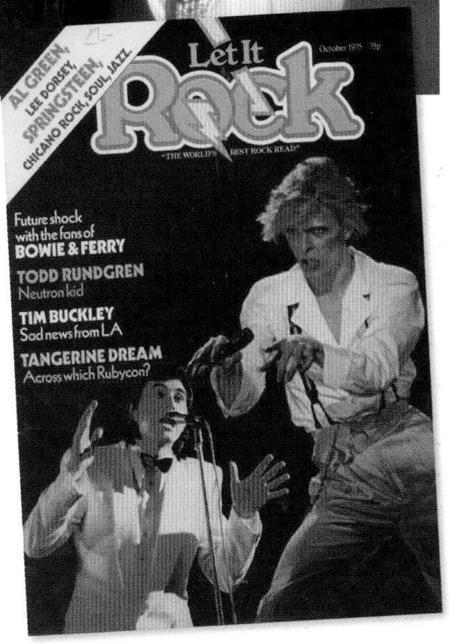
Let It Rock
October 1975 35p
"THE WORLD'S BEST ROCK READ"
AL GREEN, LEE DORSEY, SPRINGSTEEN, CHICANO ROCK, SOUL, JAZZ.
Future shock with the fans of BOWIE & FERRY
TODD RUNDGREN
Neutron kid
TIM BUCKLEY
Sad news from LA
TANGERINE DREAM
Across which Rubycon?

STATION TO STATION 1976

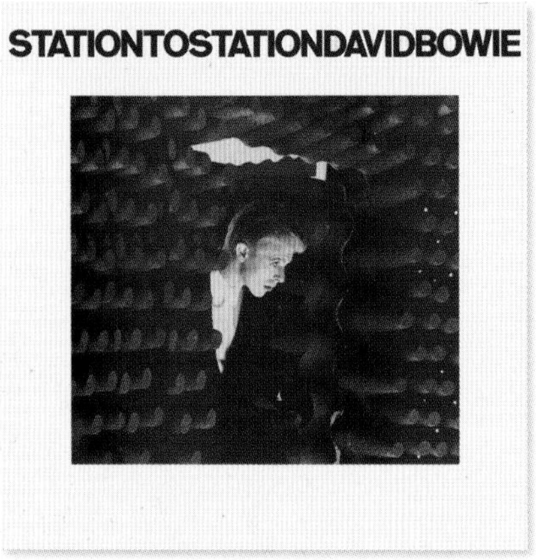

‘I WAS IN ANOTHER WORLD BY THAT TIME. A COMPLETELY DIFFERENT PLANET. I HONESTLY HAVE NO IDEA WHAT I THOUGHT BETWEEN 1975 AND 1977.’

DAVID BOWIE, 1993

1975
June
US release of 'Fame'/'Right' (1)
July
UK release of 'Fame'/'Right' (17)
September
UK re-release of 'Space Oddity'/'Changes'/'Velvet Goldmine' (1)
November
Release of 'Golden Years'/'Can You Hear Me' (UK 8, US 10)
16 November
Performs on ABC's *Soul Train*

1976
January
Dismisses manager Michael Lippman
23 January
Release of *Station To Station* (UK 5, US 3)

Previous page: Photo session arranged to promote the announcement of Bowie's role in *The Man Who Fell To Earth*, 1975.

Opposite: 'From *kether* to *malkuth*' – the kabbalistic diagram scrawled on the wall in this Steve Schapiro photo for *Station To Station* reflects Bowie's increasing mid-seventies interest in occult symbolism.

Cocaine: drug of choice for the seventies rock star. Bowie watched the *Young Americans* project increase his American success ten-fold. 'Fame' became his first number one US single and the album went top ten. Serious sales figures and, with them, serious money to burn.

Bowie moved to Los Angeles in 1975 and holed up in a mansion. Touring was over, so was his management contract. Life darkened. Along with the powder there came a deepening interest in the occult. Reports have Bowie spending hours drawing weird symbols, surrounded by black candles and obsessing over numerology. After a fantastic show the following year, he tells a reporter:

'The numbers were a bit tough for us tonight. We were a four and the audience was a four. That can sometimes mean resistance. In LA we'll be a five, in the realm of the magician – and the audience will be a six, meaning comfortable, agreeable. That should really be something.' DB, 1976

Yet, as lurid as the tales of excess, debauchery and degradation may be, and as frazzled by heavy cocaine use as he reportedly was, this fact remains: Bowie was about to create a masterpiece.

Station To Station is an album of desperation and grandeur, of spiritual discovery. It is as coherent a piece of art as any record he has released before or since, sculpted in amazing sounds, biting guitars and percussion that seem to take up the entire room. And, for a man supposedly heavily addicted to cocaine, his vocals are magisterial. Here, Bowie's sense of timing – of when to change up or down, when to colour or when to simply ride the music – is impeccable.

Guitarist Carlos Alomar recalled in 2006, 'Man, there was so much experimentation on that album, it was unbelievable! I do remember Earl Slick's inability to understand how long we wanted him to sustain notes on 'Station To Station'. We messed with different time signatures, tones, recording techniques – you name it, we did it.'

'The road of excess leads to the palace of wisdom,' William Blake wrote in his book *The Marriage Of Heaven And Hell*, and nowhere are those words more pertinent than on this record. That Bowie sometimes makes this clear and sometimes doesn't is par for the course; his best work always sways between the impulse to reveal and the impulse to conceal. On this album he is at his most oblique, and his most open.

Station To Station starts with three major Bowie compositions and the running order may have a secret significance. As a student of numerology, Bowie would have been aware of the significance of the number three. For example, earth is the third planet from the sun. Jesus rose on the third day to take his place in the Holy Trinity of the Father, Son and the Holy Ghost. The number of disciples, twelve, is a multiple of three, and some early accounts gave the number of stations of the Cross as twelve (rather than fourteen, as came to be accepted); Bowie would later insist that he had the stations of the Cross in mind when he titled the album.

Not surprising, then, that the first three songs tell his story. In song one he lays out his world of black magic, occultism and heavy cocaine use; in song two he offers himself advice; and in song three he takes that advice and finds salvation.

The album opens with the sound of a train leaving a platform, a signal of movement from dark to light, a journey beginning. The instruments enter ominously, a precise and discordant rhythm. Then, after more than three minutes, it's over to Bowie and the album's famous opening line: 'The return of the Thin White Duke throwing darts in lovers' eyes.'

It is probable that Bowie took this image from an incident concerning the occult master Aleister Crowley, whose work had long fascinated Bowie. In 1918 a young couple had been lured to a New York flat and put to death by a crowd of Crowley disciples who threw darts into their bodies until they died.

The occult references continue throughout with various allusions to oceans, circles and 'One magical movement from *kether* to *malkuth*'. The reference to the *kether* ('crown') and the *malkuth* ('kingdom') is taken from the Kabbalah, a mystical Jewish symbol system co-opted by occultists from the Middle Ages onwards.

The song switches to a second movement, far more positive, a place from which Bowie recalls a simpler time of mountains and sunbirds that took his heart. Who, he wonders, can connect him with love? Then the famous interjection: 'It's not the side effects of the cocaine,' he sings, 'I'm thinking that it must be love.'

But is it? After all, at this point in his life he is, apparently, surviving on a diet of milk and cocaine. Psychosis is upon him, despite his producer Harry Maslin's disingenuous comments to *Circus* on the album's release: 'I thought it was a little unusual for him to put that in there, but I'm glad he did. He's probably tried it, like everybody else, but I wouldn't call him a cokey or anything like that.'

It is then that he enters the third section, and posits an answer: 'The European canon is here.' Canon is defined as an ecclesiastical rule or law enacted by a council or other authority and, in the Roman Catholic Church, approved by the pope. It also refers to a body of work.

While recording *Station To Station* at the Cherokee Studios in Los Angeles, Bowie received notable visitors, including Ronnie Wood (lying down) and Bobby Womack (seated, second from left).

Part of the impetus behind the album lay with Bowie's admiration for German groups such as Kraftwerk, Neu! and Can, and their innovative use of sound and rhythm. Of course, he would take this inspiration even further with his next album.

Problem painted, 'Golden Years' follows – a single that will give Bowie yet another enormous chart hit (and is lined up to be the album's title track early in the sessions). In it, Bowie portrays himself pulling someone back into life. Although he seems to be addressing a woman, it's not hard to believe that it is himself he is singing to, the use of the feminine a mischievous play on his past image. Get up from your stupor, he tells himself, 'Look at the sky... for the nights are warm and the days are young.' He refers to his personal manifesto, 'Never look back, walk tall, act fine,' an essential code of behaviour for public figures who cannot afford to show weakness.

Trouble is, the philosophy isn't working. He knows the problem, he is lost, that's all. And stardom encourages oblivion. 'Last night they loved you, opening doors and pulling some strings.' It is then that he sings, 'I believe, oh Lord, I believe all the way.' Here then is the answer, setting us up for the third part of the trilogy, the simply stunning 'Word On A Wing'.

Again, while Bowie may often be accused of cold aloofness, here his vocal performance tells a different story.

ING
WEENEY GYM
MAIN EVENT
B FOSTER
- VS. -
BILL HARDNEY
I-FINAL EVENT
VS.
MANUEL
TORREZ

Opposite: Photographed by Geoff MacCormack while on location shooting *The Man Who Fell To Earth*, New Mexico, summer 1975.

Right: A Sonny substitute, duetting with Cher on her television show, 23 November 1975.

This is David Bowie singing of redemption through God, and it is beautiful. He later said:

'There's a song – 'Word On A Wing' – in the show and on the new album that I wrote when I felt very much at peace with the world. I had established my own environment with my own people for the first time. I wrote the whole thing as a hymn. What better way can a man give thanks for achieving something that he had dreamed of achieving, than doing it with a hymn? Yes, I do feel like I'm starting over again in a way.' DB, 1976

In three years time Bob Dylan's album *Slow Train Coming* will be widely recognised as a declaration of his belief in God. Bowie makes the same kind of statement on *Station To Station* and no one notices. Perhaps because, initially, 'Word On A Wing' sounds like a love song: someone has stepped out of his dreams and into his life – but then, 'Lord, I kneel and offer you my word on a wing/And I'm trying hard to fit among your scheme of things.'

The music is beautiful and touching, Bowie's voice tremendously moving. This is not the sound of a man addled by drugs but that of a man finding blessed peace after a nightmare.

How long this state lasted for is unclear. No one asked him much about God at this point in his life, so his thoughts on the matter remain undocumented. In an interview given shortly after the album was recorded, he is asked about a biting comment recently made by Mick Ronson. 'I've got God, who has Mick got?' he snaps back. But as his new guitarist, Earl Slick, commented, 'Who knows what he's thinking at the time?'

Theologically then, we do not have much else to go on. What we do have is three other songs on the album. 'TVC15', about a girlfriend who is swallowed up by her TV, has wonderful doo-wop backing vocals and shows Bowie's great knack for producing hit singles.

'Stay' consists of fiery funk guitars, their extreme violence offset by Bowie's tremendous vocal talents. Again, we are back in the darkened nightmare room he has been unable to leave these past few months, a place where the days fall on their knees and Bowie is forced to reach out for something to get him through. Paranoia hangs heavy: 'You can never really tell when somebody wants something you want too'.

He wants to ask for salvation, for someone to stay, but, given the dangers of his world, knows that no one will. 'This time tomorrow, I will know what to do...'.

The album finishes with a beautiful rendition of 'Wild Is The Wind'. Written in 1957 by Dimitri Tiomkin and Ned Washington, and originally sung by Johnny Mathis for the film of the same name, this song is one in which we find

Bowie realising that all life's answers lie in life itself. And that life is like the wind. All he knows is that when he touches his love he hears the sound of mandolins, and it is the sound of salvation. It is a fitting way to end a superb piece of work.

That Bowie produced anything at all, let alone a record of such emotive beauty, is remarkable considering the physical and emotional state he was in during its making. People who worked with him on the record report his incredible stamina, working from ten at night to ten in the morning, then switching studios to carry on even longer. At other times, he didn't show up at all. Or he might stay awake for five or six days at a time before stumbling into the studio to recommence work.

'At this time David was very much a nocturnal creature. Coco [Schwab] and I would try to create some kind of order by occasionally cooking at home and getting David up before noon, but one was loath to wake somebody who'd been awake for three days straight.' Geoff MacCormack, 2007

His intake of cocaine seems not to have floored him yet – he will soon be experiencing fainting fits – but rather wrung from him an album whose power touches us today just as strongly as it did on its release in January 1976.

Previous page: Port to port – on the SS *Leonardo da Vinci* about to set sail from New York for the Station to Station European tour, March 1976. One of the great advantages for Bowie of his aversion to flying was the time it gave him to read. In a 1999 interview he claimed to have packed 400 books for the filming of *The Man Who Fell To Earth*.

This page, top: Despite a serious cocaine habit during the mid-seventies, Bowie's only arrest came in March 1976, when he and Iggy Pop were detained on suspicion of marijuana possession in Rochester, New York. The case didn't make it to court.

This page, bottom: Facing the press armed with a glass of brandy, 1976.

Overleaf: 'Well, I'm not a scientist. But I know all things begin and end in eternity.' Thomas Jerome Newton scans the desert horizon.

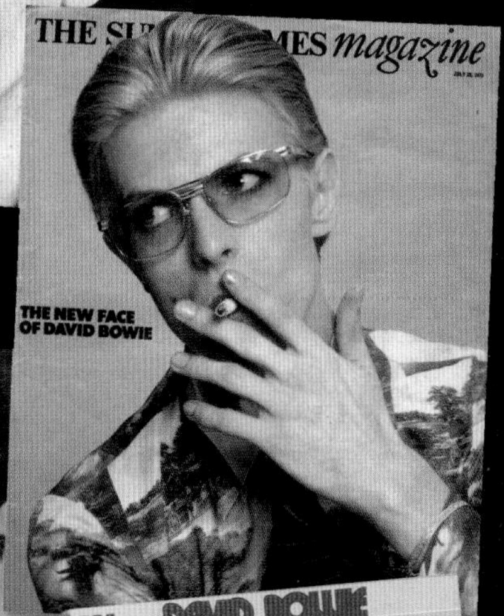

THE MAN WHO FELL TO EARTH

Prior to recording *Station To Station*, Bowie had shot his first lead role in a major film: Nic Roeg's *The Man Who Fell To Earth*.

Bowie was physically and mentally fragile. He was becoming as alienated as his on-screen character – Thomas Jerome Newton, a humanoid alien visiting earth to find water for his own drought-ridden planet. Needing money to adapt his spacecraft for the journey home, he patents inventions based on alien technology. Before he can return he succumbs to alcoholism, his true identity is revealed and he's imprisoned by the government. While he eventually escapes his physical cell, he can't escape the confines of drink and depression.

The film received mixed reviews on its release but its popularity among fans and critics alike has grown with time. Certainly, Bowie puts in a compelling performance and the whole movie is beautifully shot. If it occasionally feels cold and awkward, then possibly that is entirely appropriate given its subject matter.

'My one snapshot memory of that film is not having to act. Just being me as I was, was perfectly adequate for the role. I wasn't of this earth at that particular time.' DB, 1993

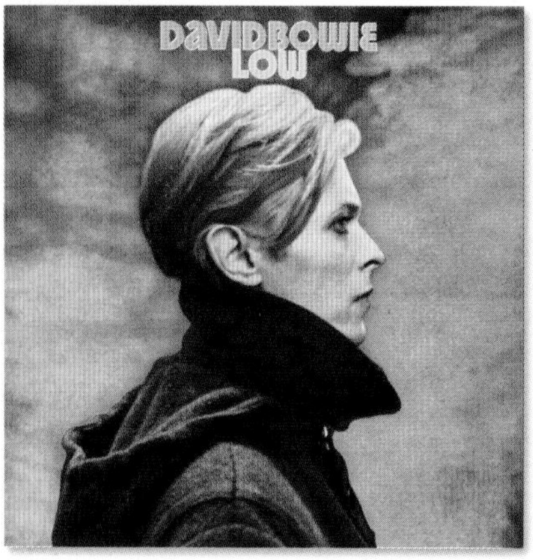

‘OVERALL, I GET A SENSE OF REAL OPTIMISM THROUGH THE VEILS OF DESPAIR FROM *LOW*. I CAN HEAR MYSELF REALLY STRUGGLING TO GET WELL.’

DAVID BOWIE, 1999

"(This book) tells one of the strangest, saddest stories
of a great comedian that there is to be told."
—Bosley Crowther, The New York Times Book Review
Rudi Blesh

1976

2 February
Station To Station tour opens at the PNE Coliseum, Vancouver

18 March
The Man Who Fell To Earth (Bowie stars as Thomas Jerome Newton)

20 March
Arrested on suspicion of marijuana possession, Rochester, New York

April
Release of 'TVC15'/'We Are The Dead' (UK 33, US 64)

2 May
A wave to photographers at Victoria Station, London, is misconstrued as a Nazi salute

18 May
Station To Station tour closes at the Pavillon, Paris

July
UK release of 'Suffragette City'/'Stay' (DNC)
US release of 'Stay'/'Word On A Wing' (DNC)

October
David moves to Berlin

1977

14 January
Release of *Low* (UK 2, US 11)

Previous page: Low profile – recreating the pose used on the album cover in this 1977 photograph by Norman Parkinson.

Opposite: Bowie's interest in Buster Keaton is particularly evident in the video for 'Be My Wife', one of the singles from *Low*, in which he wears pale make-up and mimics the silent movie star's exaggerated facial expressions.

Above: The Station To Station tour band on stage in Los Angeles, February 1976. From left to right: Carlos Alomar (guitar), David Bowie, George Murray (bass) and Stacey Heydon (guitar).

Overleaf: Like a Weimar Sinatra, the Thin White Duke commands the stage.

Fitting, really, that this next phase of Bowie's career, a time that many think of as his most creative and brilliant, should be kick-started by the man who gave him the name Ziggy in the first place. In February 1976 the Station To Station tour came to Los Angeles. Bowie had already told the press that it was a calculated attempt to make some serious money after the MainMan fiasco. 'I think I deserve it,' he told writers, 'don't you?'

For the show Bowie – always looking to do something different – screened the 1929 surrealist film *Un Chien Andalou* by Luis Buñuel and Salvador Dalí, in which an eye is sliced open with a knife; he prefaced that by playing Kraftwerk's new album, *Radio-Activity*, to the audience through the PA. The band then appeared and went straight into the title track.

Bowie took to the stage dressed in simple clothing – black trousers and waistcoat, white shirt, hair slicked back. His current fascinations included Sinatra and fascism and his dress evoked a lounge singer well versed in the starkness of German expressionism.

'He [Sinatra] is someone who is not just an actor or a singer. He transcends all those areas. He's even something of a public figure. That's what I want to be felt about me. It's the idea of seeing what you can do with the human persona, how far you can extend the ego out of the body. I think my music is never looked at as just music. You have to have one's attitude towards David Bowie in there as well. It's all very McLuhan-ish, isn't it? I'm trying to make myself the message, which is the twentieth-century form of communication.' DB, 1976

After one of the shows Bowie hooked up with Iggy Pop, the result being that Iggy was invited to travel with the band for the rest of the tour. When it ended, in Paris, Bowie proposed that he write and produce Iggy's next album. For Iggy, who had recently been forced into rehab by the courts and was still struggling with addiction, it was a chance not to be missed. For Bowie, it was a way to start work on an idea he had been mulling over – 'to experiment; to discover new forms of writing; to evolve, in fact, a new musical language.'

A new musical language. Bowie had had enough of the rock star game. It had brought him to the edge of insanity. It had engendered a frightening use of drugs that was now threatening to derail his career. In interviews he had expressed a fascination with Hitler, even suggesting that he was the first 'rock star'; the mass adulation, the manipulation of an audience through theatricality and showmanship, style over substance – the parallels aren't hard to find if you're looking for them (and it should be noted that, in 1977, Bowie went on record to assert categorically, 'I am NOT a fascist'). But still, it was time to quit the rock star game now. Time to disappear, recover and return as a brand new man, not as a character.

'I realised that I exhausted that particular environment and the effect of that environment upon my writing. I was afraid that if I continued to work in that environment I would begin repeating myself.' DB, 1977

The two men travelled out to the Château d'Hérouville, which Bowie had last visited to record *Pin Ups*. The in-house engineer and session musician (and, later, studio owner) was Laurent Thibault, the former bass player of a band called Magma whose music Bowie admired. After a couple of days there, Bowie re-booked the studio for later in the year.

Bowie then returned to his new abode in Switzerland. Los Angeles was now thousands of miles away and the singer could pursue a more peaceful life. At home, he began composing musical sketches, fragments, which he took back to France in June. There, Bowie and Iggy began work on *The Idiot*, named after the Dostoyevsky novel.

Bowie's method of recording was quite informal. He would play the drummer, Michel Santangeli, whatever rough musical sketches he had, and they would work their way through each song. Then Bowie would allow Thibault to lay bass on top.

Meanwhile, Iggy would be writing fractured lyrics, or at one point simply taking to the microphone and making up the words as he went along. Bowie was intrigued by

In Berlin, June 1977. Bowie's interest in the city had been stimulated by a meeting with one of its most famous chroniclers, novelist Christopher Isherwood.

Pop's spontaneity; he would later use the same improvisational technique himself. In August recording moved to Germany: first Munich and then Berlin.

The resulting work was hailed as one of the albums of the year; Iggy's doom-laden vocals set to a futuristic soundscape captured the mood of the decade. It certainly set Bowie up for his next album. He rushed back to the château to start work on a record of his own.

He already had some material to work with, fall-out from the aborted soundtrack to *The Man Who Fell To Earth*, which he'd begun composing after cutting *Station To Station*. However, by then he was in such a parlous state that the music he produced – with cellist and composer Paul Buckmaster (who had arranged 'Space Oddity') – was nowhere near the required standard. When he embarked on the Station To Station world tour he was, as usual, already looking to the future – as his use of Kraftwerk at his shows illustrates. And that is why his meetings with

writer Christopher Isherwood and musician Brian Eno are significant.

Isherwood was renowned for writing about thirties Berlin; one of his novels, *Goodbye To Berlin*, was the source material for *Cabaret*. Isherwood and Bowie met in Los Angeles in 1976, during the Station To Station tour; Bowie quizzed him on the city and was intrigued by what he heard. When he took up residence there he did so in a flat just ten minutes' walk from Isherwood's old house.

Bowie already knew Eno from his Roxy Music days. Since then Eno had been experimenting with a type of music that would come to be known as 'ambient'. This was an area of music ripe for Bowie to explore. He had made ten albums, but he was yet to cut an instrumental.

'I know he liked *Another Green World* a lot,' said Eno in 1999, 'and he must have realised that there were these two parallel streams of working going on in what I was doing, and when you find someone with the same problems you tend to become friendly with them. He said when he first heard *Discreet Music* he could imagine in the future that you would go into the supermarket and there would be a rack of 'Ambience' records, all in very similar covers. And – this is my addition – they would just have titles like *Sparkling* or *Nostalgic* or *Melancholy* or *Sombre*. They would all be mood titles, and so very cheap to buy you could chuck them away when you didn't want them anymore.'

When work began on *Low* at the Château d'Hérouville, Bowie and Tony Visconti reunited as co-producers (Visconti had told Bowie he had an instrument that could 'fuck with the fabric of time', the Eventide Harmonizer), and began working in their familiar way. This meant building up the songs from basic rhythms, adding the instruments and then, at the very last, adding Bowie's vocals. This allowed Bowie to use his voice much more expressively than if recorded at an earlier stage.

The music on *Low* follows its own logic. Songs seem to appear, state their case and then fade out. While many point to Kraftwerk as the album's main source of inspiration, it is a false trail. Their music works on robotic rhythms coloured by unexpected dashes of sound. What Bowie wrought here is loose and unpredictable. It carries none of the relentless rhythm that Kraftwerk thrived on. Rather *Low* is underpinned with scatter-shot drumming, funky bass lines, crying guitars, sudden time shifts.

Lyrically, the songs are brief snapshots relying on simple images, usually relating to Bowie's time in Los Angeles. 'Breaking Glass', 'Sound And Vision' and 'What In The World' all place the listener in a room where either bad things are happening or salvation is awaited. 'Always Crashing In The Same Car' is a song supposedly inspired by a drug deal gone wrong and 'Be My Wife' (title taken from Nina Simone's 'Be My Husband') finds Bowie reverting to his 'London' voice – the one that mixed Syd Barrett with Anthony Newley – to tell us that for all his success he is still an English boy at heart.

Around these songs are two instrumentals, 'Speed Of Life' and 'A New Career In A New Town'. These are short sharp shocks, often abrasive in nature. Apparently they were not planned as instrumentals, but Bowie simply could not find the appropriate words. In the free-flowing sprit of the album they were left as they were.

The remainder of the album is taken up by longer, more sombre pieces, which is hardly surprising given their subject matter.

''Warszawa' is about Warsaw and the very bleak atmosphere I got from the city.' DB, 1977

He does a disservice to the music to describe it so prosaically. In fact, at some points it seems to prefigure Ennio Morricone's scores for films such as *The Mission*. There is also a hint of the approach Walter (now Wendy) Carlos took with the music for *A Clockwork Orange*, specifically the dramatic entrance of big chords after a space of silence.

''Art Decade' is West Berlin – a city cut off from its world, art and culture, dying with no hope of retribution. 'Weeping Wall' is about the Berlin Wall – the misery of it. 'Subterraneans' is about the people who got caught in East Berlin after the separation – hence the faint jazz saxophones representing the memory of what it was.' DB, 1977

Amazingly, for such an experimental album, sales were good. Very good. The single 'Sound And Vision' went to three in the UK charts. The album went to two in the UK and eleven in the US – very impressive. Critically, there was a huge divide. Some reviewers lauded his artistic courage; others were baffled.

With expectations of a tour to accompany the album running high, Bowie of course went his own way and played keyboards for Iggy Pop to promote *The Idiot* live throughout the UK and USA. In May he made another album with Iggy, *Lust For Life*, and then in August went back into the studio to cut what many consider his greatest ever song. He was still just thirty years old.

'... a remarkable record and certainly the most interesting Bowie has ever made' ***Melody Maker*, January 1977**

Opposite: Waiting for a flight at Heathrow Airport, March 1977. Surprisingly, it's Iggy Pop who appears more uneasy.

Overleaf: Happy to concede the limelight, Bowie played keyboards on Iggy Pop's tour to promote *The Idiot*, the first of two albums he co-produced for his friend in 1976 and 1977 (the other being *Lust For Life*).

"HEROES" 1977

'I'M HAPPY NOW. CONTENT. I FEEL MORE THAN A PRODUCT ON AN ASSEMBLY LINE AND NO MORE A MEANS OF SUPPORT FOR 10,000 PERSONS WHO SEEM TO REVOLVE AROUND EVERY FART THAT I MAKE.'

DAVID BOWIE, 1977

1977

February
Release of 'Sound And Vision'/ 'A New Career In A New Town' (UK 3, US 69)

18 March
Release of *The Idiot* by Iggy Pop

March–April
Plays keyboards on Iggy Pop's Idiot tour

June
Release of 'Be My Wife'/'Speed Of Life' (DNC)

29 August
Release of *Lust For Life* by Iggy Pop

September
Release of "Heroes"/'V-2 Schneider' (UK 24, US DNC)

11 September
Sings 'Peace On Earth'/'Little Drummer Boy' duet with Bing Crosby for *Bing Crosby's Merrie Old Christmas* to be shown on ITV

14 October
Release of *"Heroes"* (UK 3, US 35)

Previous page: From the Sukita photoshoot for *"Heroes"*, April 1977.

Opposite: Portrait by Clive Arrowsmith, November 1977.

This page, bottom: 'The finest gifts we'll bring' – Bowie and Bing manage to celebrate Christmas in a TV special recorded in Elstree in September 1977.

David Bowie enters the producer's room of Studio Two in the Hansa recording studio, Berlin, and asks producer Tony Visconti if he minds leaving. He wants time alone to write lyrics to a compelling piece of music they have been working on since their arrival in July 1977. Visconti understands, and exits.

Bowie wants to write a song about two lovers set against the divisive image of the Berlin Wall. It is said that two works of art planted this idea in his ever-fertile mind. One was a short story called *A Grave For A Dolphin* by the Italian writer Alberto Denti di Pirajno; the other, a painting by the German expressionist Otto Mueller called *Lovers Between Garden Walls* (this page, top right).

As he muses on the words, Bowie looks out of the window and, to his great surprise, sees his producer kissing a jazz singer called Antonia Maass. Bowie knows Maass. He and Visconti met her at a nightclub and she has subsequently been providing backing vocals on the album they are making. Visconti is a married man and, where he and Maass stand kissing, they are hemmed in by a wall. For Bowie it is a riveting image. He later tells the *NME* (while also being discreet about Visconti's infidelity):

'There's a wall by the studio... It's about twenty or thirty metres away from the studio and the control room looks out onto it. There's a turret on top of the wall where the guards sit and during the course of lunch break every day, a boy and girl would meet out there and carry on. They were obviously having an affair. And I thought, of all the places to meet in Berlin, why pick a bench underneath a guard turret on the wall? And I – using license – presumed that they were feeling somewhat guilty about this affair and so they had imposed this restriction on themselves, thereby giving themselves an excuse for their heroic act.' DB, 1977

When Visconti appears back in the studio Bowie is ready to go, ready to lay down a vocal that will turn "Heroes" from a very good piece of music to one of the greatest songs of his entire career.

Bowie begins in an almost conversational tone, then his voice builds with the music into an epic of synthesizers, guitars and driving rhythms. The result is a grand, wonderful, triumphant song about lovers, where the shame is on the other side and love is the most powerful force of all.

Yet this title track is the only one on the album to follow something resembling a conventional path. Using the same technique that they had employed so successfully on *Low*, Bowie, Visconti and Eno joined forces once more to create an album in two distinct parts: five 'up' tracks, unsettling and brilliant, and a series of instrumentals.

If there was a sketchiness about *Low*, particularly in its lyrical content, no such complaint can be made here. Bowie writes and sings more here, the sound is fuller, the songs far more cohesive, far less elusive.

Like *Station To Station*, this album begins with a piano refrain; but unlike 'Station To Station', 'Beauty And The Beast' is a rollercoaster ride, a hectic fusion of guitars, percussion and all kinds of weird instrumentation with Bowie's vocal placed right in the centre. 'Nothing will corrupt us/Nothing will compete/Thank God heaven left us/Standing on our feet', he sings, full of hope and optimism.

Bowie's good mood was a direct result of Berlin itself where he had settled, in late 1976, in a spacious seven-room apartment. Not only had he always admired Germany, its art and its artists, but the local residents remained completely unfazed by his presence. Pop singers did not cut it in this part of the world. Bowie could walk the streets alone, undisturbed.

'Since my teenage years I had obsessed on the angst-ridden, emotional work of the expressionists, both artists and filmmakers, and Berlin had been their spiritual home. This was the nub of Die Brücke movement, Max Reinhardt, Brecht and where Metropolis *and* [The Cabinet Of Dr] Caligari *had originated. It was an art form that mirrored life not by event but by mood. This was where I felt my work was going. My attention had swung back to Europe with the release of Kraftwerk's* Autobahn *in 1974. The preponderance of electronic instruments convinced me that this was an area that I had to investigate a little further.'* DB, 2001

Bowie rented an apartment in Schöneberg, Berlin, from October 1976 to February 1978, and recorded *"Heroes"* in its entirety in the city. With Europe now his focus he also sojourned in Paris in 1977, pictured here by Christian Simonpietri.

On the album's second track, 'Joe The Lion', Bowie copied the working method he had observed Iggy Pop using on *The Idiot*; he stood in front of the microphone and, amid the cacophony of sound, sung whatever came to mind. He repeated the process, keeping the best lines each time until the song was completed. 'I thought it a very effective way of breaking normality in the lyric,' he later said of the technique.

"Heroes" follows, its majestic intro and sense of grace acting as a neat, and welcome, contrast to the turbulence before it. Bowie includes in his lyric a reference to drinking all the time. It is pertinent. Although he had started to pull himself out of the woods, Berlin had not yet solved his problem with cocaine completely. He had reduced his intake considerably but now alcohol was taking its place. Iggy Pop later revealed how the week was usually divided into two days of coke, two days of drinking and three days of sobriety visiting museums and galleries.

Certainly, Bowie was in far better shape than the previous year. On *Low* he had entered the studio still burnt by the dark days of Los Angeles and welcomed the chance to fade into the background. On *"Heroes"* his improved mood and health made for a much more rounded and confident record.

"Heroes" is followed by another memorable composition, 'Sons Of The Silent Age'. If the power of *Low* was its ability to hint at wider possibilities, 'Sons Of The Silent Age' manages to pull some of those possibilities together as Bowie closes in on his objective of creating 'a new musical language'. Once again putting on his best Newley/Barrett voice, his lyrics hark back to *Diamond Dogs*, painting a disturbing *1984*-inspired vision of the future. Amid the saxophones, the dragging rhythm and the crashing cymbals, there comes the contrasting colour of Beach Boys-style backing vocals before his own voice soars majestically over an enthralling chorus. In the hands of a lesser talent, the result would be considered simply strange, but Bowie's vocal abilities turn it into something great. Not many singers can go from 'Syd Barrett' to 'heartfelt' within a verse, that's for sure.

'Blackout' concludes the first half of the album, a song that may well have its seeds in Bowie's personal life. His marriage to Angie was now on the rocks, and would never recover. On his last visit to Berlin, he had collapsed, everyone initially believing he'd suffered a heart attack. At the military hospital he was diagnosed as simply having drunk too much. Is it too much of a stretch to believe that 'Get me to a doctor's/I've been told someone's back in town, the chips are down', refers both to his soon-to-be ex-wife and his collapse? Bowie subsequently claimed that the lyric was inspired by a power cut in New York City. Either way, 'Blackout' is weird, confrontational and dissonant.

The song that follows, 'V-2 Schneider', creates a bridge to the album's more contemplative compositions. Its languid verses and catchy chorus lead into the sombre 'Sense Of Doubt' and its haunting piano refrain and dramatic *Clockwork Orange* keyboards. Its companion piece is 'Neuköln', with a saxophone break conjuring images of Berlin's substantial Turkish community.

In between the two is 'Moss Garden'. On 'Blackout' Bowie screams 'I'm under Japanese influence'. Here he sets up a still pool of serenity amid all the discord, a tranquil musical setting using a koto, a traditional Japanese string instrument.

The album closes with 'The Secret Life Of Arabia'. The brevity of the lyrics hark back to *Low* (the phrase 'speed of life' a direct reference to the opening track of *Low*) and its up-tempo nature is a satisfying, refreshing rain after the stormy winds preceding it.

Low, *"Heroes"* and *Lodger* are commonly and collectively referred to as the Berlin trilogy, although this is a misnomer. *Low* was made in France and only mixed in Berlin; *Lodger* was recorded in Switzerland. So *"Heroes"* is the only one of the three that Bowie cut in the city. His sense of ease at having escaped the self-induced horror of Los Angeles is palpable. Certainly, the cover photo reveals him looking in better shape than he had in a long time.

'Berlin was the first time in years that I had felt a joy of life and a great feeling of release and healing. It's a city eight times bigger than Paris, remember, and so easy to "get lost" in and to "find" oneself too.' DB, 2001

A happier, healthier Bowie, having left the stresses and excesses of Los Angeles behind him. Dorchester Hotel, London, 1977.

RALEIGH

Tony Visconti, too, has fond memories of the experience, saying in 2007, '*"Heroes"* was the best of the trilogy to work on. Hansa Studio, Berlin itself and the great musicians and Eno were a magic formula. I'd go back to my hotel every evening smiling inwardly knowing that we were making a killer album. I had a sense at the time that the song "Heroes" was going to be an evergreen classic.'

He was not wrong. Incredibly, "Heroes" was not the massive hit single it should have been on its release but it has since been consistently acknowledged as one of Bowie's greatest achievements.

After completing the album, part of Bowie's promotion duties – he still was not touring – was to appear on Marc Bolan's British television show, *Marc*, where he delivered a stunning rendition of the song in front of his old pal and sparring partner from the glam rock days. Bolan looked like a man grateful to be in front of camera, while Bowie looked graceful. Looked like a hero, in fact.

'... a strange, cold, sometimes impenetrable album, but Bowie makes all these unlikely ingredients work'

***ZigZag*, October 1977**

Performing "Heroes" on Marc Bolan's TV show, *Marc*, 9 September 1977.
One week later, Bolan was killed in a car crash and the recording was broadcast posthumously on 28 September.

THE ART OF THE COVER

The cover photo for *"Heroes"* was taken by Japanese photographer Masayoshi Sukita, who first met Bowie in London in 1972, after seeing him play at the Royal Festival Hall. It was the start of a long working relationship. Principally a fashion photographer, Sukita arranged the first meeting, in 1973, between Bowie and the designer Kansai Yamamoto, who would go on to design many of Ziggy's stage costumes.

In 1977, David visited Japan with Iggy Pop while promoting *The Idiot*. Sukita photographed them at his Tokyo studio – one of Iggy's portraits appears on the cover of his 1981 album *Party*. Sukita has said Bowie's poses were completely spontaneous. The cover shot has been compared to a self-portrait by German expressionist artist Walter Gramatté, but Bowie says it was actually an allusion to another expressionist work, Erich Heckel's *Roquairol*.

Above: In the Hansa Studios in Berlin, with lead guitarist Robert Fripp (formerly of King Crimson) and Brian Eno (centre).

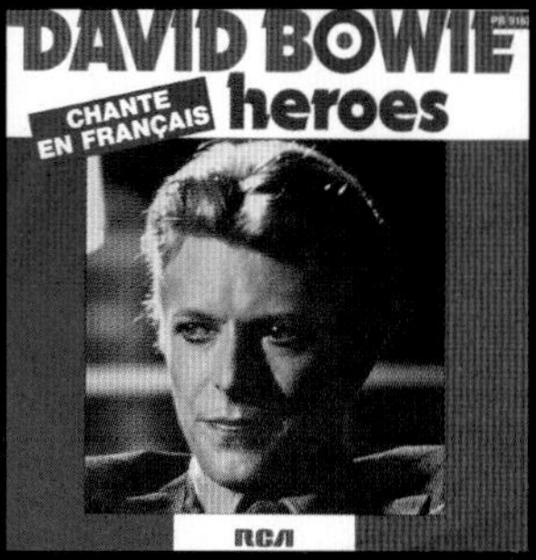

LODGER 1979

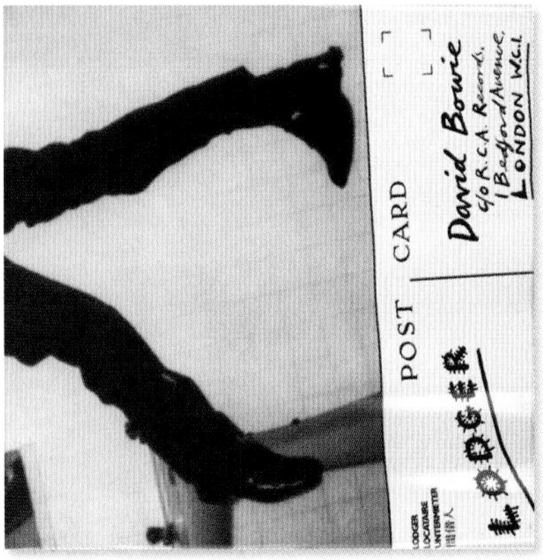

> 'I'VE OFTEN BEEN COUNTED MORE REMARKABLE FOR WHAT I'M NOT – NOT PREDICTABLE, NOT DRAB, NOT PHILISTINE, WHATEVER – THAN FOR WHAT I LIKE TO THINK I AM.'

DAVID BOWIE, 1983

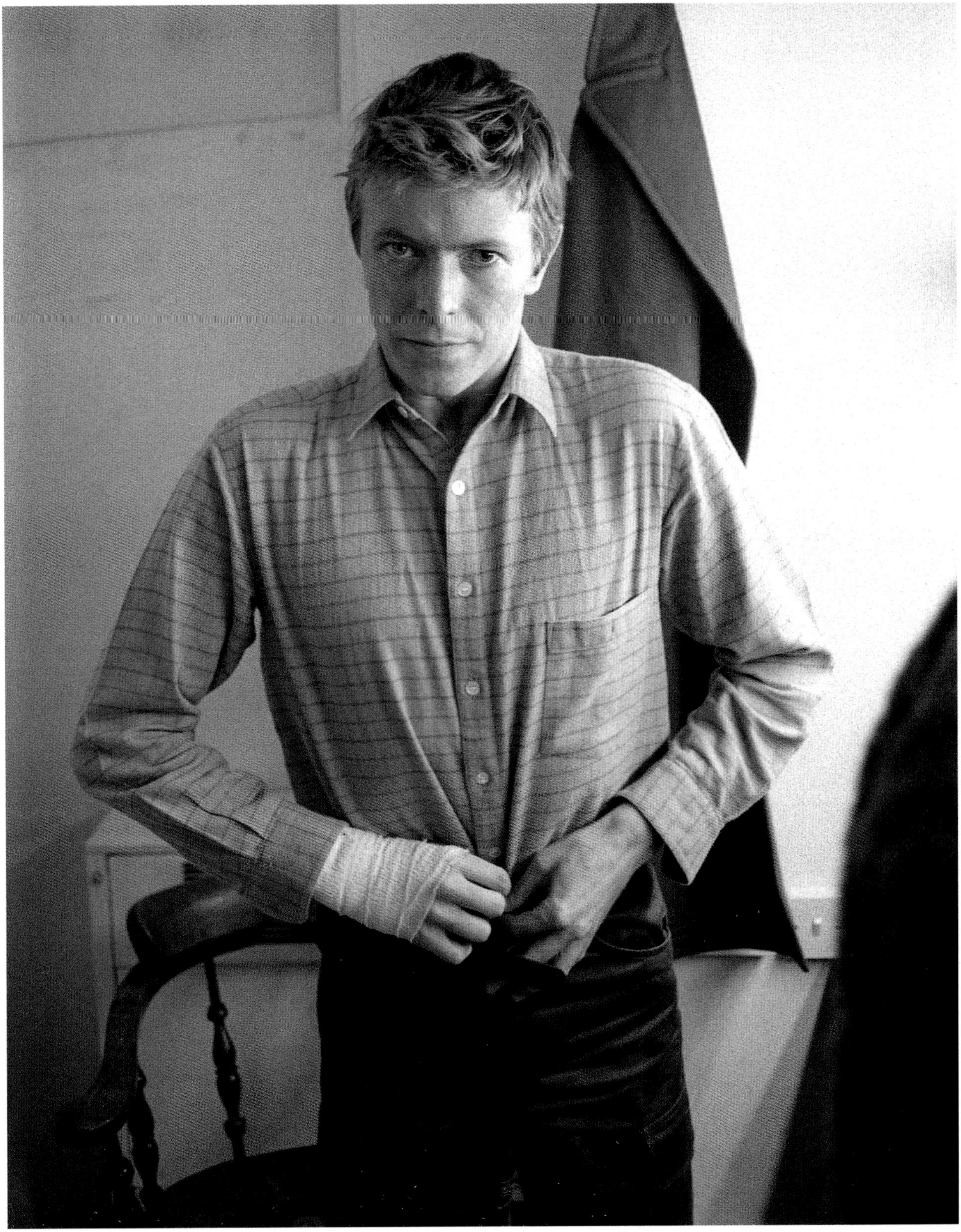

1978

January
Release of 'Beauty And The Beast'/ 'Sense Of Doubt' (UK 39, US DNC)
February
Leaves Berlin
29 March
Stage tour opens at the Sports Arena, San Diego
12 May
Release of *David Bowie Narrates Prokofiev's Peter And The Wolf*
25 September
Release of *Stage* (UK 5, US 44)
November
UK release of 'Breaking Glass'/'Art Decade'/ 'Ziggy Stardust' (54)
16 November
Just A Gigolo (Bowie stars as Paul Ambrosius von Przygodski)
12 December
Stage tour closes at the NHK Hall, Tokyo

1979

April
UK release of 'Boys Keep Swinging'/'Fantastic Voyage' (7)
18 May
Release of *Lodger* (UK 4, US 20)

Previous page: A feigned injury doesn't stop Bowie buttoning up following the *Lodger* cover shoot by Brian Duffy.

Opposite: Shortly before leaving Berlin, Bowie filmed *Just A Gigolo*, attracted by the prospect of acting with Marlene Dietrich. However, Dietrich refused to travel to Berlin, so a special set had to be created near her home in Paris, and he never met her.

In January 1978 *ZigZag* magazine asked David Bowie what he thought about his albums to date.

'Some of them I think were sketchy ideas that I didn't work on hard enough. That didn't quite cut it. It's like painting really, I mean, not every painting that you do is gonna be good but you've done them and there you are. I tend to look at albums rather like that. I admit some of the ideas didn't come off, but there's some good work in there somewhere, though. There's a logical sequence… I can just about see the year that I wrote that album, or I can say, "Yes, that describes that environment and that year very well", I think. Which is very good, sort of what I set out to do.'
DB, 1978

Which brings us to *Lodger*, the third in the so-called Berlin trilogy; although it was recorded in Switzerland, halfway through Bowie's highly successful 1978 world tour. (In fact, the 'trilogy' was held together by Bowie and Eno's collaboration rather than Berlin.)

Again, RCA were on his case, demanding another studio album. Although he thought his live album *Stage* had fulfilled the demands of his contract, RCA disagreed. They were also concerned about Bowie's new musical direction. *Low* and *"Heroes"* had sold in nowhere near the quantities that *Young Americans* and *Station To Station* had. Pressure was applied. Bowie resisted. When he entered Mountain Studios in Montreux in August 1978, during a break in his world tour, he did so again with Tony Visconti and Brian Eno. This would be the final part of the trilogy they had started back in 1976.

Artistically, the last few years of creativity had been highly beneficial for David. He would later say that of all his albums, *Low*, *"Heroes"* and *Lodger* were where his true musical DNA was.

Lodger was meant to bookend this prolific period. As it happened, it became an album that divides people and opinion; some think it a work of genius, others view it as proof of a slowing down of Bowie's creativity.

That last notion was planted when Gary Numan marched to the top of the charts with 'Are Friends Electric?' while Bowie's 'Boys Keep Swinging', the album's lead-off single,

Above: The mammoth Stage tour ran from March to December 1978, covering North America, Europe, Australia, New Zealand and Japan.

Opposite: Put on a pedestal – portrait by Snowdon in the photographer's garden, 1978.

failed to reach the top five. The cry of the town was that the pupil had usurped the master. History suggests such a proclamation may have been a little premature...

Bowie later admitted that personal issues had served to lessen his focus during the making of the album (Angie had not taken their separation well), while Visconti thought their choice of studio was poor.

Tension among the album's protagonists did not help the record, either. Bowie and Eno had not seen each other for nearly a year. Both arrived with different albums in mind and there were frequent heated discussions about what direction they should be travelling in.

'*Lodger* started off extremely promising and quite revolutionary,' Eno later recalled, 'but it didn't seem to end up that way.'

In 1975 Brian Eno and a friend had developed what they termed 'Oblique Strategies'. This was a pack of 100 small cards on which were written instructions, phrases or ideas. One would randomly pick a card and follow the edict to the letter. The idea was to unblock creativity, either by suggesting an alternative approach or occasionally lifting people out of their comfort zones. For example, one card ordered the musicians to switch instruments. Thus on 'Boys Keep Swinging' Carlos Alomar played drums, Dennis Davis moved to bass. Alomar later named it as his favourite Bowie track that he'd played on, adding, 'I can't play drums worth a shit, but it was awesome to do it.' Davis's bass part was later re-recorded by Tony Visconti. Later Visconti recalled:

'A lot more chaos was intended. Brian was doing some strange experiments like writing his eight favourite chords on a blackboard and asking the rhythm section to "play something funky". Then he would randomly point at a chord and the band had to follow. This didn't go down too well, but we were trying all sorts of different things.' Tony Visconti, 2001

It is hard to place *Lodger* within the trilogy. It carried no ambient side, as *Low* and *"Heroes"* had done. There is far less electronics, the instrumentation is far more conventional. Whereas before the emphasis was on experimentation with sound, here the emphasis was on a broader experimentation with music.

The haunting 'Yassassin', for example, sounds like a band of Turkish kids who have just heard their first ska record, backing a determined vocalist. And 'African Night Flight' (Bowie had just spent six weeks on holiday in Kenya with his son) pits Bowie's manic music-hall voice against clattering percussion, a doom-laden bass, topped off by unexpected chord changes and chanted backing vocals.

Despite all that, *Lodger* contains some great music. The album starts with the gorgeous ballad 'Fantastic Voyage', Bowie singing in that instantly warm, almost careless style of his, enticing you in. The song used the same chords as 'Boys Keep Swinging'.

Many hear 'Boys Keep Swinging' as Bowie's tongue-in-cheek attempt to undermine macho behaviour. Another reading would render it as a wonderfully uplifting tribute to youth and its ability to overcome all problems.

On 'Move On', Bowie plunders his own composition 'All The Young Dudes' – the wonderful hit single he had handed to Mott The Hoople in 1972.

'I had put one of my reel-to-reel tapes on backwards by mistake and really quite liked the melody it created. So I played quite a few more in this fashion and chose five or six that were really quite compelling. 'Dudes' was the only one to make the album, as I didn't want to abandon the "normal" writing I was doing completely. But it was a worthwhile exercise in my mind.'

DB, 2001

Other stand-out tracks include 'Repetition', a chilling tale of domestic abuse, and 'D.J.', which takes on Talking Heads and beats them at their own game.

While it is easy to overlook *Lodger* among so many other great albums in David Bowie's back catalogue, to do so is to miss out on hidden gems.

'I think Tony and I would both agree that we didn't take enough care mixing. This had a lot to do with my being distracted by personal events in my life and I think Tony lost heart a little because it never came together as easily as both Low *and* "Heroes" *had. I would still maintain, though, that there are a number of really important ideas on* Lodger. *If I had more time I would explore them for you... but... you can probably pick them out as easily.'* DB, 2001

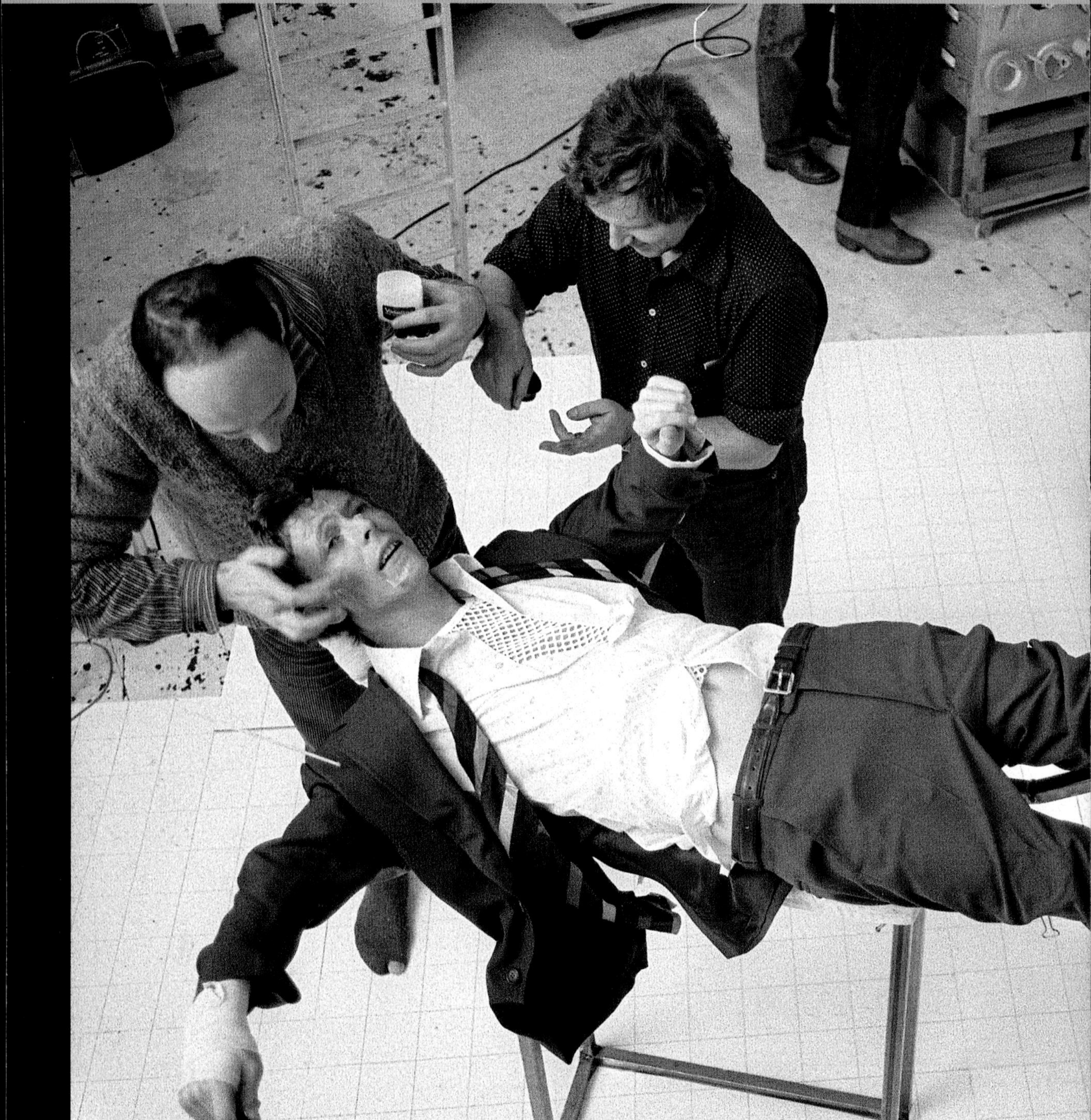

THE ART OF THE COVER

David Bowie had one of the most bankable faces in pop. So what must RCA have thought when presented with a grainy Polaroid of a pair of twisted legs?

The design was a collaboration between photographer Brian Duffy, Bowie and British pop artist Derek Boshier. Boshier had attended the Royal College of Art alongside David Hockney and shared with Bowie a passion for the writings of Marshall McLuhan who coined the theory, 'the medium is the message'.

The gatefold revealed Bowie broken and bandaged while, inside, photographs of the cover shoot sit alongside images that supposedly inspired it, including Che Guevara's corpse and Andrea Mantegna's *Lamentation Over The Dead Christ*. (These images were not included with the 1991 CD reissue.) In a twist of Marshall McLuhan's famous phrase, here the method is the message.

Left: Attending to the patient during Brian Duffy's photoshoot for the *Lodger* cover.

SCARY MONSTERS... AND SUPER CREEPS 1980

'SCARY MONSTERS HAS ALWAYS BEEN SOME KIND OF PURGE. IT WAS ME ERADICATING THE FEELINGS WITHIN MYSELF THAT I WAS UNCOMFORTABLE WITH.'

DAVID BOWIE, 1990

1979
June
UK release of 'D.J.'/ 'Repetition' (29)
August
US release of 'Look Back In Anger'/ 'Repetition' (DNC)
December
UK release of 'John, I'm Only Dancing (Again)'/ 'John, I'm Only Dancing' (12)
US release of 'John, I'm Only Dancing (Again)'/ 'Golden Years' (DNC)

1980
February
UK release of 'Alabama Song'/ 'Space Oddity' (23)
8 February
Divorces Angie Bowie (having separated *c.* 1977)
29 July
First performance of *The Elephant Man* with Bowie in the title role, Center of Performing Arts, Denver
August
UK release of 'Ashes To Ashes'/ 'Move On' (1)
September
US release of 'Ashes To Ashes'/ 'It's No Game (Part 1)' (DNC)
12 September
Release of *Scary Monsters... And Super Creeps* (UK 1, US 12)

Previous page and opposite: More than twelve years after *Pierrot In Turquoise*, Bowie strikes another Pierrot pose for *Scary Monsters* in a costume by designer Natasha Korniloff, who had previously made clothes for Lindsay Kemp's company

'He actually sat down and wrote the songs for a change; for David, this is good form.' Thus Tony Visconti on Bowie's *Scary Monsters... And Super Creeps*, the album that would deliver him great commercial success and put him back among the pop gods. Gone were Brian Eno and his 'Oblique Strategies', gone the desire to create ambient music; but what hadn't gone was the desire to keep experimenting. Two impulses were guiding Bowie at this point, one highly artistic, one very practical.

Bowie felt that the music of his last three albums represented unfinished business. There were boundaries he still wanted to break through, boundaries that *Lodger* had only leaned on.

There was also the vexed issue of MainMan and his former manager, Tony Defries. In interviews Bowie kept his cool on the subject. Yes, they had parted and badly, but that was all in the past. In private he was still fuming over what he perceived as Defries's mismanagement. Worse, to extricate himself from MainMan, Bowie had been obliged to sign over a significant percentage of his earnings on future recordings to Defries.

The albums he had delivered since that agreement (signed in 1976) had in no way matched the commercial successes of some of his earlier work and, on that level, Bowie was mightily pleased. His strategy seemed to be to write hit singles but produce very demanding albums that were unlikely to make Defries pots of money. But Bowie's deal with Defries applied only to recordings made before 30 September 1982. With this in mind Bowie began work in New York in February 1980.

Again, he turned to the familiar names who had served him so well in the past: Carlos Alomar, Dennis Davis, George Murray and former King Crimson guitarist, Robert Fripp. Bruce Springsteen's piano player, Roy Bittan – last heard on *Station To Station* – returned and Pete Townshend came in to play guitar on 'Because You're Young' ('He didn't let me do much', Townshend has since said; 'one of the more bizarre things about the album', in Visconti's view).

As work began, Bowie was made an astounding offer. Would he consider playing the lead role in the Broadway production of *The Elephant Man*?

THE
ELEPHANT MAN

The Elephant Man was the popular nickname of Joseph Merrick whose terrible physical impairments had turned him into a public freak. Only the intervention of a brilliant surgeon and a beautiful actress had helped rescue his life and enabled him to escape the taunting scrutiny of the world at large.

Bowie had always been attracted to the strange, to those whose mental or physical difficulties consigned them to the margins of society. An important book for him as a teenager was *Strange People* by Frank Edwards. The stories it contained were extraordinary: like the tale of a man who, every time he lay down on a bed, the pillow burst into flames. Of course, the chance to prove his acting chops on a Broadway stage was far too good to miss and Bowie agreed to take the role. This meant that by April, when he returned to the studio to lay down his vocals, monsters were dancing in his head.

'I think 1980s nursery rhymes will have to a lot to do with the 1880s nursery rhymes which were all horrid and had little boys getting their ears cut off.' DB, 1980

By August he had registered his first number one in the UK since the 1975 re-release of 'Space Oddity'. 'Ashes To Ashes' was defined by its compellingly unique sound and structure; Bowie's vocal ability, and his matchless knack of conjuring striking new musical effects in a catchy pop format had in no way abated. The song quickly caught the public's imagination.

It helped that the lyric centred on Major Tom, the character Bowie had introduced to the world in 'Space Oddity' in 1969. The original Major Tom song had been on Bowie's mind for some time. In September 1979 he had recorded an acoustic version for British television's *Kenny Everett's New Year's Eve Show*, which would appear on the B-side of his single of February 1980, a version of the Bertolt Brecht/Kurt Weill composition 'Alabama Song' (also covered by The Doors on their 1967 debut album).

Bowie explained that in 'Space Oddity' Major Tom had refused to come back to earth because it was in such a mess. Now, ten years later, he realises that his mission to space was meaningless. It served no purpose. His only solace is to bliss out on a space drug.

Tony Visconti summed up the song perfectly: ''Ashes To Ashes'... took everyone by surprise, because what was expected was another of those bizarre kind of things off *Low* or *"Heroes"* or *Lodger*, and here's this most conventional pop song ever written, with a cute verse, a cute chorus, and then the devastating stab where he tells the world that Major Tom's a junkie, and kills off the character he created and glorified all those years before. That was the beauty of that track, because he'd been sardonically looking for some way to get rid of Major Tom once and for all.'

Unlike Major Tom, in 1980 Bowie did do something out of the blue. His portrayal of John Merrick, the Elephant Man, was perhaps the greatest achievement of his acting career, described as 'simply electrifying' by the *New York Post* and 'one of the events of the New York theatrical season' by the *New York Times*.

The number one single was soon followed by a number one album, proving that Bowie still had much to offer as a contemporary artist, was still a vital musical force.

Scary Monsters opens and closes with the sound of a film reel spooling round and round. The first track, 'It's No Game', begins with Michi Hirota reciting the song's lyrics in Japanese, and then Bowie's voice arrives, at points screaming in pain.

On 'Up The Hill Backwards', also a single, Bowie lets Robert Fripp loose, and then changes pace with a catchy pop chorus that works in stunning contrast to the demented sounds emanating from the former King Crimson man's guitar.

'That's a very odd piece of music. What happens, by the end of it, is that it actually makes some kind of commitment. But on first hearing, it sounds as though it's a very shrugged, almost cynical, there-is-nothing-we-can-do-about-it attitude, which is thrown at you on a very MOR-voiced track so that it sounds like very much the epitome of indifference.' DB, 1980

On some of the songs Bowie used his famed cut-up technique to create the lyrics. It was an artistic device he had first experimented with when writing *Diamond Dogs* following a meeting with William Burroughs in 1973. He explained to BBC Radio One's Andy Peebles:

'If you take a couple of subject matters... someone jumping over the Berlin Wall, I would write a paragraph from the jumper's point of view. I would write a paragraph from an observer's point of view from this side of the wall, then an observer's view from that side of the wall, so you have three different viewpoints, then I would cut them up and reshuffle them. Then I pull them out in three or four word phrases and put the parts together; from that I can either use what is exactly laid out, or I can re-sort them. There are no ground rules. It is a tool of writing to promote a new perspective on something that might have got stodgy.' DB, 1980

Other highlights include the UK top-ten single 'Fashion'; a soulful version of the Tom Verlaine song 'Kingdom Come'; the insistent ferocity of the title track; and a return to 'It's No Game', this time as a ballad, using a Lou

Reed-tinged voice without Michi's input. Visconti again: "'Fashion' just proved that he could recreate 'Fame' at will, and in fact the album most definitely sums up the whole era from 'Space Oddity' up to there. It wasn't our original intention, but after the two-month break, we realised that we had ten tracks which were all very commercial, and encapsulated one period or another, like the title track was back to the Ziggy days, and 'It's No Game' was like a *Low* kind of feeling.'

Also of note was the video for 'Ashes To Ashes', shot in Hastings with director David Mallet. Bowie dressed in a Pierrot outfit made for him by costume designer Natasha Korniloff, an old friend who had previously made clothes for Lindsay Kemp's theatre company. Pierrot is a character from the Commedia dell'Arte tradition, originally established by a troupe of Italian entertainers who travelled throughout Europe. He always appears with a painted face, a blouse with big buttons, pantaloon trousers and a dunce's cap. His character is always trusting and always taken advantage of by others. Read into that what you will.

'I got the same woman who used to do all the costumes for the Lindsay Kemp mime company, Natasha Korniloff, to make this outfit for me. It was based on the Italian Pierrot. It was pretty well authentic. With a cigarette. The make-up was designed by Richard Sharah, which I smeared at the end of the video. That was a well-known drag act finale gesture, which I appropriated.

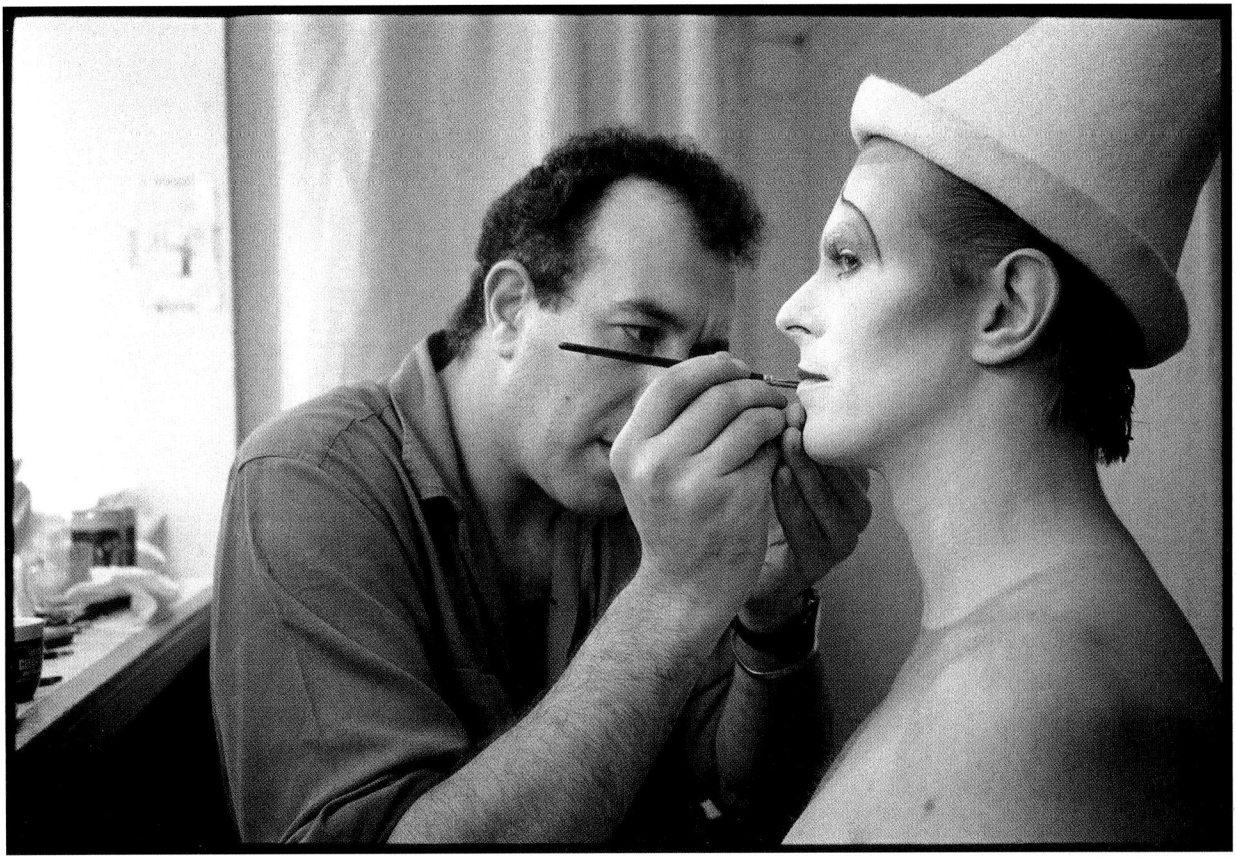

I really liked the idea of screwing up his make-up after all the meticulous work that had gone into it. It was a nice destructive thing to do. Quite anarchistic.' DB, 1993

The idea for the look may have been prompted by Bowie's visit to the famous New Romantic club Blitz in London. The New Romantic style was in direct contrast to punk. Its proponents – including Boy George, Steve Strange, Rusty Egan, Gary Kemp, et al. – adored Bowie. He had been the idol of their youth, the soundtrack of their teenage years. Many of the principles Bowie had followed when dressing up in the seventies they had adopted for themselves. Bowie recognised this and invited Steve Strange to be in the video, which featured Pierrot walking alongside an ink-black sea, talking to an old woman who represented his mother. After years apart, Bowie had recently reconciled with Peggy, who had to admit that her son had been something of a success...

'This is a time in which an intelligent person does well to be afraid. To know fear but not be conquered by it is the response that is needed now... even from a man in a clown suit.'

***NME*, September 1980**

Make-up artist Richard Sharah applies the finishing touches during the photoshoot for the *Scary Monsters* cover. Sharah also worked on the video for 'Ashes To Ashes', which, at £250,000, was the most expensive promo ever made at the time.

中出洋服店
MK
京55
い94-28

1

2

3

Previous page: While in Japan in April 1980 to shoot two TV commercials for a brand of sake, Bowie's exploration of Kyoto and Tokyo was captured by Masayoshi Sukita.

Right: On his return to Japan in October 1983, he was photographed outside a Tokyo restaurant by Denis O'Regan.

ビール、酒、他

LET'S DANCE 1983

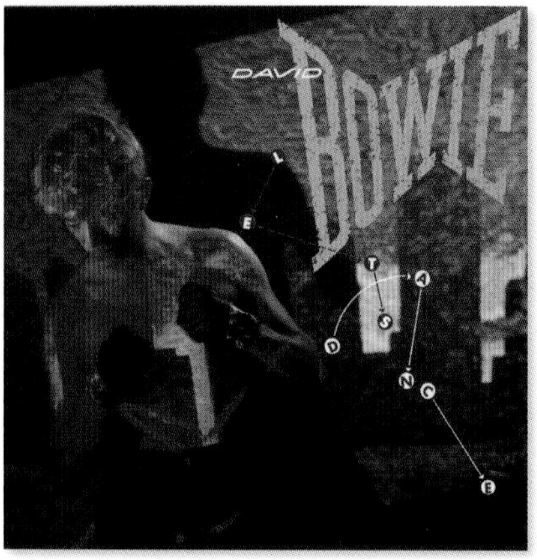

'I'M WRITING ABOUT SOMETHING THAT I'VE NEVER REALLY TOUCHED ON BEFORE... THE EMOTIONAL SITUATION BETWEEN TWO PEOPLE SEEMS TO HAVE ESCAPED ME — OR I'VE AVOIDED IT IS PROBABLY NEARER THE TRUTH.'

DAVID BOWIE, 1983

1980

October

Release of 'Fashion'/'Scream Like A Baby' (UK 5, US 70)

1981

January

UK release of 'Scary Monsters (And Super Creeps)'/'Because You're Young' (20)

3 January

Bowie's final performance in *The Elephant Man*, Booth Theater, New York

March

UK release of 'Up The Hill Backwards'/'Crystal Japan' (32)

October

Release of Queen and David Bowie's 'Under Pressure'/'Soul Brother' (Queen only) (UK 1, US 29)

November

UK release of 'Wild Is The Wind'/'Golden Years' (24)

1982

February

UK release of 'David Bowie In Bertolt Brecht's *Baal* EP' (29)

2 February

BBC adaptation of Bertolt Brecht's play *Baal* (Bowie stars in the title role)

April

Release of 'Cat People (Putting Out Fire)'/'Paul's Theme (Jogging Chase)' (Giorgio Moroder only) (UK 26, US 67)

October

UK release with Bing Crosby of 'Peace On Earth/ Little Drummer Boy'/'Fantastic Voyage' (David Bowie only) (3)

1983

March

Release of 'Let's Dance'/'Cat People (Putting Out Fire)' (UK 1, US 1)

14 April

Release of *Let's Dance* (UK 1, US 4)

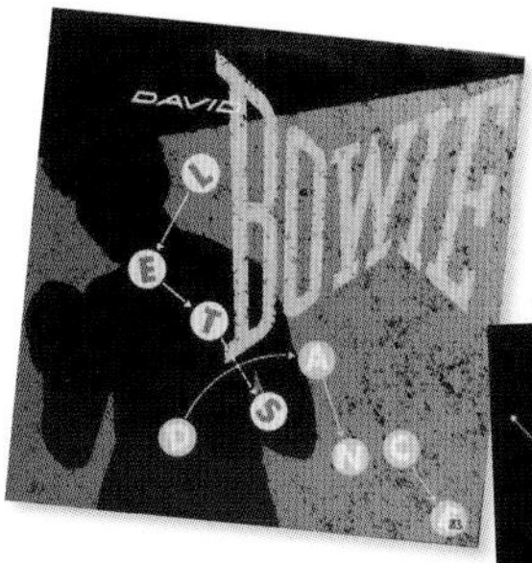

Previous page and opposite: 'Starting to enjoy growing up'. After more than a decade of pushing the boundaries, with *Let's Dance* Bowie made one of his most unpredictable moves – into the mainstream.

In the latter half of 1980, with *Scary Monsters* climbing the charts the world over, Bowie, now approaching his mid-thirties, could have been forgiven for taking the easy option: a few high-profile interviews, the odd chat show and then relax in a warm bath of critical and commercial success. Instead, he put in 157 emotionally draining appearances as the Elephant Man. He received excellent reviews, but the effort exhausted him.

In January 1981, his tenure of the part over, he returned to his home in Switzerland and effectively retreated from public life. Until July, that is, when he undertook a recording session that raised a few eyebrows.

Queen, who were considered by many as conservative purveyors of bombastic rock, were recording in Montreux and invited him to the studio. They were fronted by the flamboyant Freddie Mercury, who had Bowie to thank for creating a mainstream cultural environment that allowed his camp-rocker persona to flourish. Still, many thought the alliance strange. 'Yes, I found that quite odd,' Bowie later admitted.

In the studio, he and Queen began work on a song called 'Cool Cat' but Bowie wasn't happy with the results. Instead they ended up doing what all musicians do when put in the same room: they began to jam, 'which led to a skeleton of a song,' Bowie recalled in a 1983 *NME* interview.

'I thought it was quite a nice tune, so we finished it off. It sort of half came off but it could have been a lot better… I think it stands up better as a demo.' DB, 1983

The public disagreed. They thought 'Under Pressure' was just fine and when it was released in October 1981 it hit number one in the UK and twenty-nine in the US.

During its recording, Bowie was intrigued to hear Freddie Mercury speaking well of Queen's record label, EMI, who, according to Mercury, had given Queen complete artistic control of their material. Bowie had been unhappy with his own label, RCA, for some time. He was particularly irked by their policy of issuing Bowie compilations without consulting him first. In turn, they had been frustrated by his long experimental sojourn and kept urging him to return to making hit albums in the style of *Ziggy Stardust* or *Young Americans*. One executive actually suggested Bowie move to Philadelphia, presumably in the hope that it would lead to him recording *Young Americans II*.

With his contract approaching its expiry date, Bowie decided to seek a new deal and before long a bidding war ensued between EMI, CBS and Geffen. EMI won and, in January 1983, Bowie signed a contract giving him a £17 million advance against five albums.

Ironically, since *Scary Monsters*, and excepting his brief collaboration with Queen, music had been the last thing on Bowie's mind. Instead, buoyed by his success in *The Elephant Man*, he had spent 1982 almost entirely focused on acting. He made a cameo appearance as himself in the German film *Christiane F.*, the soundtrack to which amounted to an anthology of Bowie songs from 1976 to 1979. In February 1982 he showed up as the lead in a BBC production of the Bertolt Brecht play *Baal*; his performances of the play's five songs were released as an EP. He received mixed reviews. Just as copies of *Let's Dance* were arriving at record stores, he showed up in *The Hunger*, a horror film directed by Tony Scott. Bowie played a 250-year-old vampire and this time the reviews were terrible. Fortunately, this was immediately followed by a lead in another film, *Merry Christmas, Mr Lawrence*, by the famed Japanese director Nagisa Oshima, whose *In The Realm Of The Senses* Bowie much admired. Bowie's performance – as a British officer in a Japanese World War II prison camp – was widely praised.

Having completed filming, and with the new EMI deal under his belt, he returned to the recording studio.

One of Bowie's great strengths was always his unerring ability to pick the right man for the job. During his experimental phase he had used several musicians – Robert Fripp, Adrian Belew, Carlos Alomar, Dennis Davis and George Murray – whose improvisational talents had proved crucial in realising his musical aims. Now he had new waters to navigate. His intent was to move away from the avant-garde and into the mainstream. With that in mind, he approached Nile Rodgers of the disco group Chic and told him bluntly, 'I want a hit.'

Rodgers was the perfect choice. His stewardship of Chic, and songwriting partnership with Bernard Edwards in

the late seventies, had produced a succession of worldwide hits such as 'Le Freak', 'I Want Your Love' and 'Good Times'. Their music was disco but it was also bright, catchy and, unusually for the genre, classy. Chic were the disco band even the rock press liked.

During the peak of his experimental phase with collaborator Tony Visconti, Bowie had said:

'I'm not a big fan of disco at all. I loathe it. I really get so embarrassed that my records do so well in discos. I've had two enormous disco hits now – can't hold my head up when I go into arty clubs…'
DB, 1978

Now, with an eye on the charts and its potential riches, Bowie's tune had, quite literally, changed. He had grown up and, like all grown-ups, realised that the necessity of cold, hard cash can have a compromising effect on artistic – or other – ideals.

During the early eighties, Bowie spent more time acting than making music: he didn't perform a single concert during 1981 and 1982. As well as starring on the big screen in horror film *The Hunger* and POW drama *Merry Christmas, Mr Lawrence* (opposite), he also took the title role in a BBC adaptation of the Bertolt Brecht play *Baal* (right).

'I don't really have the urge to continue as a songwriter and a performer in terms of experimentation, at this moment. I'm of an age – and age has an awful lot to do with it – when I'm just starting to enjoy growing up.' DB, 1983

In truth, it was inevitable that Bowie would exploit his stardom. Acting was never going to make him rich and, although he had immense musical credibility, he had nowhere near the financial security of his contemporaries. He had done his bit for art, it was time to cash in.

Work on the album started at The Power Station in New York in December 1982. According to co-producer Rodgers, it was finished within a mere seventeen days. Whereas Bowie had previously entered the studio with sketches and ideas that he fleshed out with his musicians, this time around he had written the entire album in a three-day spell.

Present at the sessions was acclaimed blues guitarist Stevie Ray Vaughan, whom Bowie had met the previous year at the Montreux Jazz Festival. They had chatted about music for hours and gone their separate ways until, months later and much to the Texan's surprise, Bowie called to ask if he would work on a new album; a record of commercial dance music flavoured with the blues.

In the UK, at least, soul and dance music was starting to usurp rock in both the charts and in a proliferation of new nightclubs. The end of punk had left rock music with little to say while dance music – and later hip hop – had given black music a much stronger currency.

The album's title track, and lead-off single, fitted perfectly into these new musical developments, and not just in the UK. 'Let's Dance' was a number one single in several countries, including the US, and became one of Bowie's biggest international hits. Charles Shaar Murray, writing in the *NME*, said of it: ''Let's Dance' is easily this year's biggest single; every time it comes up it creates an instant impression of sheer scale. The sounds are huge, the emotions it contains gigantic.'

It wasn't always so. It had started off as a gently strummed folk song; Bowie knew how good it was, but he also knew that releasing a folk song in 1983 was as avant-garde as recording ambient music in 1977. Instead, he gave it to Nile Rodgers – some say 'sacrificed it' – who tried to create something out of it that you could actually dance to.

'The subject matter of 'Let's Dance' is nebulous. There is an undercurrent of commitment, but it's not quite so straightforward... It's a one-to-one thing, yes, but the danger, the terrifying conclusion, is only intimated in the piece. It is not apparent what exactly the fear is that they're running from. There's an ominous quality about it, quite definitely... it's almost like the last dance.' DB, 1983

The album was similarly successful, as were the follow-up singles 'China Girl' (a version of the song that had originally appeared on the Iggy Pop album *The Idiot*) and 'Modern Love'. Their glossy productions, large drum sound and insistent, danceable rhythms helped Bowie pay back all of his advance within a year, and then some.

'I think the music I am writing at the moment is probably going to reach a newer audience for me. But if I am going to reach a new audience then I'm going to try and reach it with something to say; which is on a very obvious and simplistic level.'
DB, 1983

The European global superstar was here.

'This album just goes straight to the heart of it: it is warm, strong, inspiring and useful. Powerful, positive music that dances like a dream and makes you feel ten feet tall. Who can ask for anything more?' ***NME*, April 1983**

Let's Dance was the first album Bowie had made since the expiration of his settlement with Tony Defries, according to which his former manager claimed a significant percentage of royalties on recordings made up to the end of September 1982. This meant that for the first time in his career he was able to enjoy full financial rewards for his achievements. Here relaxing by the pool on tour in Australia, 1983.

TONIGHT 1984

‘MY WRITING FOR SO LONG HAS BEEN TO DO WITH THE SURREAL THAT I DON’T EVEN KNOW WHETHER I COULD TAKE MYSELF SERIOUSLY AS A WRITER OF DIDACTIC STATEMENTS.’

DAVID BOWIE, 1984

1983
May
Release of 'China Girl'/'Shake It' (UK 2, US 10)
18 May
Serious Moonlight tour opens
at the Vorst Nationaal, Brussels
29 April
The Hunger
(Bowie stars as John Blaylock)
10 May
Merry Christmas, Mr Lawrence
(Bowie stars as Major Jack Celliers)
September
Release of 'Modern Love'/
'Modern Love (live)' (UK 2, US 14)
October
Release of *Ziggy Stardust: The Motion Picture*
(soundtrack) (UK 17, US 89)
November
UK release of 'White Light, White Heat'/'Cracked Actor' (46)
US release of 'Without You'/'Criminal World' (73)
8 December
Serious Moonlight tour closes
at the Coliseum, Hong Kong
23 December
Raymond Briggs' *The Snowman* broadcast on Channel 4,
introduced by Bowie

1984
21 February
Wins BRIT Award for Best British Male Artist
September
Release of 'Blue Jean'/
'Dancing With The Big Boys' (UK 6, US 8)
14 September
Wins MTV Video Music Award for Best Male Video ('China Girl')
and Video Vanguard Award
24 September
Release of *Tonight* (UK 1, US 11)

'Camouflaged face': bathed in blue light for the 'Blue Jean' video.

Following *Let's Dance*, Bowie embarked on the Serious Moonlight tour – and it made him serious money.

Ninety-six performances in sixteen countries, to a combined audience of 2.5 million people. In a typical show, Bowie played four songs from *Let's Dance* – the title track, 'China Girl', 'Modern Love' and 'Cat People' – and up to twenty-six songs from his back catalogue, from 'Space Oddity' onwards. Referred to privately as his 'pension plan tour', Bowie was also keen to remind people – including many new fans – just how good a songwriter he had been for over fifteen years.

The tour stretched from May to December 1983, Bowie's polished on-stage persona charming audiences night after night. These were not the hard-edged audiences of old – the demanding crowds excited by his artistic courage. The David Bowie Show was now an arena spectacle for upwardly mobile couples.

Bowie, to a greater degree than ever before, was in it for the money. No doubt his deepening relationship with his son had brought home to him the need to provide for his family's future. The good will he had built up over the years would now stand him in good stead. He had already made enough great music to last lesser acts three lifetimes; who could begrudge him a desire finally to get paid?

Meanwhile EMI were nudging him for another album.

Unlike during the maniacal tours of the early seventies, Bowie found himself unable – or unwilling – to write during his Serious Moonlight travels. Instead, on his return he took a quick break for Christmas and set to work in January 1984; but, perhaps for the first time ever, he was finding it difficult to locate his muse.

'I wanted to keep my hand in, so to speak, and go back in the studio – but I didn't really feel as if I had enough new things of my own because of the tour. I can't write on tour, and there wasn't really enough preparation afterwards to write anything that I felt was worth putting down, and I didn't want to put out things that "would do"...' DB, 1984

He brought in two British producers, Hugh Padgham and Derek Bramble, the former initially as engineer despite a

The immensely successful Serious Moonlight tour played to 2.5 million people, including three sell-outs at the Milton Keynes Bowl in July 1983 (main image). Flanked by Carmine Rojas (bass, left) and Carlos Alomar (guitar, right), Bowie made all the right moves (inset). However, writing his follow-up album, *Tonight*, proved to be a more difficult experience.

CV that included the huge hit album *Ghost In The Machine* with The Police. Padgham was initially irked at his 'junior' role, particularly in light of Bramble's relative inexperience. According to some commentators, Bramble was not quite ready to take on a musician of Bowie's standing and his careful handling of the recording process seemed at odds with Bowie's spontaneity. Towards the end of the five-week recording process, Bramble left the project, meaning Padgham was now in charge.

Bowie changed gears, decided to junk his own compositions and record a series of cover versions. These included The Beach Boys' 'God Only Knows', the Leiber and Stoller composition 'I Keep Forgettin'', and Iggy Pop's 'Neighbourhood Threat' and 'Tonight'.

''God Only Knows' I first did – or tried to do – with Ava Cherry and that crowd The Astronettes when I tried to develop them into a group. Nothing came of that! I still have the tapes, though. It sounded such a good idea at the time and I never had the chance to do it with anybody else again, so I thought I'd do it myself… it might be a bit saccharine, I suppose.' DB, 1984

Iggy then showed up at the studio to co-write a further two songs with David – 'Tumble and Twirl', about a holiday in Indonesia the two had recently returned from, and 'Dancing With The Big Boys'. Bowie hoped it would lead to further work together and expressed his desire to produce Iggy's next album – and two years later, with *Blah Blah Blah*, he did just that.

Two compositions solely by Bowie did make the album; indeed, 'Blue Jean' and the anti-religious 'Loving The Alien' are, perhaps, *Tonight*'s most successful tracks. 'Blue Jean' appeared as the album's second single, accompanied by a twenty-two minute promotional video shot by director Julien Temple. Temple would later bring Bowie in to work, as both musician and actor, on his debut feature film, *Absolute Beginners*.

Yet, even as he was promoting the album, Bowie had started to distance himself from it, sensing from its muted reception that it had not met the standard required of him.

'I thought it was great material that got simmered down to product level. I really should have not done it quite so studio-ly… You should hear 'Loving The Alien' on demo. It's wonderful on demo. I promise you!' DB, 1989

But, at the time, to critics who felt that *Tonight* was indicative of Bowie's well running dry, of his apparent road map to commercialism having led him up a blind alley, he was ready with his reply.

'Whenever anyone asks me what the next album is going to be like, I invariably reply "protest" because I have as little idea as anybody what comes next… I always thought I was intellectual about what I do, but I've come to the realisation that I have absolutely no idea what I'm doing half the time… That's the territory of the artist anyway: to be quite at sea with what he does, and working towards not being intuitive about it and being far more methodical and academic about it.' DB, 1984

Opposite: 'Give me your head' – the 'Cracked Actor' routine, complete with cape and skull, was a regular feature of Serious Moonlight performances.

LABYRINTH & ABSOLUTE BEGINNERS 1986

'FOR ALL THE TIMES I MAKE MYSELF LOOK A PRANNY, I ALSO DO THINGS I KNOW ARE GOOD.'

DAVID BOWIE, 1997

1984

November

Release of 'Tonight'/'Tumble And Twirl' (UK 53, US 53)

1985

16 January

Suicide of half-brother Terry Burns, aged 47

February

Release with Pat Matheny Group of 'This Is Not America'/ 'This Is Not America (instrumental)' (UK 14, US 32)

22 February

Into The Night (Bowie cameo as Colin Morris)

26 February

Wins Grammy for Best Video, Short Form, for *Jazzin' for Blue Jean*

May

Release of 'Loving The Alien (remixed)'/ 'Don't Look Down (remixed)' (UK 19, US DNC)

13 July

Performs at Live Aid, Wembley Stadium, London

August

Release with Mick Jagger of 'Dancing In The Street'/ 'Dancing In The Street (dub version)' (UK 1, US 7)

1986

March

Release of 'Absolute Beginners'/ 'Absolute Beginners (dub mix)' (UK 2, US 53)

4 April

Absolute Beginners (film) (Bowie cameo as Vendice Partners)

7 April

Release of *Absolute Beginners* (soundtrack) (UK 19, US 62)

June

Release of 'Underground'/ 'Underground (instrumental)' (UK 21, US DNC)

23 June

Release of *Labyrinth* (soundtrack) (UK 38, US 68)

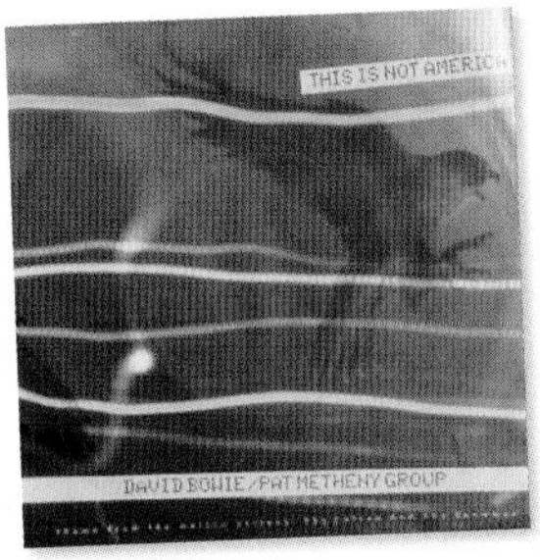

Previous page and opposite: More than twenty years after his last brush with the advertising industry, Bowie played cynical 'mad man' Vendice Partners in *Absolute Beginners*.

It was the dream ticket – Jim Henson, of *The Muppets* fame, directing; George Lucas, creator of *Star Wars*, co-directing; *Monty Python*'s Terry Jones writing the script; David Bowie starring and supplying the soundtrack. The budget was twenty-five million dollars and the film would introduce the world to the precocious talents of a fifteen-year-old Jennifer Connolly. The rest of the characters would be puppets.

Nursery rhymes and children's stories had always fascinated Bowie; in 1978 he'd narrated a version of Sergei Prokofiev's *Peter And The Wolf*. He also admired director Jim Henson; *The Muppets* is one of those brilliant pieces of work with equal appeal for both kids and adults.

Labyrinth's plot involves Bowie as a wicked goblin king, Jareth, who kidnaps a baby named Toby. Toby's sister, Sarah – played by Jennifer Connolly – then embarks on a search to rescue him.

In many ways Bowie saw his character as yet another he could add to his ever-growing collection and he approached the work as seriously as he might have when developing either Ziggy Stardust or Aladdin Sane.

'I think Jareth is, at best, a romantic, but, at worst, he is a spoilt child, vain and temperamental… like a rock 'n' roll star!'

DB, 1986

Filming began on 15 April 1985 at London's Elstree Studios and lasted five very long months, much of the time taken up with the complex puppetry. At first Bowie found this aspect of the role disquieting. 'I had some initial problems,' he admitted, 'because for one thing, what they say does not come from their mouths but from the side of the set, or from behind you.'

After a tiring and complicated shoot, Bowie entered the studio to record five songs he'd written especially for the soundtrack: 'Underground', 'Magic Dance', 'Chilly Down', 'Within You' and 'As The World Falls Down'.

The last was a lovely ballad carrying hints of one of Bowie's finest songs, 'Word On A Wing'. It was scheduled for release as a single – to coincide with the film's UK premiere in November 1986 – but, for reasons unknown, it was pulled at the last minute, despite the promotional video for it already having been shot.

'Magic Dance' – almost an eighties update of 'The Laughing Gnome' – did make it as a single in the US, as a twelve-inch dance mix featuring Bowie on baby gurgles.

'Underground' was released in June 1986 – again, a twelve-inch dance mix was available. Despite its strong, catchy gospel inflections, all-star cast – with old friend and 'Young American' Luther Vandross and Chaka Khan among a stellar line-up of backing singers and the legendary Albert Collins on lead guitar – and a Steve Barron-directed video, the single failed to chart in the US, although did make it to twenty-one in the UK.

Labyrinth was the first soundtrack for which Bowie had specifically written all the songs – not to disregard Trevor Jones' electro-orchestral score. Previous soundtracks had either culled his back catalogue (*Christiane F.*) or featured a few specially written tracks among the work of others (*Cat People*). As such, *Labyrinth* is something of an anomaly among Bowie's studio albums in that it clearly can't be judged as a reflection of him as an artist, following his instincts, choosing a muse and letting inspiration run wild. In this case, he was given the muse, and the muse happened to be a slightly muddled children's film with puppets and tight trousers. Of course, he could have declined the offer to provide a soundtrack, but then Bowie has always taken the path least trodden.

'I'd always wanted to be involved in the music-writing aspect of a movie that would appeal to children of all ages, as well as everyone else, and I must say that Jim gave me a completely free hand with it.'
DB, 1986

The film topped the box-office charts in the UK but on a global scale it failed to recoup even half its budget. Yet, with time, *Labyrinth* has become something of a cult classic. Some cinemas even hold special *Rocky Horror*-style audience-participation screenings of the movie.

With hindsight, it's enough to take the positives – 'As The World Falls Down', 'Underground' – and raise a smile for the rest. But those not smiling at the time were the executives at EMI Records. They wanted *Let's Dance II* and this, quite palpably, wasn't it.

Above: Down in the underground, as Jareth the goblin king in *Labyrinth*.

Opposite: 'That's motivation!' – selling the dream of a career in advertising to central character, Colin, in *Absolute Beginners*.

Just months before *Labyrinth*'s release, Bowie appeared as ad-man Vendice Partners in Julien Temple's film adaptation of Colin MacInnes's novel *Absolute Beginners*.

The British film industry was struggling, as usual, and up-and-coming director Temple was touted as the man to breathe life into it.

Bowie had taken an early interest in Temple. To promote the 1984 single 'Blue Jean' the two had filmed *Jazzin' For Blue Jean*. At twenty-two minutes long, it blurred the lines between 'video' – a short piece of promotional eye candy – and 'film', something lengthy enough to accommodate conflict, resolution and dialogue. It was screened in cinemas as a support feature to *The Company Of Wolves*. Even as they were filming, Bowie told the *NME*:

'I think his plans for his own film, Absolute Beginners, *should do a lot for young British filmmaking… I'd love to do a feature with him…'*
DB, 1984

Set in 1958 the film tells the story of a young photographer, Colin, vying for the affections of career-oriented fashion designer Crepe Suzette, set against a backdrop of interracial tension in London's Notting Hill. Despite a substantial amount of pre-release hype, the film bombed critically and commercially, perhaps under its weight of expectation as much as anything else.

One of the critics' biggest gripes was with the anachronistic soundtrack, linked in the film like a series of extended music videos. Ironic, then, that perhaps the best thing to come out of *Absolute Beginners* was Bowie's incredible title track. Released in March 1986, it reached number two in the UK, fifty-three in the US, and remains one of the greatest songs Bowie ever recorded.

At Live Aid, Wembley, 13 July 1985: performing his solo set (opposite); returning for the ensemble rendition of 'Do They Know It's Christmas?' (this page, bottom); and backstage with Paul McCartney (this page, centre). Bowie also teamed up with Mick Jagger to record the Live Aid single 'Dancing In The Street' (above).

'Now hear this, Robert Zimmerman': pictured at an exhibition with Bob Dylan, 1985 (this page, top).

NEVER LET ME DOWN 1987

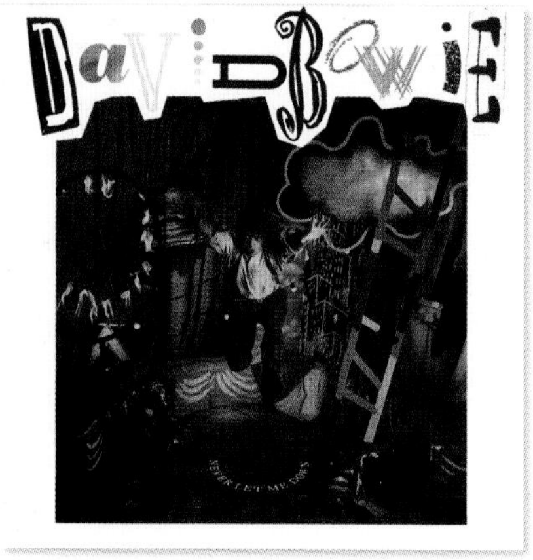

'I SUCCUMBED, TRIED TO MAKE THINGS MORE ACCESSIBLE, TOOK AWAY THE VERY STRENGTH OF WHAT I DO.'

DAVID BOWIE, 1995

Das si

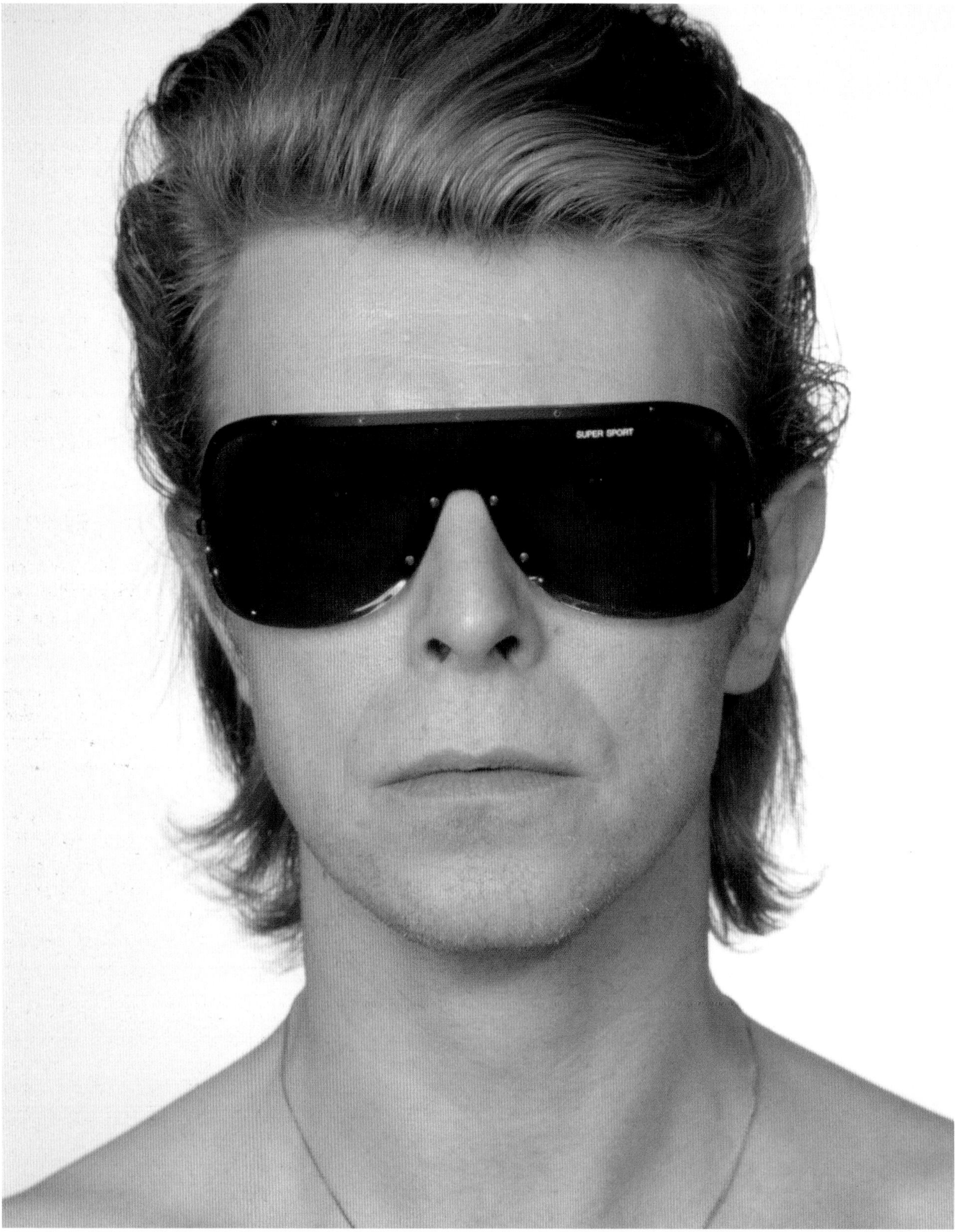
SUPER SPORT

1986
27 June
Labyrinth (film) (Bowie stars as Jareth)
23 October
Release of Iggy Pop's *Blah Blah Blah*
November
UK release of 'When The Wind Blows'/ 'When The Wind Blows (instrumental)' (44)

1987
January
US release of 'Magic Dance'/ 'Magic Dance (dub)'/'Within You' (DNC)
March
Release of 'Day-In Day-Out'/'Julie' (UK 17, US 21)
17–30 March
Promotional press tour of Glass Spider
27 April
Release of *Never Let Me Down* (UK 6, US 34)

Previous page: 'Standing by the wall' – back in Berlin on the Glass Spider tour, June 1987, two years before the fall of the wall.

Opposite: In another nod to 1977, Bowie joined up with Iggy Pop again to co-write and co-produce Iggy's *Blah Blah Blah* album… including the single 'Shades'.

When David Bowie decided to embrace global superstardom, he made one strategic error; that which had made him would now be denied him. Bowie's stature rested on his enormous talent as a songwriter, his artistic courage, his drive to experiment, his mission to expand rock's boundaries to encompass theatre and literature. His multimedia and multi-genre career had seen him embraced by fans from widely differing backgrounds; Bowie's appeal had started on the council estates and stretched right through to academics.

Such imagination would not now be needed. Bowie had spent 1986 refusing EMI's request to put out an album and tour with it; by 1987 he had no choice but to follow orders. What was needed was an album that appealed to the pop masses and could be performed in huge arenas. The days spent cutting up lyrics or pulling cards out of Brian Eno's 'Oblique Strategies' pack were in the past.

This left him somewhat confused. As gratifying as it was to see the zeros on the end of his bank balance and be known from London to Laos, it left him artistically inert. This was a new career in a new town that he didn't know his way around.

Bowie's long-time guitarist Carlos Alomar told biographer David Buckley, 'The man didn't want to go into the studio to record an album. When you let the political agenda of a record company infiltrate your mood, there's no inspiration.'

Never Let Me Down was written and recorded in a three-month period in Switzerland. Bowie used a mix of the old and the new. The ever-faithful Carlos Alomar reappeared, and Peter Frampton was a first-time guest (Frampton's father had been Bowie's art teacher at school).

The songs signified a shift in Bowie's lyrics towards socio-political statements – something he'd previously resisted. The album's lead single, 'Day-In Day-Out' typified this approach, taking a hard look at the plight of America's homeless. Its video – again directed by Julien Temple – was a misguided foray into social commentary featuring an attempted rape and Bowie on roller-skates; it would later be banned by both the BBC in the UK and MTV in the US.

The follow-up single, 'Time Will Crawl', was inspired by the 1986 nuclear disaster at Chernobyl.

The title track, and third single, was more personal. It was written about Bowie's long-serving personal assistant Coco Schwab, who had worked for Bowie since the mid-seventies. Although David always insisted their relationship was platonic, he also said:

'There is romance in it, I guess, in as much as it's hard for two people to feel totally at ease in each other's company for that period of time and not expect too much from each other.'
DB, 1987

Elsewhere there was the now-customary Iggy Pop cover, 'Bang Bang', and Mickey Rourke made an effort at rapping on 'Shining Star (Makin' My Love)'.

'My biggest up was when I met Mickey Rourke for the first time and he said, "Oh man, in 1973, man, I was dressing just like you, man, I had green hair and stack-heeled boots and leather trousers." And I'm trying to see Mickey Rourke wearing all this gear. I said, "You were a glam-rocker?" He said, "Yeah, man, in Florida nobody had seen anything like it!" I found that absolutely great. I felt so encouraged by that.' DB, 1989

One huge problem David had with the album was to do with its sound. In the eighties, drum machines and synthesizers took centre stage on many an artist's records, turning their songs into glossy artefacts, and robbing the music of its soul. Bowie's vocals have always worked best set to music that is as interesting as his voice – be it the crazed cacophony of *"Heroes"* or the clipped funk of *Station To Station*.

The mainstream sound of the eighties had become inflexible; it lacked the capacity to shock or surprise. While Bowie expressed a desire to return to rock 'n' roll, the resulting blandness in sound production disguised much of the good in Bowie's new songs.

Yet real sonic experiments were happening all around if one cared to listen. In hip hop, Public Enemy were forging fiery, intelligently dissonant music based around samples. House music was taking off and already influencing UK guitar bands such as The Happy Mondays and The Stone Roses. Singles such as 'Beat Dis' by Bomb The Bass and 'Pump Up The Volume' by MARRS suggested fruitful areas for Bowie to explore. Instead, he made an album he would later come to regret.

On its release *Never Let Me Down* sold far less than expected. In America it reached thirty-four in the Billboard charts; and in the UK it climbed to number six. It did very well in Scandinavia.

Although, at the time, Bowie defended the album vigorously – and performed most of it on his infamous Glass Spider tour – he later expressed severe doubts about its worth and his position as a mainstream artist.

'Let's Dance *was an excellent album in a certain genre, but the next two albums showed that my lack of interest in my own work was really becoming transparent. My nadir was* Never Let Me Down. *It was such an awful album. I've got to a place now where I'm not very judgemental about myself. I put out what I do, whether it's in visual arts or in music, because I know that everything I do is really heartfelt. Even if it's a failure artistically, it doesn't bother me in the same way that* Never Let Me Down *bothers me. I really shouldn't have even bothered going into the studio to record it. In fact, when I play it, I wonder if I did sometimes.'* DB, 1995

If anything *Never Let Me Down* served a purpose: it showed Bowie that happiness did not lie in arena tours and populist appeal, but in artistic brilliance. The question was, would he now be able to relocate that instinct?

Now a fully fledged member of the jet set, but *Never Let Me Down* never left the ground. Although in songs such as 'Day-In Day-Out' and 'Time Will Crawl' he tackled current social and political issues, for the first time in his career Bowie seemed out of touch.

TIN MACHINE 1989

‘I HAD TO GET PASSIONATE AGAIN. I COULDN’T KEEP GOING THE WAY I WAS GOING. IT WAS SHIT OR GET OFF THE POT.’

DAVID BOWIE, 1989

1987
30 May
Glass Spider tour officially opens at the Stadion Feyenoord, Rotterdam
June
Release of 'Time Will Crawl'/'Girls' (UK 33, US DNC)
August
Release of 'Never Let Me Down'/''87 And Cry' (UK 34, US 27)
28 November
Glass Spider tour closes at the Western Springs Stadium, Auckland

1988
1 July
Collaborates with avant-garde dance troupe La La La Human Steps in performance of 'Look Back In Anger' at an ICA benefit concert, London
12 August
The Last Temptation Of Christ (Bowie cameo as Pontius Pilate)

1989
22 May
Release of *Tin Machine* (UK 3, US 28)

Previous page: On stage during the Glass Spider tour, 1987. His next project was to be a far more stripped down affair.

Opposite: The stockbroker attire belied the raw, visceral songs on *Tin Machine*.

The Glass Spider tour: hugely ambitious and hugely profitable. Between May and November 1987, the tour covered Europe, North America and Australasia reaching an estimated three million people – but still did little to sell copies of *Never Let Me Down*. By the end of it David Bowie was very rich, very tired and very hurt.

'There was too much responsibility on the last tour. I was under stress every single day… I just had to grit my teeth and get through it, which is not a great way of working.' DB, 1989

The tour had been ripped apart by the critics. It was seen as hysterically excessive and unbecomingly theatrical for an artist of Bowie's stature. What's more, by performing all but two songs from his new album every night, Bowie was forced to forsake past gems and the usual praise for his established canon. Instead he was pilloried for providing entertainment rather than 'art', for avoiding a meaningful musical exchange between artist and audience.

Stung by the criticism, Bowie decided enough was enough. He had the money now, he had the fame; it was time to stop playing Bowie the superstar and return to Bowie the artist – always a much more interesting creature to look at in the morning mirror.

Reeves Gabrels was an extraordinary guitarist devoted to exploring sonic extremes. His wife, Sarah, worked as a publicist on the Glass Spider tour and handed Bowie a tape of his work. Bowie was impressed and in mid-1988 the two began collaborating, decamping to Bowie's favourite Montreux studios with producer Tim Palmer, originally to explore a concept album based on Steven Berkoff's play *West*. That idea was quickly scrapped but their experiments yielded promising new material, including early versions of 'Heaven's In Here' and 'Baby Universal'. Still ostensibly contemplating a David Bowie solo project, the pair realised they needed a rhythm section.

The Sales brothers – drummer Hunt and bass player Tony, the sons of stand-up comic Soupy Sales – had been the rhythm section on Iggy Pop's *Lust For Life*, co-written and co-produced by Bowie. Rock 'n' rollers in the raw with attitudes to match, their arrival in Montreux marked a dramatic shift in the tone of the sessions. Working spontaneously, as a democratic unit, new songs began to pile up – hard-rock music over which Bowie improvised lyrics with little revision.

Licking the numerous wounds inflicted on him by the critics, Bowie saw a chance to slip the shallow currents of the mainstream that flowed towards sequinned jumpsuits and Las Vegas residencies; he would lose Bowie the entertainer and re-emerge as a singer in a rock band called Tin Machine playing small theatres and clubs.

'This is the first band that I've been in – as opposed to led or directed – since The Konrads, in 1963! I thought that we'd just get on musically, but the fact that it evolved very quickly into a band format was just great, and that it's become what it's become is just wonderful, but it wasn't a preconceived idea.'

DB, 1991

After a break, the band members reconvened in Nassau, in the Bahamas, quickly knocking together more than thirty songs, catching a raw live sound without fuss or frills and almost no overdubs. Fourteen of these songs were assembled into an album and aired to the press at a playback in New York.

Initial critical feedback was reassuringly positive. On first hearing, *Q* magazine described it as 'mercifully quite splendid... raw, hysterical and crackling with life'. More positive reviews followed and the album quickly went to number three in the UK charts. The backlash came later.

In hindsight, *Tin Machine* is raw, aggressive and wayward, but there were some genuine highlights. Opening track, 'Heaven's In Here', set the tone and pace to follow, charging in with wild guitars and fast-paced vocals; 'Crack City' combined Bo Diddley and Bob Dylan; 'I Can't Read' could have been placed on *Lodger*; and the version of 'Working Class Hero' is one of Bowie's better covers, replacing Lennon's sneering cynicism with a disarming air of defiance.

In the spirit of starting over, of going back to basics, the band embarked on a tour of tiny venues – certainly compared to the arenas and stadiums of Glass Spider – travelling together in a van, their set list completely ignoring Bowie's back catalogue.

'I've never been moved by an artist in a stadium, except maybe the wrong way: towards the exits and out... the spontaneity and the interaction go as well: you're ruled by the confines of the choreography.'

DB, 1991

However, many fans and critics could not accept Bowie – the supreme individualist – submerging himself within a band. It's also possible that he was slightly too far ahead of the game. At the time he was absorbing emerging American noise-experimentalists like The Pixies and Sonic Youth, bands yet to break into the mainstream. Traditional Bowie fans were, perhaps, taken by surprise by his new direction while younger audiences resented a mainstream 'oldie' co-opting the sounds of the underground.

'I've never been worried about losing fans. I just haven't bothered to put that into practice recently. My strength has always been that I never gave a shit about what people thought of what I was doing... I'm sort of back to that again...'

DB, 1989

But EMI were worried. They weren't thrilled with the album's financial returns and when the band signalled they wanted to cut a follow-up, the label opted out, leaving Bowie to secure a deal elsewhere. Bowie didn't care. He was shedding another skin.

Join the gang: For the first time since the sixties, Bowie played the role of the singer in a rock band. The other members of Tin Machine were bassist Tony Sales (left), drummer Hunt Sales and guitarist Reeves Gabrels (right).

Ludwig
UNT

TIN MACHINE II 1991

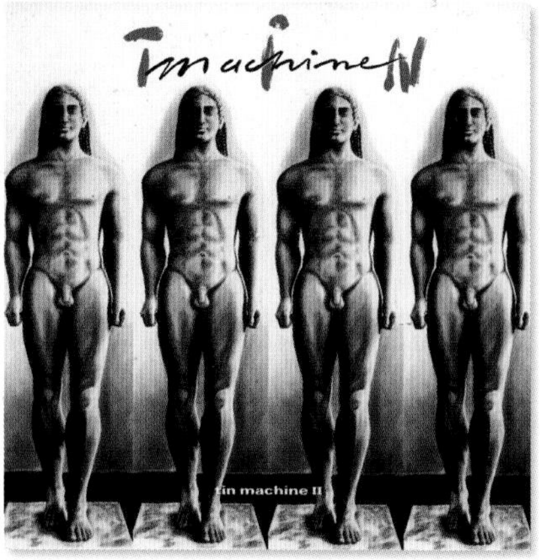

'TIN MACHINE WAS THE BEST THING I COULD HAVE DONE TO SOLVE MY MID-FORTIES CRISIS.'

DAVID BOWIE, 1994

1989
June
Release of Tin Machine's 'Under The God'/
'Sacrifice Yourself' (UK 51, US DNC)
14 June
1989 Tin Machine tour opens at the World, New York
3 July
1989 Tin Machine tour closes at the Forum, Livingston, Scotland
(an additional gig added, 4 November, Moby Dick's, Sydney)
September
Release of Tin Machine's 'Tin Machine'/
'Maggie's Farm (live)' (UK 48, US DNC)
October
Release of Tin Machine's 'Prisoner Of Love'/
'Baby Can Dance (live)' (DNC)

1990
March
Release of 'Fame '90'/
'Fame '90 (Queen Latifah's rap version)' (UK 28, US DNC)
4 March
Sound+Vision tour opens at the Colisée, Quebec
2 April
Wins Ivor Novello Award for Outstanding Contribution to British Music
May
Release of Adrian Belew's 'Pretty Pink Rose'/
'Neptune Pool'/'Shoe Salesman'/'Oh Daddy'
(featuring David Bowie on track one) (DNC)
29 September
Sound+Vision tour closes at the River Plate Stadium, Buenos Aires

1991
7 July
Appears as Sir Roland Moorcock in two episodes of HBO's *Dream On*
August
UK release of Tin Machine's 'You Belong In Rock 'n' Roll'/
'Amlapura (Indonesian version)' (33)
2 September
Release of *Tin Machine II* (UK 23, US DNC)

If many felt Bowie's musical imagination had temporarily been put on hold – though it would soon return in splendour – he retained the capacity to surprise.

In March 1990 he embarked on the Sound+Vision tour. This, he explained, would be the last time he sang his old hits on stage; one last outing for the songs that had made him famous, after which his past would remain just that – the past. He hoped that by doing so, he'd open up his future.

'Knowing I won't ever have those songs to rely on again spurs me to keep doing new things, which is good for an artist.'
DB, 1990

The tour was also a way of promoting a career-spanning box set of the same name, full of rarities and curios. And this, in turn, was designed to drum up interest in an ongoing programme of album reissues with EMI and Rykodisc.

Ahead of the tour, in an effort to break the wall between performer and audience, Bowie set up a phone line for fans to request their favourite songs to be played live. The British music paper *NME* quickly realised the potential for making mischief and the line was overrun by readers requesting 'The Laughing Gnome'.

In the US, 'Fame', 'Let's Dance' and 'Changes' were requested most often, while in Europe it was "Heroes" and 'Blue Jean'.

This time, Bowie lost the accoutrements of the Glass Spider extravaganza. Dressed like the Thin White Duke he made imaginative use of video screens – designed by Édouard Lock – to bridge the gap between the performer and an arena audience. Lock explained: 'You can amplify sound to reach large areas, the problem is that the technology hasn't extended itself to visuals. You can still go to a stadium and see a pea on stage… Rock's traditional answer has been to extend the stage set, which actually makes the problem worse. It just underlines how small the human being is… I wanted to build an architecture based around the person as opposed to the set. Make the person into the building; use bits of the face, etc. to create a more spherical architecture.'

The tour was incredibly successful. Between March and September 1990 it included 108 performances in twenty-seven countries. Almost as soon as it was over, Bowie announced that he was leaving his record label, EMI.

EMI were less than enthusiastic about Tin Machine. So, in March 1991, Bowie and band jumped ship to the newly formed Victory Music and set about completing their second album. They'd already recorded a hatful of songs in Sydney, Australia, at the end of their first tour in 1989. Reconvening in Los Angeles with Hugh Padgham (last seen on *Tonight*), only another three songs were needed.

The result was a record even louder and more inaccessible than the first. This was the sound of Bowie letting off steam, shouting, screaming, embedding himself in heavy rock. On its release, Reeves Gabrels revealed the ethos behind *Tin Machine II*: 'Within this band there's a total mistrust of a comfortable thing. As soon as it starts to feel like it's our mode of operation, then we have to change the parameters.'

There are some notable high points on the record – 'Baby Universal', 'Goodbye Mr. Ed', 'One Shot', 'Shopping For Girls' – but there are also some very low points. On the whole it was an album that set itself against contemporary music. House music now dominated; clubs all over the world were filled with dancers high on hope and ecstasy. Rap had reached new heights, thanks to bands such as A Tribe Called Quest, De La Soul and Gang Starr. In the UK, guitar music was still dominated by the dance-influenced 'Madchester' scene led by the likes of The Happy Mondays. The only link between Tin Machine and contemporary music was the rise of 'grunge', spearheaded by Nirvana, Pearl Jam, Soundgarden and Alice In Chains. But the difference was one of age.

In many ways Tin Machine was Bowie's hiding place, somewhere to lie low while he reignited his creative furnace. As just one quarter of a whole, if people pointed fingers any blame could be deflected onto others. Yet it also kept him in the game. Bowie always denied this was his intention and, despite the second album's generally downbeat reviews, he showed his commitment to the cause by undertaking a seven-month world tour.

Once again playing small venues and encouraging an atmosphere of spontaneity – 'we have no set list whatsoever', Bowie claimed – Tin Machine played sixty-nine shows in twelve countries and recorded a live album in the process – *Tin Machine Live: Oy Vey, Baby*.

Bowie professed his loyalty to the band to the very end, but as the tour closed the wheels in his head were turning once more and he would soon be heading back to the studio as a solo artist.

Today, critical opinion on Tin Machine is less dogmatically negative than it once was. They were an anachronism for sure, and maybe their peculiarity blinded contemporary critics to their true worth. Others disregard the music entirely and see Tin Machine purely in terms of how it served David Bowie, solo artist, allowing him to destroy his own myth while he found himself again. It also brought about a valuable relationship with guitarist Reeves Gabrels, who would become an important collaborator as Bowie embarked on a stunning return to form.

'It freed me up musically and sometimes you have to go back to something before you work through certain ideas. Tin Machine has been that sort of work-in-progress, although it has met with complete hostility. But I remember exactly the same response to Low*... and now it's considered a milestone in art rock, according to the critics.'* DB, 1993

Previous pages and opposite: After taking time out in 1990 for his solo Sound+Vision arena tour, Bowie returned to Tin Machine to record a second studio album. The band also toured extensively from autumn 1991 to spring 1992, playing much smaller venues than he had visited since the seventies – Bowie even dusted off his trusty saxophone (opposite). This tour gave rise to a live album, *Oy Vey, Baby*, which was to be Tin Machine's final release.

BLACK TIE WHITE NOISE 1993

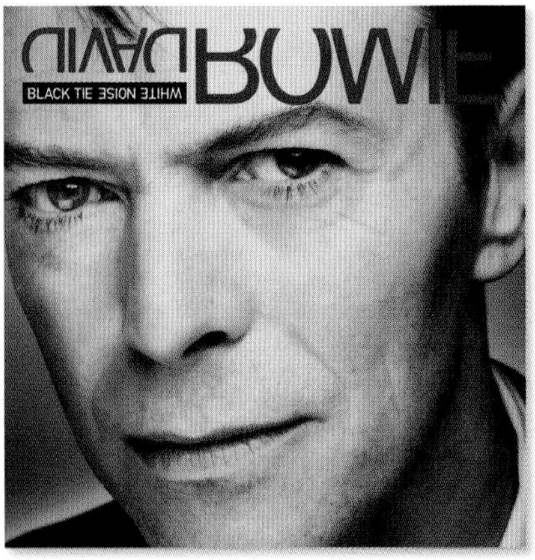

'I'M REALLY COMING INTO MY OWN NOW. TOOK A WHILE, DIDN'T IT?'

DAVID BOWIE, 1993

1991

October

Release of Tin Machine's 'Baby Universal'/ 'You Belong In Rock 'n' Roll (extended version)' (UK 48, US DNC)

5 October

Tin Machine 'It's My Life' tour opens at the Teatro Smeraldo, Milan

30 October

The Linguini Incident (Bowie stars as Monte)

1992

17 February

Tin Machine 'It's My Life' tour closes at the Budokan Hall, Tokyo

20 April

Performs at the Freddie Mercury Tribute Concert, Wembley Stadium, London

24 April

Marries Iman (Iman Mohamed Abdulmajid)

3 June

Twin Peaks: Fire Walk With Me (Bowie cameo as Phillip Jeffries)

27 July

Release of *Tin Machine Live: Oy Vey, Baby* (DNC)

August

Release of 'Real Cool World' (various editions) (UK 53, US DNC)

30 August

Symphony No. 1 *'Low'* by Philip Glass (based on the *Low* album) premieres in Munich

1993

March

Release of 'Jump They Say' (various editions) (UK 9, US DNC)

5 April

Release of *Black Tie White Noise* (UK 1, US 39)

While his appearance at the Freddie Mercury Tribute Concert (above, right) underlined his membership of the rock establishment, Bowie was no dinosaur. A new generation of British bands such as Blur, Oasis and, in particular, Suede (above, left) were keen to associate themselves with him.

'There's quite a bit of you on this one,' Brett Anderson told David Bowie, as he played a song off the debut album by his band, Suede – a moment arranged by the *NME* in March 1993.

Bowie was back in critics' good books. The Sound+Vision tour and box set had forcibly reminded the world of his immense talents. New, young voices formed a queue to sing his praises: Blur were obvious fans, as was Morrissey, and even Oasis later expressed their admiration, covering "Heroes" as a B-side to 'D'You Know What I Mean?' in 1997. Without lifting a finger, Bowie was hip again, and he would stay hip.

With impeccable timing, Bowie released an album that was undeniably fresh sounding, experimental and modern. *Black Tie White Noise* was the result of Bowie returning to one of his most fruitful musical sources: contemporary black American music.

Black music always brought out the best in Bowie. He had grown up under its spell; soul was vibrant, sexy, worldly. He was not alone. Most of the great white British male vocalists of the sixties and seventies – John Lennon, Mick Jagger, Ray Davies, Steve Marriott, Bryan Ferry, Rod Stewart – wanted to sing like Otis Redding, dance like James Brown. Although Bowie had built his kingdom on Ziggy's rock 'n' roll, some of his most rewarding records were immersed in rhythm rather than Rickenbackers: *Station To Station*, *Young Americans*, even the best songs from the so-called 'Berlin' period – the clipped funk of 'Sound And Vision', or the pumping dance beat of "Heroes" – have some link to R&B.

'The first artist I really sort of dug was Little Richard when I was about eight years old. I found it all very exciting... It was like breaking up the sky – his voice broke out of the skies – an extraordinary voice. That's what triggered my interest in American black music.' DB, 1993

In this spirit, and ten years since they'd worked on *Let's Dance*, Bowie reconnected with producer Nile Rodgers. That collaboration had helped make Bowie's millions and turned him into a pop star. It was not a road he wanted to

Left: Performing 'Under Pressure' with Annie Lennox at the Freddie Mercury Tribute Concert, Wembley, 20 April 1992. Later, after a rousing rendition of "Heroes", Bowie also memorably – and spontaneously – knelt to recite the Lord's Prayer.

Opposite: 'Really quite paradise' – with new wife Iman at the premiere of *Exit To Eden*, October 1994. Bowie and Iman met at a dinner party in 1990 and married two years later, shortly before the recording of *Black Tie White Noise*.

travel again and Rodgers would find that, this time around, Bowie was very much in control of the sessions.

Shortly before recording commenced, Bowie married the supermodel Iman in Switzerland. Days later they flew to Los Angeles to look at new homes, arriving as the city erupted in riots. The couple settled in New York instead. This backdrop of personal contentment and contrasting civil strife would inform much of his new work.

In June, the couple publicly celebrated their marriage in Florence, with a celebrity guest list and a helicopter full of cameras hovering above. Bowie had composed a piece of music especially for the occasion and 'The Wedding' both opens and closes the album, an acknowledgement, perhaps, that his life now began and ended with his new wife. The song is dominated by David's first instrument, the saxophone. It seems important, as if love has helped him find his true self again.

Thereafter the album maintains this high standard. 'You've Been Around', written with Reeves Gabrels (and originally considered for *Tin Machine II*) could happily sit on any of the 'Berlin' albums. The clever arrangement sees Bowie's vocal take the lead, the instrumentation added in supporting layers as the song progresses.

'What I like about it is the fact that for the first half of the song, there's no harmonic reference. It's just drums and the voice comes in out of nowhere…' DB, 1993

After its portentous growling intro it becomes positively funky, sexy, full of swaggering bass runs and trumpets.

'It's the texture of a song, for me, that almost comes above the lyrical content. The sex is in the rhythm, and being a very sexual person, that's very important for me, that it moves me.'

DB, 1993

'You've Been Around' is followed by Cream's 'I Feel Free', the original's psychedelic-tinged jazz-rock updated with a modern dance thrust and edge that gradually gains in intensity. Bowie had long admired Cream, as had his old musical foil Mick Ronson. It's fitting, then, that this sees the two together on record for the first time since *Pin Ups*. It would also be the last time.

Cancer had invaded Ronson's body. His contribution to Bowie's career between 1970 and 1973 is immeasurable. The fact that, when success grabbed Bowie by the throat and shook him down, Ronson's was a lone voice of warning as the singer slipped into potentially fatal habits, demonstrated his essential goodness. He was to die a few weeks after the release of this final collaboration, but his reputation as a musical giant continues to grow.

The inclusion of 'I Feel Free' was also partly a result of Bowie, a new man with a new vision of the future, reconciling himself to elements of his past; in this case, his half-brother Terry Burns, who had committed suicide in 1985 and who was also the inspiration for 'Jump They Say' – *Black Tie White Noise*'s first single.

Growing up, Terry had been a significant influence on Bowie; he showed him great books, played him great music, gave him the tools of Beatnik culture before slipping away into heart-breaking mental problems. 'Jump,' says the world; 'watch your arse,' says Bowie.

'One of the few times I went out with my late half-brother, Terry, was to a Cream concert and it had a devastating effect on him in terms of opening him up to another kind of music. And 'Jump They Say' deals with my feelings about Terry to a certain extent. That had been a difficult relationship in my life because we were so very similar in many ways.' DB, 1993

In fact, the whole album sees Bowie re-mixing the past for the future; from Ronson and brother Terry, the return of pianist Mike Garson on 'Looking For Lester', through back-catalogue references aplenty ('Ch-ch-ch-ch-ch-ch-changed' he sings on 'You've Been Around') to Marvin Gaye's eternal question – 'what's going on?' – receiving its ominous answer on the album's title track: 'There'll be some blood…'.

'Black Tie White Noise' was inspired by the Los Angeles riots he had witnessed first hand. They followed the beating of a black man, Rodney King, by policemen and, for Bowie, the violence and anger brutally confirmed the huge rifts in society. The song is dripping in cynicism, images of Benetton adverts of black and white couples lit up by the riots' fires.

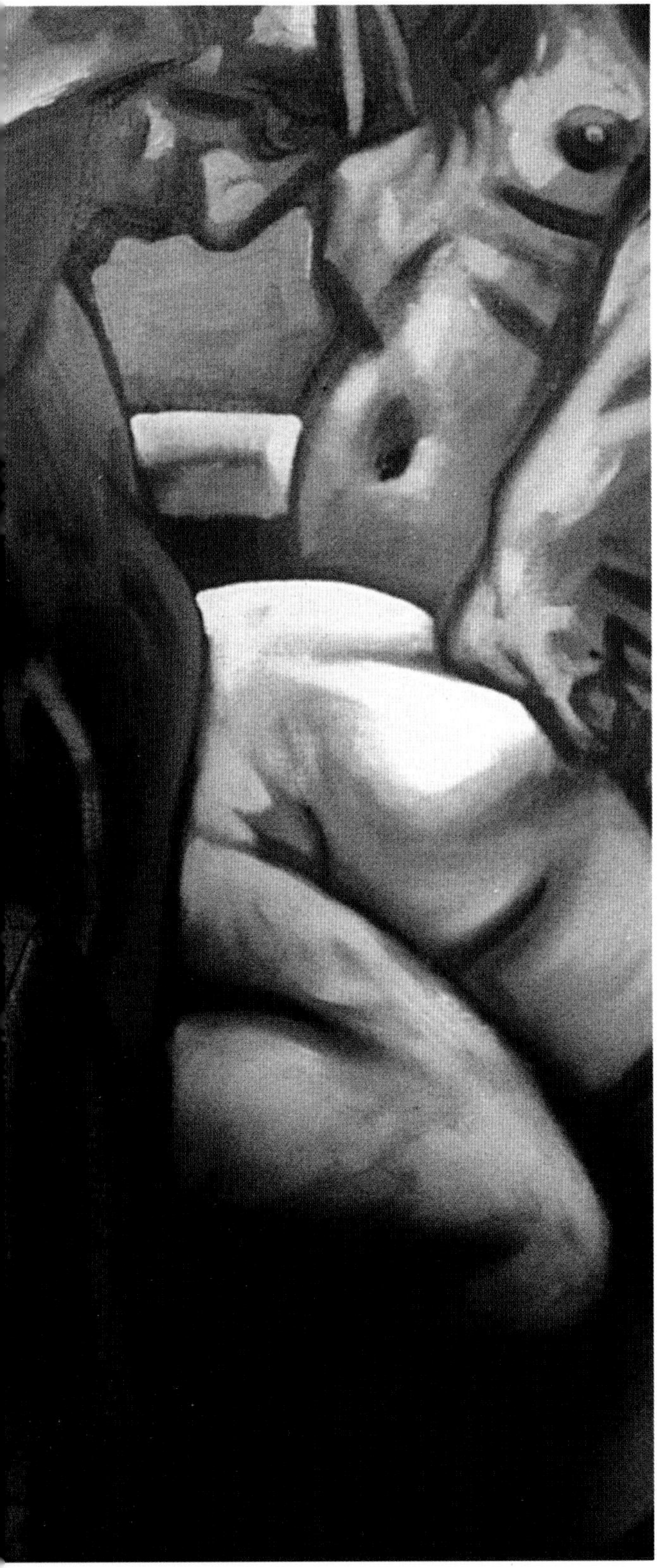

'It felt as if innocent inmates of some vast prison were trying to break out – break free from their bonds.' DB, 1993

With 'Nite Flights', Bowie pays tribute to Scott Walker – an artist he'd long admired, and whose vocal style he'd borrowed more than once previously – while 'Pallas Athena' shows that his experimental instincts are still very much intact.

'Miracle Goodnight' is a tribute to his new wife, unadorned and understated – and all the better for its simplicity. 'Morning star you're beautiful/Yellow diamond high/Spins around my little room/Miracle, goodnight'. Bowie's voice is perfectly pitched, somehow distant and present simultaneously.

'Looking For Lester' is about an unrelated namesake – Lester Bowie, the legendary trumpet player. Originally brought in to work on 'Don't Let Me Down & Down', he ended up playing on six tracks, contributing one of the record's defining sounds.

In recognition of his new status, Bowie then gives a nod to one of his disciples with a cover of Morrissey's 'I Know It's Going To Happen Someday'. This is Bowie singing Morrissey as Morrissey sings Bowie.

Then the album comes full circle with 'The Wedding' – Bowie reasserting his happiness with images of heaven in a wedding dress.

Bowie was forty-six years old and true love had brought a new realisation of himself. On *Black Tie White Noise*, Bowie relaxes and channels his ideas more fluently than he did with the angry energy of Tin Machine. Mostly inviting and friendly, even its darker rooms are painted in warm shadow rather then harsh blackness. Bowie's fans certainly had few problems with it. In the US it went to number thirty-nine and might have gone higher had Bowie's new American label, Savage, not gone into administration. In the UK it went straight to number one replacing, with delicious irony, the debut album by his young acolytes, Suede.

'... if any collection of songs could reinstate his godhead status, then this is it' **Q, May 1993**

Standing in front of a painting by Peter Howson, the official war artist of the Bosnian Civil War, 1994.

THE BUDDHA OF SUBURBIA 1993

> ‘THIS ALBUM MAY WELL HAVE BEEN ONE OF THE MOST ENJOYABLE PROJECTS THAT I’VE BEEN INVOLVED WITH.’

DAVID BOWIE, 1993

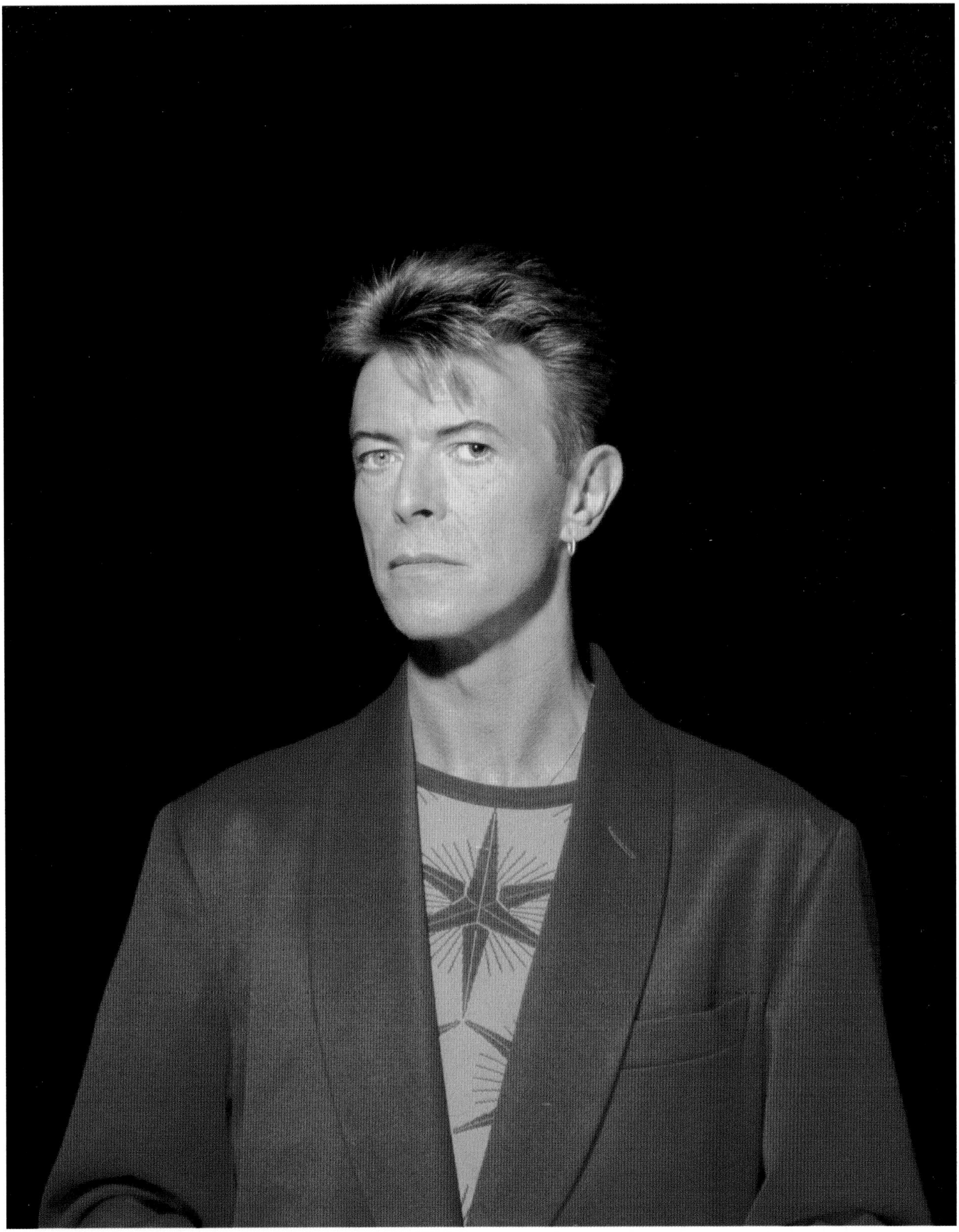

1993
29 April
Mick Ronson dies, aged 46
June
Release of 'Black Tie White Noise' (various editions) (UK 36, US DNC)
October
Release of 'Miracle Goodnight' (various editions) (UK 40, US DNC)
November
UK release of 'Buddha Of Suburbia'/ 'Dead Against It' (35)
8 November
UK release of *The Buddha Of Suburbia* (87)

Previous page: Portrait by Albert Sanchez, 1993.

Opposite: Limbering up for the 'Miracle Goodnight' video, Los Angeles, May 1993.

Bowie considered it to be one of the best albums of his career and he may have had a point. Certainly, on *The Buddha Of Suburbia* he moves effortlessly and confidently through an impressive array of styles, just as comfortable with dreamy sixties pop as he is with modern pop, acid house, jazz and ambient.

The Hanif Kureishi novel on which the album is based deals with a boy growing up in seventies-era Bromley, with a mother named Margaret, struggling with issues of race, religious belief and sexuality while his best friend forges a career as a rock star; enough there for Bowie to identify with certainly.

And Bowie and Kureishi shared many biographical similarities. Both were raised in the suburbs feeling like outsiders, and that feeling of alienation presented in their work. Both had used shock tactics to leapfrog into the spotlight; Bowie had played with gender roles using make-up and costumes, Kureishi had written a film (*My Beautiful Laundrette*) in which a skinhead boy falls in love with a young Asian guy. And both men's lives were consumed by art, especially music and literature.

Approached to write the soundtrack to the novel's dramatisation for the BBC, Bowie created over forty discrete pieces of incidental music that helped link the television series' more obvious choice of classic seventies hit singles. That score – which remains unreleased – was good enough to be nominated for a BAFTA. However, the process sparked in him a larger set of ideas that evolved into something quite different – a collection of songs that had little to do with the television series other than some shared themes and the title track.

Excited to have found his muse once again, Bowie spent a mere six days writing and recording the album – a further fifteen mixing it (this would have been less, Bowie suggested on the liner notes, were it not for 'some technical breakdowns'). Working with multi-instrumentalist Erdal Kizilcay – last heard on *Never Let Me Down* – he entered the studio determined to avoid cliché (a lifelong passion for Bowie), taking the musical motifs from the original soundtrack and spontaneously nurturing them as they grew into something else entirely.

'I would often pull down the faders leaving just the percussive element with no harmonic information to refer to. Working in layers, I would then build up reinforcements in the key of the composition totally blind, so to speak. When all faders were pushed up again a number of clashes would make themselves evident. The more dangerous or attractive ones would be isolated and repeated at varying intervals so giving the impression of forethought.' DB, 1993

The only song from the album used in the television show was the title track, a wonderful sixties-infused pop song in which Bowie cleverly inserted hints of his former classics – 'Space Oddity', 'Starman' – songs that had helped him out of suburbia into the life of his teenage dreams. With lines about 'living lies by the railway line', 'screaming in south London', and a fear that the whole world is 'queer', the song softly catches the chimerical nature of suburbia, a space of silence and silent dreams.

What to follow it with? Some acid house, of course. 'Sex And The Church' conjures a trance-like electronic riff topped with Bowie's robotically intoned lyrics.

Another change of direction follows: 'South Horizons' starts as a jazz-led instrumental, Mike Garson giving the full range of his genius on the piano, until halfway through when it suddenly turns into acid house again, before all the elements come together in a heady, genre-defying mix. And why not? It works beautifully.

'The Mysteries' is ambient music at its finest, as good as or better than anything on either *Low* or *"Heroes"*. It's haunting, mature music with depth and meaning, instruments dripping notes into a lake of sound, setting off musical ripples.

'Bleed Like A Craze, Dad' is a full-on dance number perfectly in tune with the times – with echoes of the Stereo MCs' 1992 hit 'Connected' – which again blends jazz piano, this time with a heavy funk riff and some impressive rock guitar work. Garson's contributions were improvised alone in California, then shipped to Bowie to play with as he wished.

Next comes the rousing 'Strangers When We Meet'. With its foot-stomping bass line taken straight from The Spencer Davis Group's 'Gimme Some Lovin'', it is powerful and compelling in both structure and sound. The way it builds in intensity recalls "Heroes", although here the lyrics are far more elliptical and introspective. If it had been a single it would have surely charted everywhere. Instead Bowie re-recorded it for his next album and got nowhere near the organic push of this version.

'Dead Against It' plays the Pet Shop Boys at their own game, while 'Untitled No. 1' floats Bowie's cool, perfectly restrained voice above a wash of synthesizers.

'Ian Fish, UK Heir' (an anagram of Hanif Kureshi) is, perhaps, the album's comparative weak spot: an instrumental that lacks the focus, the presence or evocative nature of 'The Mysteries'. The album closes with a reprise of the title track, Lenny Kravitz guesting on guitar.

In a short essay in the liner notes Bowie listed some of the influences that had been at play during the album's creation, including: free-association lyrics, Pink Floyd, Harry Partch, blues clubs, Unter den Linden, the Brücke Museum in Berlin, *Pet Sounds*, Roxy Music, T. Rex, casserole, Neu!, Kraftwerk, Bromley, prostitutes and Soho, Philip Glass playing in London in 1970/71, and acid house. Tellingly, he also listed 'Eno'. His old sparring partner did not feature on the record, but Bowie gives him plenty of credit for inspiring his working methods.

Opposite: Hanif Kureishi, author of *The Buddha Of Suburbia*, and David Bowie both grew up in the south London suburb of Bromley and even attended the same secondary school. Bowie tackled the task of writing music based on Kureishi's novel with enthusiasm – which was rewarded with critical appreciation but minimal sales.

Right: Portrait by Albert Sanchez, 1993.

'Brian Eno… in my humble opinion occupies the position in late twentieth-century popular music that Clement Greenberg had in art in the forties or Richard Hamilton in the sixties. In general, Brian's perceptions on form or purpose within culture leave most critics tap-dancing on the edge of the abyss spouting virtually nothing but fashionable blathering.' DB, 1993

If he was trying to woo him, it worked, and the two would soon be back working together on Bowie's next album.

Meanwhile, *The Buddha Of Suburbia* was released to almost utter indifference. Only hardcore fans instantly saw its worth. Despite the fact that only the title and title track had any real connection to the BBC television drama, it was marketed as a soundtrack with a clumsily assembled cover that made little of Bowie's presence. In the US it wasn't released at all until two years later – finally with a cover worthy of the contents. One would have thought Bowie's previous excursions into cinema and sonic landscapes might have prompted a more interested investigation into the work, but EMI's *The Singles Collection* was released just a week after, putting people further off the scent.

Sadly, *Buddha* remains in the suburbs of Bowie's immense canon of work. History, surely, will not leave it there.

1.OUTSIDE 1995

'IT REALLY IS LIKE PAINTING AND SCULPTING; WHERE YOU'RE NOT QUITE SURE WHAT IT IS YOU'RE DOING, BUT WHEN YOU'VE DONE IT, YOU RECOGNISE IT.'

DAVID BOWIE, 1995

1994
25 April
Release of *Santa Monica '72* (UK 74, US DNC)
***c.* September**
Joins the editorial board of art magazine *Modern Painters*

1995
18–29 April
Holds first solo art exhibition, at the Kate Chertavian Gallery, 28 Cork Street, London
14 September
Outside tour opens at the Meadows Amphitheater, Hartford, Connecticut
September
Release of 'The Hearts Filthy Lesson' (various editions) (UK 35, US 92)
25 September
Release of *1.Outside* (UK 8, US 21)

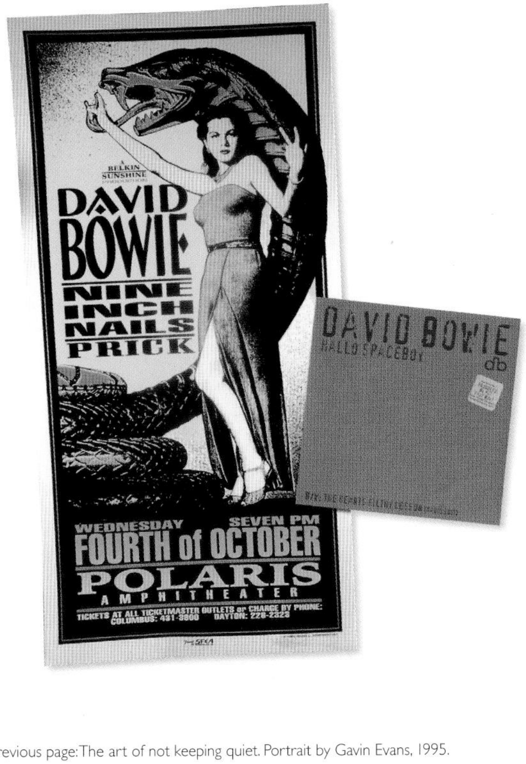

Previous page: The art of not keeping quiet. Portrait by Gavin Evans, 1995.

Opposite: The Outside tour was Bowie's first since Tin Machine in 1992. The support act for the North American leg was industrial-rock group Nine Inch Nails. In a typically unorthodox move, the headliner decided to come on stage before the end of the Nine Inch Nails set (as shown here), joining his support for renditions of songs such as 'Scary Monsters' and 'Hallo Spaceboy'.

Emboldened by the commercial success of *Black Tie White Noise*, energised by the artistic achievement of *The Buddha Of Suburbia*, David Bowie now decided to embark on a journey marked once more by incredible imagination and bravado.

Bowie possessed something many of his peers did not: a desire – or rather a *need* – to create and subvert, to express himself without resorting to the obvious methods. It gave his career longevity, allowed him to grow apart from his contemporaries, plough different fields and continually arouse our admiration, whatever we might have thought of some of the harvests.

He was now forty-eight years old. Musicians of such an age and stature do not generally look to make state-of-the-world music. They are normally to be found lolling in the Florida sunshine, creating pastiches of their past to reap riches in the future. But, if anything, Bowie was even more galvanised, even more driven to sculpt that which had not been sculpted before.

In terms of this album's conception, his wedding to Iman was again crucial. At the reception in Florence, Bowie found time for a chat with Brian Eno and their mutual admiration was rekindled.

'We both felt excited about the fact that neither of us was excited about what was happening in popular music.' DB, 1995

A year later came Bowie's praise for Eno in *The Buddha Of Suburbia* liner notes, and Eno publicly decried the fact that the album had been overlooked by press and public as a mere soundtrack. Collaboration was inevitable.

In March 1994, the two men convened at the Mountain Studios in Montreux, scene of their last previous work together on *Lodger* sixteen years earlier. The band, Reeves Gabrels, Mike Garson, Erdal Kizilcay and Sterling Campbell, were also all Bowie veterans.

Again, Eno had his 'Oblique Strategies' cards with him. These had now evolved into role play. One Christmas, Eno explained, he had been fascinated by a family game of charades. 'It occurred to me that the great thing about games is that they in some sense free you from being yourself,

you are allowed forms of behaviour that otherwise would be gratuitous, embarrassing or completely irrational.'

He devised detailed, fictional character studies for each musician and asked them to play in the style of their character, be it 'an ex disgruntled member of a South African rock band', or 'the last survivor of a catastrophic event'.

Meanwhile, Bowie had not written a note of music before entering the studio. Instead, he brought with him his easel, paints, brushes, papers and charcoal.

Art and music were now equally important in Bowie's life. In 1994 he joined the editorial board of *Modern Painters* magazine. He had become increasingly interested in modern art's obsession with blood and morbidity: the mutilation and despair of artists like Rudolf Schwarzkogler and the carefully dissected animals of Damien Hirst. In April 1995, Bowie held his first solo art exhibition at the Kate Chertavian Gallery, Cork Street, London, titled *New Afro/Pagan And Work 1975–1995*.

Eno's 'Oblique Strategies' were not the only artistic methods at play. Since the seventies, Bowie, inspired by William Burroughs, had used a cut-up technique for lyric writing and he now had a specially designed computer program to help him.

'I would type in three different subjects into the computer, and then the computer has a randomising program, and it would take each sentence and divide it into three or four and then remix it with one of the other sentences, so you get an extraordinarily weird juxtaposition of ideas. Some of the sentences that came back out were so great that I put them straight into the songs, and some of them just sparked off further ideas.' DB, 1995

Through these improvisational experiments, all the backing tracks were written and recorded in just ten days. For the rest of the year, Bowie and Eno embellished, developing themes, weaving conceptual threads.

'Once we started actually exploring the piece, we realised we had formed a very loose non-linear narrative with this small cast of characters and there was a thread of a story that kept running into conflicts. Like real life, there were no tidy endings, no tidy beginnings, the whole thing was very messy and we thought, well, that is how it should be. Let's not clean it up.'

DB, 1995

So *1.Outside* became a concept album, of sorts, starring Detective Professor Nathan Adler investigating the murder of a fourteen-year-old girl found on the steps of a museum. Yet, crucially, the album defined the concept, not the other way round, and to believe that *1.Outside* is contained by something as limiting as a 'story' is to severely underestimate it.

'The subject of the album may be the story of Nathan Adler. The content is actually the texture of 1995. The story is the skeleton and the flesh and blood are the feeling of what it's like to be around in 1995.' DB, 1995

That meant a messy, fragmented, hectic, frantic, powerful, urgent, deliberately antagonistic and energetic record that roared out at the listener; a dense, unforgiving sound filled with a sense of danger, unease and, indeed, gloom. The listener never knows where they are in the sonic landscape, which is precisely the unnerving experience its creators were hoping for. It is not an easy album by any stretch of the imagination.

The songs rarely go where you anticipate, but veer off in crazy tangents. The title track, for example, features a melody that might have been played by the Glenn Miller Orchestra, set against a clattering backdrop of drums and dramatic strings.

'Hallo Spaceboy' is held together by a furious, riveting guitar riff. 'The Motel' is archetypal Bowie and Eno but also recalls, in some strange way, *Aladdin Sane*. 'I Have Not Been To Oxford Town' is classic Bowie funk, while 'A Small Plot Of Land' starts as freeform jazz until Bowie enters, singing like a Russian monk impersonating Scott Walker in an empty tower.

Yet this is to describe the songs' styles, not their texture. Bowie was intending to encapsulate the feeling of the world as it prepared to enter a brand new millennium, to reflect a fragmented, postmodern society of relentless and unfiltered information, lacking hierarchical structure or linear narrative.

'There's no absolute religion, no absolute political system, no absolute art form, no absolute this no absolute that. There are so many contradictions and conflicts that when you accept them for what they are, when you accept that this is a manifestation of the chaos theory that's been put forward, that it really is a deconstructed society, then contradiction almost ceases to exist. Every piece of information is as unimportant as the next.'

DB, 1995

Opposite: At the beginning of the European leg of the tour, including this Wembley Arena concert from November 1995, Bowie was supported by Morrissey. However, the former Smiths frontman left the tour early because, he claimed, he wasn't prepared to share his set in the way that Nine Inch Nails had.

Right: 'Thank you, Tony, thank you everyone else. I think I'll go and sing at you.' Bowie's low-key acceptance speech at the 1996 BRITs, where he received an Outstanding Contribution award from Tony Blair.

All seventy-five minutes of *1.Outside* demand much of the listener. But even if it meets with disapproval you can't fault the creators' artistic bravery. In its original form, it would have been longer and even more demanding. Under the working title of *Leon*, it was set to be a double, perhaps triple, CD. 'It would have been a very serious musical statement,' Reeves Gabrels commented.

Predictably, such a record terrified label bosses, so between January and February 1995, Bowie and Eno entered New York's Hit Factory joined by a new group of musicians including Carlos Alomar, reporting for work on his ninth Bowie album – 'I was surprised he called me back. It was great sliding back into my role as the electric heartbeat.' As well as editing and re-shaping existing material, they recorded new tracks more easily recognisable as 'songs', including 'Thru' These Architects Eyes', 'We Prick You' and 'I Have Not Been To Oxford Town'.

In June 1995, Bowie signed new deals with Virgin America and BMG in the UK and three months later *1.Outside* was finally released to an almost unanimously positive reception from critics and paying public alike.

At the time Bowie expressed an intention to continue the story of Nathan Adler with an album a year until the advent of 2000. Unfortunately that never happened, but Bowie found himself back at that happy crossroads where critical and commercial success coincides.

Above: Promoting *1.Outside* at the HMV store on Herald Square, New York, 1995.

THE ART OF BOWIE

'The only thing that I considered changing my professional motivation to was painting, the visual arts, and I was very close to that in the eighties.' DB, 1995

David Bowie's entire career was a multimedia artistic experiment, from the consciously theatrical and costumed Ziggy Stardust and Aladdin Sane to the cut-up lyrics, experimental videos and the magpie appropriation of musical genres.

In 1975 he began to apply himself seriously to painting, but it took twenty years before he was confident enough to display his work publicly, most notably by choosing a self-portrait for the cover of *1.Outside*.

In 1994 he contributed a multimedia narrative, titled *We Saw A Minotaur*, to Brian Eno's Warchild fundraising exhibition, *Little Pieces From Big Stars*. It was subsequently included alongside works by Francis Bacon and Pablo Picasso in the *Minotaurs, Myths and Legends* exhibition at Berkeley Square Gallery, London.

In 1995, the year of his first solo exhibition, he also collaborated with Damien Hirst and designed the poster for the Montreux Jazz Festival. In 1996 collaborative installations with Tony Oursler were included at the Florence Biennale and further collaborations with the likes of Laurie Anderson and Beezy Bailey followed, as did several more shows including two at the Rupert Goldsworthy Gallery in New York.

In 1997 Bowie co-founded 21, a fine-art publishing company and, in 1998, used it to stage an impressive situationist prank by launching a monograph on the work of 'Nat Tate'. Several critics were left red-faced when they finally noticed the 'artist' was in fact a conflation of two of Britain's most famous galleries, the National and the Tate.

In the nineties, as an editorial board member of *Modern Painters*, Bowie was responsible for a number of insightful interviews with iconic artists, including the last ever with Roy Lichtenstein.

Opposite: Slightly apprehensive prior to the opening of his first solo art exhibition – *New Afro/Pagan And Work 1975–1995* – at the Kate Chertavian Gallery in Cork Street, London, April 1995. Bowie is leaning on a coffin-shaped sculpture titled 'District 6', inspired, like much of his work for the show, by a recent visit to South Africa.

EARTHLING 1997

'I DON'T WANT TO THROW MY CHANCE TO EXPERIMENT AWAY. YOU SEE, ONCE YOU'VE GONE SO FAR, YOU CAN'T TURN BACK. AND I'VE COME THAT FAR. I'M IN MY LAND, I'M DOING IT.'

DAVID BOWIE, 1997

1995

24 October
US release of *The Buddha of Suburbia* (DNC)

31 October
Wins Inspiration Award at the Q Awards

November
Release of 'Strangers When We Meet' (various editions) (UK 39, US DNC)

1996

17 January
Inducted into the Rock and Roll Hall of Fame

February
Release of 'Hallo Spaceboy' (various editions) (UK 12, US DNC)

19 February
Tony Blair presents Bowie with Outstanding Contribution award at the BRIT Awards

20 February
Outside tour closes at the Palais Omnisports, Paris

9 August
Basquiat (Bowie plays Andy Warhol)

November
UK release of 'Telling Lies' (various editions) (DNC)

1997

January
Release of 'Little Wonder' (various editions) (UK 14, US DNC)

9 January
Fiftieth birthday concert at Madison Square Garden, New York

3 February
Release of *Earthling* (UK 6, US 39)

Previous page: Portrait by Michael Benabit, New York, 1997.

Opposite: Performing at his fiftieth birthday concert, Madison Square Garden, New York, 9 January 1997.

In the late eighties, Britain was gripped by acid house; clubs were filled with teenagers in thrall to a four-to-the-floor drum beat and little white pills. 1988 was declared the second summer of love.

But then the pills got diluted and times turned darker. Money got tight and American bombs dropped on the Middle East. Club music turned on itself. Drum 'n' bass emerged, the music speeded up to over 160 beats per minute and aggression spilled from the speakers.

Drum 'n' bass was always bound to be of more interest to Bowie than the simple linearity of acid house. The music's ability to shatter pop songs into little splinters must have thrilled and intrigued him. 'Who could not be influenced by it?' he said, 'It's the most exciting rhythm of the moment.'

Earthling, then, is David Bowie's drum 'n' bass album. Actually... not really. A few songs feature its distinctive rhythms, but Bowie had merely added drum 'n' bass to his musical armoury; it had not become the heart of that unique store. For example, drummer Zachary Alford worked out various drum patterns and recorded them at 120 beats per minute. Speeding them up to 160bpm, he then improvised further rhythms on top to create a techno-organical hybrid.

Vocally, Bowie resurrected his old Anthony Newley voice, which dragged against the drums, creating a fresh new tension in the music.

Earthling is shorter and thinner than *1.Outside*, but no less intense. Stripping away the layers of its predecessor, its only concession to melody is channelled through the vocals and the occasional instrument – the brass riff on 'Seven Years In Tibet', for example, or the choruses that carry 'Battle For Britain (The Letter)' and 'Dead Man Walking'. For the most part, musical dissonance and lyrical abstraction are paramount.

'We're living in an age of chaos and fragmentation, and we should grab it positively and not be scared of it and not see it as the destruction of a society but the material from which we rebuild a society. It is discomforting to see people sorting through the wreckage and trying to pull out absolutes again.'

DB, 1997

Just me and a few friends: The fear of Americans Bowie confessed to on *Earthling* was not apparent during his all-star fiftieth birthday concert at Madison Square Garden. His guests included Frank Black, Robert Smith and Dave Grohl (top, performing 'Seven Years In Tibet'). The highlight of the show was the appearance of Lou Reed (bottom) for renditions of 'Queen Bitch', 'Waiting For The Man', 'Dirty Blvd.' and 'White Light/ White Heat'.

Recording started on completion of the Outside tour, a tour that lasted five months despite Bowie originally announcing he would play only six dates. Bowie again refused to play a greatest hits set, although he did radically rework a few songs from his back catalogue, including 'The Man Who Sold The World'. Inevitably the shows drew some criticism but Bowie rode the harsh words; he was too exhilarated by his new band to care. The tours had honed them as a unit and he wanted to take a 'sonic photograph' of just how good they were.

In August 1996 he entered New York's Looking Glass Studios with Reeves Gabrels, bassist Gail Ann Dorsey, Mike Garson and Zachary Alford on drums. Engineer Mark Plati, a veteran of Prince's *Graffiti Bridge*, was brought in to provide samples and loops.

In a matter of weeks, seven new compositions were written and recorded, while a leftover from *1.Outside* was given new life as 'I'm Afraid Of Americans'; 'Telling Lies' Bowie had recorded alone in April.

'Can't tell them apart at all': Nearly a quarter of a century after writing a song about Andy Warhol and then meeting him, Bowie relished the opportunity to portray him on the silver screen in Julian Schnabel's biopic of the American artist Jean-Michel Basquiat, released in 1996. Posing with his co-stars (left): Jeffrey Wright (in the title role), Gary Oldman (as fictional artist Albert Milo) and Dennis Hopper (as art dealer Bruno Bischofberger).

The album opens with 'Little Wonder', Bowie applying a laconic cockney vocal against frenetic drum 'n' bass. Continuing *1.Outside*'s theme that texture is more important than detail, he later explained that the obliqueness of the lyrics was wholly intentional.

'Something I noticed way, way back – of which the best example is probably 'Warszawa' off the Low *album, is that so much of what musical information is, is just the sound of the words, the phonetics, against the musical context, it can give you quite strong, emotive feelings without having to have rational sense.'*
DB, 1997

'Looking For Satellites' follows, the story of a man gazing at the sky, searching for answers; the satellite a metaphor for how far the human race has advanced set against our eternal need to find something spiritual in life before death comes knocking. A chant provides the opening melody then the band shuffle in, allowing space for Bowie's ghostly vocal before the chant is taken up again.

'What I need is to find a balance, spiritually, with the way I live and my demise. And that period of time, from today until my demise, is the only thing that fascinates me.' DB, 1997

'Battle For Britain (The Letter)' relates to the album's cover photo of Bowie in a Union Jack tailcoat. Once seen as the symbol of far-right nationalism, in mid-nineties Britain the national flag was increasingly being planted in the liberal centre-ground. British culture had found new confidence through an exciting young crop of artists, writers and designers while Britpop re-energised rock music and reclaimed it from the Americans. Bowie stood apart from this liberal nationalism, but he still wrestled with notions of identity. After all, he had been a world citizen for many years now.

'It probably comes from a sense of, "Am I or am I not British?" An inner war that wages in most expatriates. I've not lived in Britain since 1974, but I love the place, and I keep going back. I find London, especially, as exciting now as at any time I've ever known it. At a creative level, there's so much energy there. It's as if we've finally understood that we don't have the rest of the Commonwealth, or the world, to support and comfort us, that we have to do things on our own now to prove who we are.'
DB, 1997

On the wonderful 'Seven Years In Tibet' Bowie's vocal influence on singers like Blur's Damon Albarn is particularly apparent. It's a piece of music that rears up unexpectedly, guitars and drums crashing in, held together by a catchy brass refrain. It returns Bowie to his teenage fascination with Eastern mysticism. In an interview with *Mojo*, he stressed the effect that Heinrich Harrer's 1952 book of the same name had had on him; it had made him want to be Tibetan, to wear robes and live like a monk.

The lyrics of 'Dead Man Walking' were inspired by Neil Young and Crazy Horse's performances at the Bridge School benefit concerts, at which Bowie also appeared in October 1996. Bowie creates a delicious harmonic clash, positioning himself as a man 'older than the movies', tunefully vocalising over the contrastingly energetic and hard-faced backing track.

'The Last Thing You Should Do' is Bowie's attempt at 'grand advice'. 'What have you been doing to yourself?' he asks, as the drums clatter in the background, 'It's the last thing you should do.'

'I'm Afraid Of Americans' lays bare America's cultural paradox: the Mickey Mouse and McDonald's corporate disposability that threatens to obscure the singular and enduring beauty of great American achievements in fields such as music, cinema, literature and clothes design.

On the whole, though, *Earthling* saw Bowie returning home, both geographically and spiritually. A returning refugee, re-assimilating himself with the sights and sounds of his homeland, re-evaluating his place on earth, he plays counterpoint to his former Americana-obsessed, cold, alien selves.

'Bowie seems more energised by the passing years, moving faster and faster to accommodate the ever-growing sum of influences and cultural contradictions operating on his muse… wouldn't it be wonderful if all 50-year-old rockers retained such an interest in the future?'
Mojo, March 1997

'HOURS...' 1999

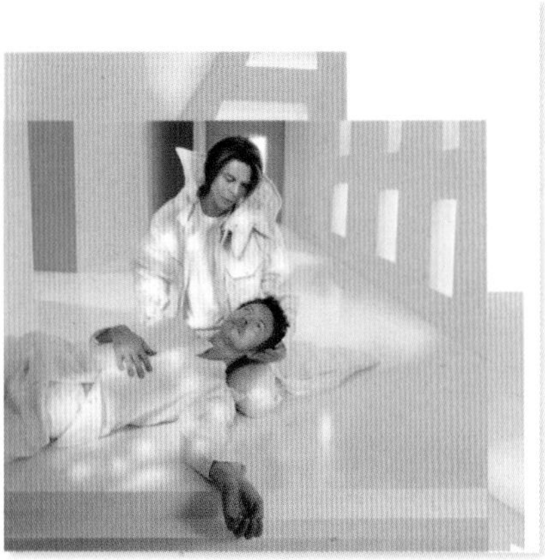

'I DON'T HAVE REGRETS. IF I AM CAJOLED INTO LOOKING AT THE PAST, WHICH I DO VERY INFREQUENTLY, I TEND TO LOOK ON IT AS NOT SO MUCH LUGGAGE AS WINGS...'

DAVID BOWIE, 1999

1997
February
Launches 'Bowie Bonds'
12 February
Awarded a star on the Hollywood Walk of Fame
April
Release of 'Dead Man Walking' (various editions) (UK 32, US DNC)
May
Becomes founding director of 21 Publishing
15 May
Symphony No. 4 *"Heroes"* by Philip Glass (based on the *"Heroes"* album) premieres in London
7 June
Earthling tour opens at the Flughafen Blankensee, Lübeck, Germany
August
Release of 'Seven Years In Tibet' (various editions) (UK 61, US DNC)
UK release as Tao Jones Index of 'Pallas Athena (live)'/'V-2 Schneider (live)' (DNC)
October
US release of 'I'm Afraid Of Americans' (various editions) (66)
November
UK release, with various artists, of 'Perfect Day '97'/ 'Perfect Day '97 (female version)'/'Perfect Day '97 (male version)' (1)
7 November
Earthling tour closes at the Ferrocarril Oeste Stadium, Buenos Aires

1998
February
UK release of 'I Can't Read (short version)'/ 'I Can't Read (long version)'/'This Is Not America' (73)
31 March
Participates in an elaborate art hoax by holding a launch party for the biography, written by William Boyd, of an invented artist, Nat Tate
1 September
Launches BowieNet, the 'first artist-created Internet Service Provider'
18 December
Il Mio West (Bowie plays Jack Sikora)

1999
March
Everybody Loves Sunshine (Bowie plays Bernie)
July
Mr Rice's Secret (Bowie stars as William Rice)
August
UK release by Placebo featuring David Bowie of 'Without You I'm Nothing' (various mixes) (DNC)
September
Release of 'Thursday's Child' (various editions) (UK 16, US DNC)
21 September
Release of *'hours...'* as a download (CD released 4 October) (UK 5, US 17)

Previous page and opposite: Having launched his own Internet Service Provider in 1998, Bowie now created music for a computer game, and the resulting album, *'hours...'*, was the first by an artist on a major label to be sold as a download. Portraits by Jill Greenberg, 1999.

Bowie always enjoyed springing a surprise, catching the world sleeping. In 1997 he issued a financial product the press dubbed 'Bowie Bonds'. The man who once sang about floating in space floated himself on the stock market.

He took a loan of fifty-five million dollars secured against his back catalogue's royalty earnings, to be repaid over a period of ten years, at which point the rights reverted to him. Prudential Insurance Securities purchased every bond while Bowie also resold his back catalogue to EMI for nearly thirty million dollars. He was now a very rich man, able to do what he liked – including buy back the publishing rights still owned by Tony Defries.

'The branding of David Bowie! Well it's been done to artists after they're dead... It's sort of pioneering and it's not an acceptable way to go. And that I always find subversive enough.'
DB, 1999

With three ingenious, artistically satisfying and commercially successful albums behind him, he now made another unexpected move: he went and wrote some songs. Songs with catchy verses and straightforward arrangements that you could sing in your head.

'hours...' was started in late 1998. For much of the year Bowie's focus had been elsewhere – setting up a fine-art publishing company, appearing in three films and establishing the BowieNet ISP.

During this time, he received an offer to supply music for a computer game called *Omikron: The Nomad Soul*. Such games traditionally use dissonant industrial music as soundtracks; Bowie, of course, went in a different direction entirely.

His most recent albums had marked a return to the spontaneous working methods of his Berlin period, writing and recording fast in the furnace of the studio. With *'hours...'* he and Reeves Gabrels settled in Bermuda and undertook the actual process of songwriting. In early 1999, they demoed their work to the games company Eidos in Paris, and by the time they returned to Bermuda all the songs were written and ready to record.

As well as allowing Gabrels his first co-writer's credit, Bowie also asked his fans, via the Internet, to submit their own lyrics. Alex Grant was the winning wordsmith and he was subsequently flown to New York to help sing backing vocals on the co-written track 'What's Really Happening?'

What is striking about *'hours...'* is how many songs look backwards, quietly, anxiously picking over the past, analysing old relationships with lovers and family.

'It was really an exercise in finding remorse and self-recrimination and regrets and I wanted to explore that as a theme for the album.' DB, 1999

Why were such feelings surfacing now, within this relentlessly future-facing artist? Had his highly successful financial dealings induced a feeling of safe contentment that allowed for rich retrospection? Or was it the dawn of a new millennium? Was this his idea of forward thinking, to look unexpectedly backwards? Or was it just a question of advancing years? At the time of recording, Bowie was fifty-two years old, an age when a man is likely to realise there are probably more years behind him than in front. Accordingly, the past becomes a fascinating country that tempts exploration, if only for clues to understanding present behaviour.

Bowie was far more content in his present self than he'd ever been. The angst that accompanied him throughout the seventies was now dormant. He had nothing left to prove. He knew, now, who David Bowie really was and with that knowledge came liberation.

One of the key songs from this album, then, is 'Seven', a lovely, melodic meditation on his father, mother and brother. 'I forgot what my brother said', he sings, but 'I remember how he wept/On a bridge of violent people/I was small enough to cry.'

In earlier years, Bowie had been haunted with worry that his brother's mental problems would affect him too. Maybe they had. Maybe that was the root of his songwriting genius, the creative schizophrenia that produced so many dizzyingly disparate musical worlds.

'It's a more personal piece but I hesitate to say if it's autobiographical. In a way, it self-evidently isn't... The progenitor of this piece is obviously a man who is fairly disillusioned. He's not a happy man. Whereas I am an incredibly happy man! So what I was trying to do, more than anything else, was capture some of the angst and feelings of guys of my age.' DB, 1999

With his knowledge of numerology, Bowie would have seen seven as a highly significant number. Someone on life path seven (derived from a calculation based on one's date of birth) is described as 'the searcher and the seeker of the truth'. The numerological profile continues: 'You have a clear and compelling sense of yourself as a spiritual being. As a result, your life path is devoted to investigations into the unknown, and finding the answers to the mysteries of life. You are well equipped to handle your task. You possess a fine mind; you are an analytical thinker, capable of great concentration and theoretical insight. You enjoy research, and putting the pieces of an intellectual puzzle together. Once you have enough pieces in place, you are capable of highly creative insight and practical solutions to problems. You enjoy your solitude and prefer to work alone.' Remind you of anyone?

'Survive' and 'Something In The Air' are ruminations on past relationships, with whom it's impossible to say. As with the rest of the album's lyrical content, Bowie paints in broad, diluted strokes, details left to the listener's interpretation. Fifteen years earlier he had told the *NME*:

'So much of the subconscious comes through with the melody and the placement of a particular word on a particular note. For better or for worse, the information is inherent in the song, not in the writer or his intentions or even in the lyrics.'

DB, 1984

Opposite: Performing 'Thursday's Child' on French music show *Les Années Tubes*, October 1999.

Overleaf, left-hand page: Appearing on the VH1 programme *Storytellers*, August 1999. An album and DVD of the performance, which included songs selected from the whole of his career to that point, was released ten years later.

Overleaf, right-hand page: On stage at the BRIT awards, February 1999. Bowie joined the British band Placebo in a version of T. Rex's '20th Century Boy' and later that year sang on their single 'Without You I'm Nothing'.

The vagueness of the outlines presented on *'hours...'* was partly a result of its relationship with the *Omikron* computer game. As with the *Labyrinth* soundtrack previously, Bowie was working within a framework not strictly of his own definition; but this context – a grown-up, non-linear, multi-layered experience – provided a bigger room in which to work.

'Perhaps we ended up with songs that are fairly receptive to personal interpretation, and generate a kind of emotional momentum... It seems obvious to me that, in a successful game, game players are forced to draw on their own real experiences, all the while slipping seamlessly into the game world. The music, in its relationship to both 'hours...' *and* Omikron, *should help to bridge the gap and maintain the suspension of disbelief.'*

DB, 1999

The rocked-up romp of 'The Pretty Things Are Going To Hell' (candidate for best-ever Bowie title) expresses the confusion sometimes brought by age, the blurring of previously certain lines, who to trust, who to hurt, what to do, where to go?

Also of interest is the touching 'Thursday's Child', the album's first single. Its 'Monday, Tuesday, Wednesday' refrain recalls Bowie's young fascination with the Frank Loesser song 'Inchworm', sung by Danny Kaye in the 1952 film *Hans Christian Andersen*.

Bowie himself suggested the album represented a search for spiritual answers. Organised religion had never been of much interest to him but the idea of finding something to hang your soul on was.

'A belief system is merely a personal support system really. It's up to me to construct one that isn't carved in stone, that may change overnight.'

DB, 1999

The album was steeped in religious imagery, from the lyrics through to the cover, a homage to *La Pietà*. The title itself can be read as a reference to *The Book Of Hours*, the ancient prayer book that allocates prayers and devotions to

different hours of the day. It is also, Bowie pointed out, a pun on 'ours', a suggestion that our individual experiences through time are also shared.

As such, *'hours…'* is an album of midlife crisis, the vague, quietly intense worries of a man fearing the future, peering myopically backwards to reconcile the present; a metaphor for all mankind on millennium eve.

'I've actually had quite a few midlife crises, most of them when I was in my twenties. It wasn't a particularly happy time of my life… So, crazily, I found myself drawing on my experiences from that time when I wanted to write an album on my present age.' DB, 1999

Bowie had one more unexpected trick up his sleeve. *'hours…'* would be the first complete album by a major artist available to download over the Internet, two weeks before the CDs hit the shop shelves.

He may have been looking back but he was very much seeing the future too.

THE ART OF THE COVER

The cover of *'hours…'* is a direct reference to *La Pietà*, a common image in Renaissance and medieval art of the Virgin Mary cradling the dead Christ. Photographed by Tim Bret-Day, the Bowie of *'hours…'* cradles the *Earthling*-era Bowie (photographed by Frank Ockenfels). The overtly religious imagery is continued on the back cover with a triptych of Bowies with a serpent; and the juxtaposition of Gothic typeface for 'David Bowie' and modern sans-serif lettering for the album title reinforces the general theme of the songs: a spiritual examination of the past in order to face the future; the confession of sin to find redemption; the death of feckless youth and resurrection through self-awareness.

The reference to the *Pietà* pose is clear when the *'hours…'* front cover is viewed next to Michelangelo's *Pietà* (St Peter's Basilica, the Vatican, Rome).

HEATHEN 2002

'WHAT I LIKE MY MUSIC TO DO TO ME IS AWAKEN THE GHOSTS INSIDE OF ME. NOT THE DEMONS, YOU UNDERSTAND, BUT THE GHOSTS.'

DAVID BOWIE, 2002

1999
9 October
Performs at NetAid, Wembley Stadium, London
10 October
'hours...' tour opens at the HQ, Dublin
14 October
Named a *Commandeur* in France's Ordre des Arts et des Lettres
28 October
Receives 'Legend' award at Warner Brothers' WB Radio Music Awards
7 December
'hours...' tour closes at the Vega, Copenhagen
1999–2000
Appears as Julian Priest in nine episodes of *The Hunger* TV series

2000
January
Release of 'Survive' (various editions) (UK 28, US DNC)
25 June
Headlines Glastonbury Festival
27 June
Records performance at BBC Radio Theatre, London, for BBC broadcast on 24 September
July
Release of 'Seven' (various editions) (UK 32, US DNC)
15 August
Birth of daughter Alexandria Zahra Jones
13 September
Release to BowieNet subscribers of *liveandwell.com*

2001
26 February
Performs with Moby and Philip Glass at Tibet House Trust benefit concert, Carnegie Hall, New York (again in 2002 and 2003)
2 April
Death of mother, Margaret Mary 'Peggy' Jones, aged 88
28 September
Zoolander (Bowie cameo as himself)
20 October
Opens The Concert For New York City, Madison Square Garden, New York

2002
10 June
Release of *Heathen* (UK 5, US 14)

Previous page: *Toy*-like portrait by Sukita, 2002.

Opposite: The last time Bowie had played Glastonbury, in 1971, the festival went by the quaint name of Glastonbury Fayre and his set had started at five in the morning. On his triumphant return in 2000 he was a headliner, playing in front of up to 100,000 fans on the main Pyramid Stage.

On Sunday June 25 2000, Bowie took to the Pyramid Stage and delivered a landmark performance to close that year's Glastonbury Festival. For the first time in ages he delivered a set of greatest hits reminding both the world, and himself, of the brilliance of his back catalogue. These were songs that had stood the test of time, that sounded as vitally relevant now as at any time before. A month later he started work on a new album. It was called *Toy*. Or it was going to be.

His plan was to update songs he'd written in the sixties including 'The London Boys', 'Liza Jane' (his first single, with The King Bees), 'I Dig Everything', 'Can't Help Thinking About Me', 'You've Got A Habit Of Leaving', 'Baby Loves That Way', 'Conversation Piece', 'Let Me Sleep Beside You', 'Silly Boy Blue', 'In The Heat Of The Morning' (a play on the Sidney Poitier film *In The Heat Of The Night*) and 'Karma Man'.

There were also tracks he'd written but never got round to recording – rumoured to be 'Hole In The Ground' and 'Miss American High' – as well as a few new compositions: 'Toy' would later be retitled 'Your Turn To Drive' while 'Afraid' and 'Uncle Floyd' resurfaced on *Heathen*, the latter as 'Slip Away', while 'Toy', retitled as 'Your Turn To Drive', eventually appeared on the 2014 compilation *Nothing Has Changed*.

Halfway through recording *Toy*, Bowie halted proceedings and on 15 August was by his wife Iman's side as she gave birth to a daughter – Alexandria Zahra Jones. Bowie himself cut the umbilical cord.

Bowie took the next two months off to be a father. He did not want to repeat a previous mistake. When his son, Duncan, was born in May 1971, Bowie had found the twin jobs of creating and performing music and raising a child problematic. With the arrival of Alexandria, Bowie determined to be present. 'And my soul feels complete,' he said of her arrival.

'I certainly wasn't there that much for him... I was ambitious, I wanted to be a real kind of presence, I wanted to be something... Fortunately, everything with us is tremendous now. But I would give my eye teeth to have that time back again to have shared it with him as a child.' DB, 2003

He returned to the studio and by early 2001 delivered the tapes to EMI/Virgin. They had a busy schedule, they said, but would issue it at some point, perhaps in May.

By the time summer came around, the album's prospects looked decidedly shaky. EMI/Virgin came back with a different proposal. Would David deliver an album of new material instead?

Bowie was quietly furious. He had already whetted his fan's appetite by stating that *Toy* was, 'not so much a *Pin Ups II* as an Update I'. By March 2002 he had left the label, set up his own – ISO – and signed a marketing and distribution deal with Columbia Records. *Toy* remains unreleased although several of the recordings have since appeared as B-sides.

With the *Toy* master tapes still sitting on executives' desks at EMI/Virgin, Bowie re-entered the studio to record a new album. The dust of the past was still settling around him, but he had invited an old friend to bring a new broom.

Bowie and Tony Visconti had fallen out since they last worked together on *Scary Monsters*. Word on a wing had it that Bowie had been upset by Visconti's openness in interviews about their time together. But they were older now and love was buried deep between them.

'I wrote to him several times and said, "Whatever I did, let's talk it over",' Visconti confided in 2006. 'Then one day I got a phone call from him. I just started to cry, because I'd really missed him. And he just glazed over the problem. It only took minutes to catch up on the past and we were talking about the future.'

Since 1998 the two had collaborated on several one-off projects – a single here, some string arrangements there – courtship ahead of a full reunion that Bowie described as 'perfect… as though we had just come from the previous album into this one. It was quite stunningly comfortable to work with each other again.'

2 October 2002: Back at the Hammersmith Odeon (now Apollo), scene of Ziggy's retirement, for the last European date of the Heathen tour. For the first time ever in a formal concert, Bowie performed the much-analysed *Hunky Dory* closer, 'The Bewlay Brothers'.

Bowie's artistic aim, now, was not dissimilar to that on *'hours…'*, to examine the spiritual, to ask 'the big questions without being too grand'. Only this time, the mood was darker, more serious.

In April 2001 his mother died, aged 88. His old friend, the designer Freddie Burretti, followed a month later. Whereas with *'hours…'* he'd admitted to slipping into a role in order to convey a sense of uncertain unease, to confront the contraction of life's years, now he was no longer acting and his melancholic sense of morbidity was palpable.

'We create so many circles on this straight line we're told we're travelling. The truth, of course, is that there is no journey: We are arriving and departing all at the same time.' DB, 2002

Work began in New York's Looking Glass Studios, where Philip Glass had recorded his symphonic versions of Bowie and Visconti's masterpieces *Low* and *"Heroes"*, in 1992 and 1996 respectively.

Bowie arrived with some forty pieces of music – not whole songs, but starting points to build on. Nothing began to be set in concrete until the crew, including the steadfast Carlos Alomar and new arrival, guitarist David Torn, moved to the newly opened Allaire Studios in the Catskill Mountains in upstate New York. Set in a luxurious twenties estate, high-perched with fifty-mile views in all directions, it had a profound effect on Bowie.

'One reads about encountering epiphany, a Damascene experience. Giddy at the tranquillity and the pure gravitas of the place, everything that I had written became galvanised somehow, into an unwavering focus.' DB, 2002

Within a day he was writing new songs with passionate urgency, including what is perhaps the album's finest track, 'Sunday'.

Set on a blanket of ethereal voices, Bowie puts on his best Scott Walker voice to sing of a world destroyed – 'We could look for cars or signs of life' – before ominously evoking the eternal truth, as expressed in Giuseppe Tomasi di Lampedusa's novel *The Leopard*, that everything must change for it to remain the same. 'Nothing has changed and everything has changed', he sings. Rising through the clouds to face God, Bowie fearfully insists 'we must find peace, we must find love', concluding that 'All my trials, Lord, will be remembered'.

He's speaking to the heavens again in 'A Better Future' and 'I Would Be Your Slave', angrily, impatiently, questioning God's ways and means, frustrated at His elusiveness to a man not naturally fortified by simple faith.

The lyric to 'Afraid' has a light-hearted cheekiness, yet remains a serious dissection of the source of inner peace. 'Things really matter to me', he sings, 'But I put my faith in tomorrow', before evoking his old friend John Lennon's letter of spiritual rejection, 'God', with, 'I believe in Beatles/I believe my soul has grown.' Yet despite it all, he remains 'so afraid'. Instead, he turns inward, drawing strength from experience: 'If I put faith in medication/If I can smile a crooked smile/If I can talk on television/If I can walk an empty mile/Then I won't feel afraid.'

'When I become philosophical, in those 'long lonely hours', it's the source of all my frustrations, hammering away at the same questions I've had since I was nineteen. Nothing has really changed for me. This daunting spiritual search. If you can make the spiritual connection with some kind of clarity then everything else would fall into place. A morality would seem to be offered, a plan would seem to be offered, some sense would be there. But it evades me. Yet I can't help writing about it.'

DB, 2003

Many people, of course, thought the album reflected the terrible events of 11 September 2001 when New York's Twin Towers were attacked by terrorists. But, as Bowie astutely pointed out, half a dozen of his albums, if released in the aftermath of that event, might have led people to the same conclusion. Angst, worry, fear, isolation, rejection are recurring themes in Bowie's work. Mortality could now be added to that mix.

'When you're young, you're still "becoming", now at my age I am more concerned with "being". And not too long from now I'll be driven by surviving, I'm sure… I've kind of knocked on the door and heard a muffled answer. Nevertheless, I still don't know what the voice is saying, or even what language it's in.'

DB, 2002

Bowie had children, a soul mate, an understanding of his place in the world. He hated that death would take that away from him but he had no choice in the matter. All he had was his love of life. Hence, he turned his head to the skies, looking for answers from a God he was not sure existed. The sound of his questioning is the sound of *Heathen*.

THE ART OF THE COVER

Heathen's cover is one of the most visually dramatic in Bowie's catalogue. Bowie's eyes, windows to the soul, are terrifyingly blank, his face iron-set in emotionless resolution.

Inside the CD booklet, the desecrated religious artworks represent not disbelief in, but a rejection of God – the defining act of a heathen. The use of Guido Reni's *Massacre Of The Innocents* carries a strong echo of the then-recent 9/11 terror attacks. The three books shown are significant. Nietzsche's *The Gay Science* contains the infamous statement, 'God is dead'; Einstein's *The General Theory Of Relativity* and Freud's *The Interpretation Of Dreams* are pivotal works in which humanity seeks, and finds, understanding without resort to deities. The booklet also sees Bowie walking determinedly down a staircase, away from the light. The cumulative message is one of conscious rejection of a God who has apparently deserted us, in favour of the cold comfort of secular knowledge.

Right: Religious themes featured at various points in Bowie's musical career – notably in the song-prayer 'Word On A Wing' from *Station To Station* and, more recently, in the overtly Christian imagery of the *'hours…'* cover artwork. And as an actor he even played Pontius Pilate in Martin Scorsese's *The Last Temptation Of Christ*. With its images of desecration and turning away from the light, the *Heathen* cover artwork appears to represent a rejection of religion.

REALITY 2003

'IT'S A FAST-RECEDING PAST, AN INCREDIBLY UNCERTAIN FUTURE AND A DIMINISHING PRESENT. THERE'S A GREAT BLURRING OF EVERYTHING IN OUR LIVES NOW. IT'S FAR MORE ABOUT HOW ME AND MY FAMILY ARE GOING TO GET THROUGH THE DAY.'

DAVID BOWIE, 2002

2002

June
Curates the Meltdown festival programme, Royal Festival Hall, London
29 June
Heathen tour opens with Bowie's own Meltdown concert, during which he performs *Low* and *Heathen* in their entirety
September
Release of 'Everyone Says Hi' (various editions) (UK 20, US DNC)
23 October
Heathen tour closes at the Orpheum Theater, Boston

2003

September
Release of 'New Killer Star' (video version and various editions) (UK 38, US DNC)
15 September
Release of *Reality* (UK 3, US 29)
7 October
A Reality Tour opens at the Forum, Copenhagen

2004

June
UK release of 'Rebel Never Gets Old (radio mix)'/ 'Rebel Never Gets Old (7th Heaven edit)'/'Rebel Never Gets Old (7th Heaven mix)'/'Days (album version)' (47)
25 June
A Reality Tour closes prematurely at the Hurricane Festival, Scheessel, Germany
26 June
Bowie undergoes emergency heart surgery in St Georg Hospital, Hamburg
November
UK release of 'Band Aid 20: Do They Know It's Christmas?'/ 'Band Aid: Do They Know It's Christmas?'/ 'Band Aid: Do They Know It's Christmas? (live at Live Aid)' (1)

2005

8 September
Performs with Arcade Fire at the Fashion Rocks concert, Radio City Music Hall, New York
November
Release of 'Arcade Fire & David Bowie Live At Fashion Rocks EP' on download: 'Life On Mars?'/'Five Years'/'Wake Up' (DNC)

2006

8 February
Receives (in absentia) a Lifetime Achievement Award at the Grammys
29 May
Makes a guest appearance at a David Gilmour concert at the Royal Albert Hall, London
21 September
Appears as himself in an episode of BBC TV comedy *Extras* and contributes the song 'Pug Nosed Face'
17 October
The Prestige (Bowie plays Nikola Tesla)
November
Voted fourth on a BBC *Culture Show* list of Britain's Top Ten Living Icons
9 November
Final live appearance, at the Black Ball benefit concert, Hammerstein Ballroom, New York
December
UK release by David Gilmour featuring David Bowie of 'Arnold Layne' (various editions) (19)
29 December
Arthur And The Invisibles (Bowie provides voice for Maltazard)

2007

May
Curates New York's High Line Festival
3 June
Receives Lifetime Achievement Award at the International Academy of Digital Arts and Sciences' annual Webby Awards
25 June
Release of DVD/CD set *Glass Spider* (DNC)
12 November
SpongeBob SquarePants: Atlantis SquarePantis shown on Nickelodeon (Bowie provides guest-star voiceover)

2008

22 January
August (Bowie cameo as Cyrus Ogilvie)

2009

6 July
Release of DVD/CD set *VH1 Storytellers* (DNC)
August
Bandslam (Bowie cameo as himself)

2010

25 January
Release of *A Reality Tour* (UK 53, US DNC)
27 September
Re-release of *Station To Station* as deluxe package with *Live Nassau Coliseum '76*

2011

March
Unreleased album *Toy* leaked onto the Internet

Previous page: Facing the Australian press to promote A Reality Tour, Sydney, February 2004.

Opposite: All smiles at the Hartwall Areena, Helsinki, October 2003.

Overleaf: In blistering form at the MEN Arena, Manchester, November 2003, the first UK stop on A Reality Tour.

In October 2002, as the Heathen tour finished in Boston, Bowie was ecstatic, proclaiming his touring group as 'one of the strongest bands I've ever worked with'. He was keen to get back in the studio, record new tracks and get back on the road again.

In November, Bowie and Visconti began planning an album that would translate directly and easily to live performance. '*Heathen* consisted of very broad strokes and a grand sonic landscape,' Visconti later explained, 'there were layers and layers of overdubs – whereas for *Reality* he [Bowie] wanted to change to something that he and his live band could play on stage with great immediacy…'.

Accordingly, having carefully prepared demos of the new material in January 2003, Bowie and Visconti naturally turned to the musicians who had performed so well on the Heathen tour for recording proper.

The isolated mountain retreat of Allaire Studios had exerted enormous influence over *Heathen*, but *Reality* demanded a different setting. Designed for visceral live communication, *Reality*'s tight pop-rock needed an urban environment and recording took place in the heart of New York at Looking Glass Studios. '*Reality* is the sense of New York,' Bowie commented, and the city cuts its way through the album like Broadway through Manhattan.

'I can't imagine living anywhere else... I realised the other day that I've lived in New York longer than I've lived anywhere else. It's amazing: I am a New Yorker. It's strange; I never thought I would be.' DB, 2003

Less conceptual, less thematically unified than previous albums, *Reality*'s songs divide themselves into various, yet familiar, categories. He muses again on mortality ('Never Get Old') and on anxiety, isolation and belonging in a world post 9/11 ('Fall Dog Bombs The Moon'); there are elliptical lyrics that resonate in their vibrancy ('Bring Me The Disco King') and a return to character acting with excursions into the lives of those who roam only in his head ('The Loneliest Guy' and 'She'll Drive The Big Car').

'I write mainly about very personal and rather lonely feelings, and I explore them in a different way each time. You know, what I do is not terribly intellectual. I'm a pop singer for Christ's sake. As a person, I'm fairly uncomplicated.' DB, 2002

As ever, in contemplating mankind's future, Bowie's instincts had led him towards darkness. But he later revealed that parenthood had left him in a quandary.

'I can't talk about the negativity in the same way that I would have done before she was born – every time I say the world is fucked up and not worth living in she is going to say, "Well, thanks for bringing me into it."' DB, 2003

Musically, the songs are again more streamlined, more accessible than the ones on, say, *1.Outside*. On a track like Jonathan Richman's 'Pablo Picasso', Bowie lets rip, edging towards punk, Stooges-style. On 'Fall Dog Bombs The Moon', he is Neil Young and Crazy Horse, conjuring the fear and horror of 9/11. On 'Days' he confesses a debt of friendship over a bed of striking, haunting acoustic guitars. 'Do I need a friend? Well, I need one now,' he sings before adding plaintively, 'All the days of my life, all the days I owe you.'

Underlying all the songs on *Reality* is a sense of Bowie's great restlessness; he's unsure whether to dance or try to answer the 'idiot questions' he can't help asking himself, day after day.

'I don't think I write about a terribly wide range of subjects. My excitement is in finding a new way of approaching that same subject, and at heart I think that is what most writers do... I invariably deal with the same senses of isolation and lack of communication and all these kinds of negatives, and I'll probably deal with them to the end of my life. There'll be certain spiritual questionings and all that, and it won't change very much, because it never has, it appears, from Major Tom to Heathen.*'* DB, 2003

The album's closing track is 'Bring Me The Disco King', an extraordinary composition of avant-garde nightclub jazz. Nearly forty years in the business and still pushing the boundaries.

Written in 1992, the song was originally destined for *Black Tie White Noise*, Bowie intending it as an up-tempo cheesy disco number. Wisely, he held back and ten years later moulded it into a classic, which features his deep, resonant vocal – the ghost of Sinatra – and Mike Garson's beautifully wandering piano set against Sterling Campbell's insistent, hesitant and unnerving drums. Through misty images of his past, of excess, desire and doubt, he sings, 'Close me in the dark, let me disappear/Soon there'll be nothing left of me/Nothing left to release.'

And there was nothing to release for another ten years.

Before *Reality* was even in the shops, as it gathered near-unanimous glowing reviews, Bowie was already on the road, his concerts selling out within minutes. A new album in the can, a new tour with a tight band, all was good. And then, in Oslo, on 18 June 2004, an ominous accident: a fan throws a lollipop and hits him in the eye. 'Do remember, I've only got one!' he shouts back.

Five nights later in Prague, nine songs into the set, Bowie feels a pain shoot across his chest. He leaves the stage and is attended to straight away. The prognosis? A trapped nerve in his shoulder. Relief all round.

Two more days pass and, after playing the Hurricane Festival in Scheessel, Germany, Bowie feels the pain again. But this time it gets worse. The next day he is rushed to the St Georg Hospital in Hamburg and given emergency heart surgery. The road, the life, the demands, the pressure, the striving, all of it had caught up with him.

In his first statement after the operation, Bowie said:

'I'm so pissed off because the last ten months of this tour have been so fucking fantastic. Can't wait to be fully recovered and get back to work again. I tell you what, though, I won't be writing a song about this one.' DB, 2004

Bowie returned to New York, to Iman, his daughter and his family and that is where he stayed.

Ever the cool one, he never issued a word on his plans or his professional status. Had he retired? Was he writing, recording? No one knew.

There were occasional cameos. In 2005 he performed at Fashion Rocks, a fundraiser for the victims of Hurricane Katrina, appearing on stage with a bandaged hand and blackened eye (just make-up) to sing 'Life On Mars?'. He left to thunderous applause and then returned with Arcade Fire in tow – a band he had championed vociferously – to perform 'Five Years' (and the Arcade Fire song 'Wake Up'). Questioned afterwards he told reporters he was attending the gym and had loved being on stage. So much so, he appeared with Arcade Fire again, just four days later, at their gig in Central Park.

In 2006 he received a Grammy lifetime achievement award but failed to show up for the ceremony. In May that year, he strolled on stage in London to join Pink Floyd's David Gilmour for versions of 'Arnold Layne' and 'Comfortably Numb'. On 9 November 2006, he sang at a charity gig hosted by his wife, Iman, and Alicia Keys to raise money for Aids education and medicine in Africa. He turned up in the popular British television show *Extras*, written by and starring Ricky Gervais, and he campaigned to save BBC's publicly funded 6Music radio station from the axe in the face of budget cuts.

According to some, his life now had one focus, and it was no longer art. It was his family. Perhaps so, but with Bowie, nothing was ever obvious. Maybe, just maybe, within his self-imposed silence, his muse would again flourish.

Below: On 23 June 2004 Bowie had to cut short this performance at the T-Mobile Arena in Prague owing to excruciating chest pains. After one more show in Germany, the rest of A Reality Tour was cancelled and the next day Bowie underwent emergency heart surgery.

Opposite: 'Just gonna have to be a different man'. David Bowie's final live performance was at the Black Ball benefit concert, Hammerstein Ballroom, New York, on 9 November 2006, where he sang 'Changes' with Alicia Keys.

THE NEXT DAY 2013

"HE SAID, "KEEP IT A SECRET, AND DON'T TELL ANYBODY. NOT EVEN YOUR BEST FRIEND." I SAID, "CAN I TELL MY GIRLFRIEND?" HE SAYS, "YES, YOU CAN TELL YOUR GIRLFRIEND, BUT SHE CAN'T TELL ANYBODY.""

TONY VISCONTI, 2013

2012

27 March

Plaque unveiled on Heddon Street, central London, to commemorate the location where Bowie was photographed for *The Rise And Fall Of Ziggy Stardust And The Spiders From Mars*

12 August

Turns down an invitation to perform "Heroes" at the London 2012 Olympics closing ceremony, but the song still becomes an unofficial anthem of Team GB at the Games

31 August–2 September

Bowiefest, a festival celebrating Bowie's film career, is held at the Institute of Contemporary Arts (ICA), London

14 November

Release of Soulwax's *Radio Soulwax Presents DAVE*, an hour-long video homage to the music of David Bowie

2013

8 January

Releases single 'Where Are We Now?' (UK 6, US DNC) on his sixty-sixth birthday and announces first new album in ten years

25 February

Release of 'The Stars (Are Out Tonight)' (DNC)

11 March

Release of *The Next Day* (UK 1, US 2)

23 March–11 August

David Bowie is, the first international Bowie retrospective exhibition, is held at the Victoria and Albert Museum, London

25 May

David Bowie – Five Years documentary broadcast on BBC television

Brilliant, just brilliant. On the morning of his sixty-sixth birthday, 8 January 2013, David Bowie issued his 108th single, 'Where Are We Now?' And it came from nowhere. No one in the world, except those involved, had any idea that Bowie had been writing new music, let alone recording it.

That he had been able to keep his movements so secret can be explained by the identity of the musicians he had chosen for the project. Bowie veterans like Earl Slick, Gail Ann Dorsey, Gerry Leonard and – the longest-serving of them all – producer Tony Visconti, maintained fierce loyalty and respect for their man.

What then of the single that the world woke up to with such happy surprise? Stately and elegiac, 'Where Are We Now?' finds Bowie looking back to his Berlin days. So compelling was the song's simplicity and yearning, many suspected that the album (announced at the same time) would be in a similar vein – that *The Next Day* would find Bowie ruminating over and coming to terms with his past. This idea was strengthened by previews of the album artwork, which featured a large white square plastered over the iconic *"Heroes"* cover. Again, the idea of nostalgia had been placed in the ether.

Naturally, he had wrong-footed everyone. Bowie had no intention of wallowing in the past.

The Next Day builds on Bowie's unique artistic legacy. Hewn from his vivid imagination, the songs are set in an unspecified time and place, from which Bowie reports back with scatter-gun lines, detailing his observations, his stories, his characters.

What the album does not reveal much of is Bowie himself. With self-revelation comes categorisation, which all true artists fear like the antelope fears the leopard. Instead, Bowie again makes music that shoots across the landscape with energy and ambition. On first hearing, *The Next Day* sounds jagged, ragged, disjointed, dissonant. Like on many of his previous albums – *1.Outside* springs to mind – he creates a layered sound that fully reveals itself only after repeated plays.

The album starts with four 'up' tracks and any concern over Bowie's health appears to be dispelled by their energy

and power. Bowie sounds robust, purposeful, in control. It is thrilling to hear.

The title track features a lynching, a baying crowd who 'can't get enough of that doomsday song', a purple-headed priest, and people who work for Satan but dress like saints. Visconti revealed that Bowie had been reading a lot of medieval English history and that this explains the macabre imagery deployed in this assertive opening salvo.

Next comes 'Dirty Boys' – musically staccato, punctuated by outbursts of baritone sax, a song that would not sound out of place on *"Heroes"*, in fact.

Released as the second single from the album, 'The Stars (Are Out Tonight)' starts with a curling guitar riff, before Bowie introduces a catchy vocal line, which remains constant amid the shifting backdrop of guitars, the singer likening celebs to vampires, who burn us with their radiant smiles and trap us with their beautiful eyes. It is a song delivered by a man who is probably one of the biggest celebs on the planet.

'Love Is Lost' describes a beautiful woman of twenty-two, whose country, friends, house, and even eyes, are new, but whose fear is as old as the world – a person who will cut out her soul and all thought, and by doing so jolts Bowie into shouting, 'Oh, what have you done? Oh, what have you done?'

The music is menacing, fragmented in parts (like the woman's soul?), and so the tranquil chords of 'Where Are We Now?' come as a welcome relief. This appears to be the most straightforward track on the album, a song of questioning and hope that is elevated by the introduction halfway through of a military drum beat to emphasise Bowie's affirmation that 'as long as there's me and as long as there's you' – then there's ... well, he doesn't say. And that's the closest Bowie will come to revelation or reflection. He remains a Modernist, looking forwards, never backwards.

'Valentine's Day' does, however, remind us of Bowie past – it's a song that could join 'The Prettiest Star' on

Aladdin Sane, a song that Bowie sings like it's 1973. 'If You Can See Me' is another track that one could imagine featuring on a previous Bowie album, in this case *Earthling*. Using the drum 'n' bass style he explored so well on that work, the song is filled with paranoia and urgency, Bowie switching between different types of vocal to indicate different characters.

Above: With a surprise new album and a major V&A retrospective (shown here), Bowie-mania was back.

Opposite: In the promo for 'The Stars (Are Out Tonight)', Bowie and Tilda Swinton play a comfortable middle-aged couple. Swinton was a close friend of Bowie and gave a memorable speech at the opening of the *David Bowie is* exhibition.

Featuring a sublime chorus, 'I'd Rather Be High' is written from the perspective of a young recruit sent to war, a man who would rather be high than shoot other men. It is one of the many highlights of this album. 'Boss Of Me' follows a similar route, with a circular, jagged guitar riff again balanced out by a memorable chorus.

'Dancing Out In Space', with its mix of nagging guitar and otherworldly noises, is the best-sounding song on the album, gritty but ethereal, irresistibly danceable, a teenage rock 'n' roll workout from the future. In contrast, 'How Does The Grass Grow?' is perhaps *The Next Day*'s least attractive song. However, its quoting of the famous Shadows instrumental 'Apache' takes us back to the time of Bowie's first ever band, The Konrads.

Staying in the early 1960s, '(You Will) Set The World On Fire' locates us in the Greenwich Village folk scene where Pete Seeger, Bob Dylan and Joan Baez move in and out of focus, the central character being an unnamed talent whose lines 'Kennedy would kill for' – yet the music is rock to its core.

'You Feel So Lonely You Could Die' is one of the most intriguing tracks, full of disturbing images of murder, with Bowie actually wishing death on the song's subject. Who does he have in mind? Someone he was once close to, maybe? The song ends with the drum outro from 'Five Years', a clue perhaps to the identity of the person?

The closing track, 'Heat', starts languidly but turns up the temperature as it progresses – Bowie finishing this remarkable album with the repeated line, 'My father ran the prison'. This is a fitting image to end with, for on *The Next Day* Bowie evades every attempt to capture him.

The album shot to number one in more than twenty countries. In London, a major V&A Bowie retrospective (which, by coincidence, or perhaps not, opened two weeks after the album's release) broke all records for advance ticket sales and was planned to travel on to several key locations around the world. Internationally, magazines carried Bowie's face on their cover, and, in the absence of any interviews from the man himself, eagerly speculated about whether he would take *The Next Day* on the road. It was a stunning comeback, leading to considered reflection on Bowie's remarkable achievements and intense speculation about his future.

BLACKSTAR 2016

'HIS DEATH WAS NO DIFFERENT FROM HIS LIFE – A WORK OF ART. HE MADE BLACKSTAR *FOR US, HIS PARTING GIFT. I KNEW FOR A YEAR THIS WAS THE WAY IT WOULD BE. I WASN'T, HOWEVER, PREPARED FOR IT. HE WAS AN EXTRAORDINARY MAN, FULL OF LOVE AND LIFE. HE WILL ALWAYS BE WITH US.'*

TONY VISCONTI, 2016

2013
17 June
Release of 'The Next Day' (DNC)
19 August
Release of 'Valentine's Day' (DNC)
25 September–19 November
The *David Bowie is* exhibition tours the world, starting with a residency at the Art Gallery Ontario in Toronto
4 November
Release of *The Next Day Extra*, a three-disc collectors' edition featuring remixes, bonus tracks and promo videos
16 December
Release of 'Love Is Lost' (James Murphy remix) (DNC)

2014
31 January–20 April
The *David Bowie is* exhibition visits the Museu da Imagem e do Som, São Paulo
19 February
Bowie wins a Brit Award for Best Male Solo Artist, the oldest recipient in the history of the awards
20 May–24 August
Next stop for the *David Bowie is* exhibition: the Martin-Gropius-Bau, Berlin
23 September–4 January 2015
The *David Bowie is* exhibition visits the Museum of Contemporary Art in Chicago; the opening is marked by the release of a documentary called *David Bowie Is Happening Now*
17 November
Release of 'Sue (Or In A Season Of Crime)', recorded with the Maria Schneider Orchestra (UK 81, US DNC)
18 November
Release of *Nothing Has Changed* compilation (UK 9, US 57)

2015
2 March–31 May
David Bowie is becomes one of the first exhibitions to be held at the newly built Philharmonie de Paris
16 July–1 November
The exhibition moves to the ACMI in Melbourne
20 November
Release of 'Blackstar' (DNC)
7 December–20 January 2016
Bowie's musical play *Lazarus*, co-written with Enda Walsh, runs at the New York Theatre Workshop
11 December–10 April 2016
The *David Bowie is* exhibition returns to Europe – to the Groninger Museum, Groningen, in the Netherlands, and is announced to open in Japan in Spring 2017
17 December
Release of 'Lazarus' (DNC)

2016
8 January
Release of *Blackstar* (UK 1, US 1)
10 January
David Bowie dies, two days after his sixty-ninth birthday

On 10 January 2016, David Bowie lost a battle with cancer that he had been fighting in private for the previous eighteen months. He died just two days after his sixty-ninth birthday and the release of *Blackstar*, his twenty-ninth studio album. When the news broke the following day shortly before 7 a.m. GMT, the world stood shocked and numbed at the loss of a cultural icon.

The sadness felt by so many millions stemmed from various sources. Remembered joy was a primary factor. Many testified that Bowie had provided the soundtrack for their generation. As we had grown, so Bowie's music had grown with us – from *Ziggy* to *Young Americans*, from *"Heroes"* to *Scary Monsters*, we had travelled with him from station to station, a journey of immense proportions ingrained in our collective consciousness: London, New York, Berlin, Kyoto – anywhere in the ether, in fact.

Yet there was a stronger force at work here, powered by a deep recognition of his immense artistic courage. All his life, Bowie had pushed himself to create a body of work that all could benefit from. New Romantics, heavy rockers, modernists, intellectuals, avant garde lovers, all found music and principles and ideas that corresponded closely to their worlds or pushed them towards rich and significant changes. Bowie and his art were beautifully positioned to open minds as well as hearts.

No other artist has been so generous in his reach.

Blackstar does nothing to alter this view of Bowie's fluid artistic greatness. And although cancer claimed him, it also pushed him into astonishing activity ahead of the album's release.

He had been diagnosed in the summer of 2014. By November 2015, he knew it was terminal. At this point he was deep into a new theatrical project, a musical named *Lazarus*, co-written with Enda Walsh, the Tony award-winning Irish playwright.

Lazarus was inspired by Walter Tevis's 1963 novel *The Man Who Fell To Earth*. Bowie had, of course, famously starred as Thomas Jerome Newton in the 1976 film version directed by Nicolas Roeg. The play picks up Newton's story thirty years later. Why this character at this time? Maybe because Newton is, as he describes himself in the play, 'a dying man who can't die'.

The two-hour production features fourteen songs from Bowie's back catalogue, some presented in startling new ways. For example, there's a synthpop version of 'The Man Who Sold The World' and a stripped-down "Heroes", to go with straighter takes on 'Changes', 'All The Young Dudes' and 'This Is Not America'.

Heavyweight names came on board, including veteran producer and longtime friend Robert Fox, and the actor Michael C. Hall, who played Newton.

When Bowie met Hall for the first time, he apparently said, 'What is it with you?' referring to the vivid and off-beat characters Hall had portrayed in the TV hits *Six Feet Under* and *Dexter*. Hall would later remember Bowie thus: 'He was so generous, and so palpably kind.' Not the first to describe him in this way.

On the opening night, 7 December 2015, Bowie gave the actor an artefact from his past. Out of respect for Bowie's 'intense privacy', Hall will not reveal the nature of the gift.

Robert Fox described Bowie's active participation in rehearsals – all the more remarkable given the advanced stage of his illness. 'Some days he just wasn't able to be around but whenever he could be, it [the cancer] didn't interfere with his contribution. It was just horrible for him, rather than difficult for us.'

The play's director, Ivo Van Hove, confided to *Lazarus*'s choreographer, Annie B. Parson, that Bowie had told him 'this was the saddest piece he had ever worked on'. Van Hove added, 'I saw a man fighting. He fought like a lion and kept working like a lion through it all. I had incredible respect for that.'

Lazarus features one new song, the play's title song, which also appears on *Blackstar*. Sessions for the album had begun in January 2015 at the Magic Shop studio near Bowie's Lower Manhattan home. They ran from 11 a.m. until 4 p.m. By April, the seven tracks had been recorded and producer Tony Visconti then moved to his studio to mix them. Following the pattern set by *The Next Day*, the music had been made in total secrecy.

Later that year, after recording had finished, Bowie agreed to supply the theme music to a Sky TV series called *The Last Panthers*, loosely based on the exploits of a gang of Balkan jewel robbers called the Pink Panthers. Bowie met the show's director, Johan Renck. 'The piece of music he laid before us embodied every aspect of our characters and the series itself,' Renck said. 'Dark, brooding, beautiful and sentimental (in the best possible incarnation of this word). All along, the man inspired and intrigued me and as the process passed, I was overwhelmed with his generosity.'

Bowie now revealed to Renck that the music he had given him was the opening section of a longer song called 'Blackstar', and enlisted the director to shoot the accompanying video. In their discussions for the shoot, Renck suggested filming strange rituals suggestive of occultism. In return, Bowie sent him a sketch of a character called Button Eyes that he wanted to portray. Bowie's health was such that his part had to be shot in just one day, in September 2015.

In November, Renck and Bowie reconvened to make another video – this time for 'Lazarus', the second single released in advance of the album. This featured Bowie, again as Button Eyes, writhing in a hospital bed. There were also shots of Bowie dressed in a striped outfit very similar to one he wears in a promo shot from the mid-1970s in which he is shown drawing a kabbalistic diagram. In the video he dances, then writes frenetically – like a man running out of time – before finally stepping backwards into a wardrobe (going back into the closet, as Bowie joked).

Two months later, on the day of his sixty-ninth birthday, *Blackstar* was released and was met with great critical acclaim by reviewers as yet unaware of Bowie's grave illness. This is a vibrant work, humming itself to life with ideas and energy. Creativity abounds. It is ten steps on from *The Next Day*.

On *Blackstar* (the first mainstream Bowie album not to carry a picture of him on the cover) Bowie collaborates with the Donny McCaslin quartet, a jazz band he saw playing in a New York club in 2014 upon the advice of his friend the jazz musician Maria Schneider. The results are thrilling, outstanding.

Bowie appropriates a genre, free jazz, and moulds the form to the contours of his songwriting. Some artists use musical styles outside their normal range as a signifier of their versatility – look at me, ma, I've got an exotic instrument in my song. No such dilettantism here. The spirit of adventure that runs deep in jazz taps straight into Bowie's artistic drive, the force that gave us pioneering albums such as *Young Americans*, *Station To Station*, *Low*, *"Heroes"*, *1.Outside*, and so many other diverse treasures.

The title track opens the album, an epic work, dense, allusive, Gothic, disturbing. According to producer Tony Visconti, 'Blackstar' is a marriage of two separate compositions. The song's first movement is a statement of ominous darkness, dominated by a chanted incantation and images of executions and candles, which then gives way to a light and beautiful melody.

Much has been made of 'Blackstar', starting with McCaslin's assertion that Bowie had told him the song was his response to the deeds of Islamic State. Bowie's representatives swiftly denied this interpretation, leaving fans to explore other avenues in the days and weeks after his death. These have included occultism (analysts have suggested references to Aleister Crowley in the song), oncology ('black star' being a type of cancerous lesion) and astronomy ('black star' as the transitional state between a collapsed star and an infinite quantity). Or do we follow the path of Bowie expert and archivist Kevin Cann, who points us towards Elvis Presley?

In 1960, Elvis recorded a song entitled... 'Black Star', a rare alternative version of 'Flaming Star'. These are the opening lines. 'Every man has a black star, a black star over his shoulder and when a man sees his black star he knows his time has come...' Was this Bowie joining up the dots, referencing one of his earliest musical heroes (with whom, incidentally, he shared a birthday) to make sense of his imminent death?

Bowie, of course, refused to elucidate. To reveal meaning would be to strip him of mystery, and mystery has always been a crucial aspect of his artistic integrity. It had been nearly a decade since his last interview. This stance helped create a frenzy among his many devotees, a furore that recalls the pressure on Bob Dylan in the 1960s, a similar yearning from his audience for clarification in the hope of liberation.

If, for example, we believe that Bowie was referring to the medical meaning of 'black star' as a form of cancerous lesion, then is there anything sadder in music than Bowie insisting halfway through this majestic song that he is not

'At the centre of it all': scenes from the astonishing ten-minute 'Blackstar' video, directed by Johan Renck.

a film star, a pop star or a gangstar, but instead a blackstar, a man defined only by his illness, his achievements eclipsed by the virulent disease?

I think not. Yet his elliptical lyrics, impressionist and allusive to the last, compel us to invest ourselves in his music, to create our own meaning around them. Bowie's words and images have to be strong, rock hard, to withstand such collective pressure from his audience. And they are. And when they are not the music takes the strain.

On ''Tis Pity She Was A Whore', for example, Bowie opens with the humorous line, 'Man, she punched me like a dude' and then throws various other lines at us which, frankly, do not add up to much (the *New Yorker* referred to Bowie's 'willingness to embrace nonsense' in its review of *Blackstar*). But the music, oh the thrilling music, Bowie at one point literally whooping in delight at the sound of this band at full, marvellous tilt.

In 'Lazarus', he sings, heartbreakingly, of being in heaven, having 'scars that can't be seen', being free like a bluebird. He foresees the impact of his death with the line, 'Everybody knows me now' – which, of course, we do not and never will.

'Lazarus' is built on repetition and power, the song's dramatic guitar chords eventually giving way in volume to Bowie's voice which dominates at the end. It is just one of the many sonic wonders that Tony Visconti achieves on the album. The sound of *Blackstar* is magnificent, every song realised to its full potential. In his final chapter Bowie could not have wished for a better collaborator.

The next track, 'Sue (Or In A Season Of Crime)', was originally recorded with the Maria Schneider Orchestra in 2014 and included in the compilation *Nothing Has Changed*, released in November of that year. The version on *Blackstar* was rerecorded with McCaslin's group.

With its use of Nadsat, the language invented by Anthony Burgess for *A Clockwork Orange*, 'Girl Loves Me' obliquely evokes the spirit of Ziggy – the film adaption of Burgess's novel being a key inspiration for the Ziggy look. Bowie also sings in Polari, a slang used by gay men in 1950s London to keep their interactions secret, and a linguistic form he knew all too well. The song's unsettling effect, achieved by the use of multiple voices and astute sonic layering, delights and surprises.

Certainly the album's two closing statements – 'Dollar Days' and 'I Can't Give Everything Away' – raise *Blackstar* to classic status. 'Dollar Days' began as a simple yet affecting guitar line which Bowie found in the studio. This melody is used as a springboard, the song elevated and sustained by waves of synthesizers, changing musical landscapes, and a wonderful vocal, impassioned and open and human and honest. Bowie sings from the soul: 'Don't believe for just one second I'm forgetting you, I'm trying to, I'm dying to...'

The song ends with a modern-day equivalent of the 'Five Years' drum outro, which ushers us into 'I Can't Give Everything Away', Bowie's final message to us. The title appears to be self-explanatory (although, of course, with Bowie one can never be certain). It also brings to mind his first ever solo single, 'Can't Help Thinking About Me', in which he sang of packing his bags and leaving home, hoping he could 'make it on his own'. Now the prodigal son seems to have completed his journey.

Throughout his career, Bowie was forever throwing us oddballs, challenging his audience, seeking to open us up to new ways, to new experience. He stood on the outside and ushered us in. *Blackstar* follows in this wonderful tradition, Bowie's unique combination of generosity and rare talent. Intriguingly, Visconti has revealed that days before the album's release Bowie told him he had five new songs demoed and ready to go. Creativity surged through him right until the end.

'David Bowie had everything. He was intelligent, imaginative, brave, charismatic, cool, sexy and truly inspirational both visually and musically. He created such staggeringly brilliant work, yes, but so *much of it and it was* so *good. There are great people who make great work but who else has left a mark like his? No one like him. ... Whatever journey his beautiful soul is now on, I hope he can somehow feel how much we all miss him.'*

Kate Bush, 2016

When news of Bowie's death broke, this 2013 mural in Brixton, Bowie's birthplace, by Australian artist Jimmy C became a shrine. The local Ritzy cinema changed its hoarding to 'David Bowie, our Brixton boy, RIP' and hundreds of fans gathered outside for an impromptu street party to celebrate a remarkable man.

STAR MAN!
GOBLIN KING
David
You influenced my life
from my teenage years
Thank you
TO THE STARMAN

‘MUSIC HAS GIVEN ME OVER FORTY YEARS OF EXTRAORDINARY EXPERIENCES. I CAN’T SAY THAT LIFE’S PAINS OR MORE TRAGIC EPISODES HAVE BEEN DIMINISHED BECAUSE OF IT. BUT IT’S ALLOWED ME SO MANY MOMENTS OF COMPANIONSHIP WHEN I’VE BEEN LONELY AND A SUBLIME MEANS OF COMMUNICATION WHEN I WANTED TO TOUCH PEOPLE. IT’S BEEN BOTH MY DOORWAY OF PERCEPTION AND THE HOUSE THAT I LIVE IN.’

DAVID BOWIE, 1999

STUDIO ALBUMS

DAVID BOWIE 1967

Recorded at Decca Studios
165 Broadhurst Gardens, West Hampstead, London, UK
Produced by Mike Vernon

Personnel
David Bowie – Vocals, Guitar, Saxophone
Derek Boyes – Organ
John Eager – Drums
Derek Fearnley – Bass

Cover Art
Gerald Fearnley – Photography
Kenneth Pitt – Sleeve notes

Side One
'Uncle Arthur'/ 'Sell Me A Coat'/ 'Rubber Band'/ 'Love You Till Tuesday'/ 'There Is A Happy Land'/ 'We Are Hungry Men'/ 'When I Live My Dream'

Side Two
'Little Bombardier'/ 'Silly Boy Blue'/ 'Come And Buy My Toys'/ 'Join The Gang'/ 'She's Got Medals'/ 'Maid Of Bond Street'/ 'Please Mr Gravedigger'

Release Dates
UK 1 June 1967, US August 1967

Label and Catalogue Numbers
UK Deram SML 1007, US Deram DES 18003

Highest Chart Position on Release
UK and US: did not chart (DNC)

Notes
All tracks written by David Bowie.
Original US version omits 'We Are Hungry Men' and 'Maid Of Bond Street'. Two tracks also mis-spelled on cover: 'Little Bombardier' as 'Little Bombadier'; 'Silly Boy Blue' as 'Silly Boy Blues'.
Reissued on vinyl on Deram in 1984 (DOA-1). First released on CD in 1983 in Germany on London (800 087-2); in 1989 in UK on Deram (800 087-2); in 2010 on Deram (531 79-5) as Deluxe Edition including stereo and mono mixes plus bonus disc with contemporary singles, a 1968 version of 'London Bye Ta-Ta', and a 1967 BBC *Top Gear* session: 'Rubber Band (mono)'/ 'The London Boys (mono)'/ 'The Laughing Gnome (mono)'/ 'The Gospel According To Tony Day (mono)'/ 'Love You Till Tuesday (mono)'/ 'Did You Ever Have A Dream (mono)'/ 'When I Live My Dream (mono)'/ 'Let Me Sleep Beside You (mono)'/ 'Karma Man (mono)'/ 'London Bye Ta-Ta (mono)'/ 'In The Heat Of The Morning (mono)'/ 'The Laughing Gnome (stereo)'/ 'The Gospel According To Tony Day (stereo)'/ 'Did You Ever Have A Dream (stereo)'/ 'Let Me Sleep Beside You (stereo)'/ 'Karma Man (stereo)'/ 'In The Heat Of The Morning (stereo)'/ 'When I'm Five'/ 'Ching-A-Ling (stereo)'/ 'Sell Me A Coat (1969)'/ 'Love You Till Tuesday (BBC)'/ 'When I Live My Dream (BBC)'/ 'Little Bombardier (BBC)'/ 'Silly Boy Blue (BBC)'/ 'In The Heat of the Morning (BBC)'.

DAVID BOWIE/SPACE ODDITY 1969

Recorded at Trident Studios
17 St Anne's Court, Wardour Street, Soho, London, UK
Produced by Tony Visconti ('Space Oddity' by Gus Dudgeon)

Personnel
David Bowie – Vocals, Guitar, Stylophone, Kalimba, Organ
Paul Buckmaster – Cello
John Cambridge – Drums
Terry Cox – Drums
Keith Christmas – Guitar
Herbie Flowers – Bass
John 'Honk' Lodge – Bass
Benny Marshall – Harmonica
Tim Renwick – Guitar, Flute, Recorder
Tony Visconti – Bass, Flute, Recorder
Rick Wakeman – Mellotron, Electric Harpsichord
Mick Wayne – Guitar

Cover Art
Vernon Dewhurst – Photography
Victor Vasarely – Front cover artwork
George Underwood – Back cover illustration

Side One
'Space Oddity'/ 'Unwashed And Somewhat Slightly Dazed'/ 'Don't Sit Down'*/ 'Letter To Hermione'/ 'Cygnet Committee'

Side Two
'Janine'/ 'An Occasional Dream'/ 'Wild Eyed Boy From Freecloud'/ 'God Knows I'm Good'/ 'Memory Of A Free Festival'

Opposite: Promoting the Sound+Vision tour, Tokyo, 12 May 1990.

Release Date
14 November 1969

Label and Catalogue Numbers
UK Philips SBL 7912, US Mercury 61246

Highest Chart Position on Release
UK and US: did not chart (DNC)

Notes
All tracks written by David Bowie.
Originally *David Bowie* (UK) and *David Bowie: Man Of Words, Man Of Music* (US). Re-titled *Space Oddity* since its 1972 re-release.
*Original US release omits 'Don't Sit Down' as do all re-releases of the album until 1990. The original US cover was also different, zooming in on Bowie's face and losing the Victor Vasarely polka-dot background. Reissued on vinyl as *Space Oddity* on RCA in 1972 (LSP 4813), with a new cover featuring a Mick Rock Ziggy Stardust portrait without 'Don't Sit Down'; in 1984 on RCA in UK (PL 84813); in 1990 in USA as clear-vinyl double LP on Rykodisc (RALP 0131-2) and UK as single black-vinyl LP on EMI (EMC 3571) with 'Don't Sit Down' reinstated to track list and bonus tracks: 'Conversation Piece'/ 'Memory Of A Free Festival (Part 1)'/ 'Memory Of A Free Festival (Part 2)'; in 2000 in UK as part of the Virgin/EMI Simply Vinyl Series (SVLP 263). Reissued on CD in 1985 on RCA (PD 84813); 40th Anniversary two-CD edition released 2009 (EMI DBSOCD 40) included bonus disc with: 'Space Oddity (demo)'/ 'An Occasional Dream (demo)'/ 'Wild Eyed Boy From Freecloud (B-side)'/ 'Let Me Sleep Beside You (live)'/ 'Unwashed And Somewhat Slightly Dazed (live)'/ 'Janine (live)'/ 'London Bye Ta-Ta (stereo version)'/ 'The Prettiest Star (stereo version)'/ 'Conversation Piece (stereo version)'/ 'Memory Of A Free Festival (Part 1)'/ 'Memory Of A Free Festival (Part 2)'/ 'Wild Eyed Boy From Freecloud (alternate album mix)'/ 'Memory Of A Free Festival (alternate album mix)'/ 'London Bye Ta-Ta (alternate stereo mix)'/ 'Ragazzo Solo, Ragazza Sola (full-length stereo version)'.

THE MAN WHO SOLD THE WORLD 1970

Recorded at Trident Studios
17 St Anne's Court, Wardour Street, Soho, London, UK
and Advision Studios
23 Gosfield Street, London, UK
Produced by Tony Visconti

Personnel
David Bowie – Vocals, Guitar
Ralph Mace – Synthesizer
Mick Ronson – Guitar, Vocals
Tony Visconti – Bass, Piano, Guitar
Mick 'Woody' Woodmansey – Drums

Cover Art
Keef (Keith MacMillan) – Photography (UK release)
Mike Weller – Illustration (US release)

Side One
'The Width Of A Circle'/ 'All The Madmen'/
'Black Country Rock'/ 'After All'

Side Two
'Running Gun Blues'/ 'Saviour Machine'/
'She Shook Me Cold'/ 'The Man Who Sold The World'/
'The Supermen'

Release Dates
US 4 November 1970, UK April 1971

Label and Catalogue Numbers
UK Mercury 6338 041, US Mercury 61325

Highest Chart Position on Release
UK and US: did not chart (DNC)

Notes
All tracks written by David Bowie.
Original US release featured Mike Weller's cover cartoon of a cowboy outside Cane Hill Hospital. Reissues in 1972, 1983 and 1984 featured a black-and-white cover photo taken by Brian Ward, of a high-kicking Ziggy. Reissued on vinyl in 1972 by RCA (LSP 4816); in 1983 on RCA (INTS 5237); in 1984 on RCA (NL 84654); in 1990 as a double LP in US on Rykodisc (RALP 0132-2 2LP) and in UK on EMI (EMC 3573); in 2001 in UK as part of Virgin/EMI Simply Vinyl Series (SVLP 264). Reissued on CD in 1984 (PD-84654); in 1990 in US on Rykodisc (RCD 10132) and in UK on EMI (CDP 79 1837 2) with the bonus tracks: 'Lightning Frightening'/ 'Holy Holy'/ 'Moonage Daydream (Arnold Corns)'/ 'Hang On To Yourself (Arnold Corns)'.

HUNKY DORY 1971

Recorded at Trident Studios
17 St Anne's Court, Wardour Street, Soho, London, UK
Produced by Ken Scott and David Bowie

Personnel
David Bowie – Vocals, Guitar, Saxophone, Piano
Trevor Bolder – Bass, Trumpet

Mick Ronson – Guitar
Rick Wakeman – Piano
Mick 'Woody' Woodmansey – Drums

Cover Art
Brian Ward – Photography
Terry Pastor – Colouring

Side One
'Changes'/ 'Oh! You Pretty Things'/ 'Eight Line Poem'/ 'Life On Mars?'/ 'Kooks'/ 'Quicksand'

Side Two
'Fill Your Heart'/ 'Andy Warhol'/ 'Song For Bob Dylan'/ 'Queen Bitch'/ 'The Bewlay Brothers'

Release Date
17 December 1971

Label and Catalogue Numbers
UK RCA SF 8244, US RCA LSP 4623

Highest Chart Position on Release
UK 3, US 93

Notes
All tracks written by David Bowie except side two, track one: Biff Rose/Paul Williams.
Reissued on vinyl in 1981 on RCA (INTS 5064); in 1984 in UK as limited-edition picture disc (BOPIC2); in 1984 on RCA (NL 83844); in 1990 as a double LP in US on Rykodisc (RALP 0133-2) and in UK on EMI (EMC 3572) with bonus tracks 'Bombers'/ 'The Supermen (alternate version)'/ 'Quicksand (demo)'/ 'The Bewlay Brothers (alternate mix)'; in 2001 in UK as part of Virgin/EMI Simply Vinyl Series (SVLP 265). Reissued on CD in 1985 in Germany on RCA (RCA PD-84623); in 1990 in US on Rykodisc (RCD 10133) and in UK on EMI (CDP 79 1843 2) with bonus tracks (see above).

THE RISE AND FALL OF ZIGGY STARDUST AND THE SPIDERS FROM MARS 1972

Recorded at Trident Studios
17 St Anne's Court, Wardour Street, Soho, London, UK
Produced by Ken Scott and David Bowie

Personnel
David Bowie – Vocals, Guitar, Keyboards, Saxophone
Trevor Bolder – Bass
Dana Gillespie – Backing Vocals ('It Ain't Easy')
Mick Ronson – Guitar, Piano, Vocals
Rick Wakeman – Harpsichord, Keyboards ('It Ain't Easy')
Mick 'Woody' Woodmansey – Drums

Cover Art
Brian Ward – Photography
Terry Pastor – Colouring

Side One
'Five Years'/ 'Soul Love'/ 'Moonage Daydream'/ 'Starman'/ 'It Ain't Easy'

Side Two
'Lady Stardust'/ 'Star'/ 'Hang On To Yourself'/ 'Ziggy Stardust'/ 'Suffragette City'/ 'Rock 'n' Roll Suicide'

Release Dates
UK 6 June 1972, US 1 September 1972

Label and Catalogue Numbers
UK RCA SF8287, US AFL-1 4702

Highest Chart Position on Release
UK 5, US 75

Notes
All tracks written by David Bowie except side one, track five: Ron Davies.
Reissued on vinyl in 1981 on RCA (INTS 5063); in 1984 in UK as limited edition picture disc on RCA (BOPIC 3); in 1984 on RCA (NL 83843); in 1990 as a double LP in US on Rykodisc (RALP 0134-2) and in UK on EMI (EMC 3577) with bonus tracks: 'John, I'm Only Dancing (remix)'/ 'Velvet Goldmine'/ 'Sweet Head'/ 'Ziggy Stardust (demo)'/ 'Lady Stardust (demo)'; in 2001 as part of the Virgin/ EMI Simply Vinyl Series (SVLP 275). Reissued on CD in 1985 in Germany on RCA (PD-84702); in 1990 in US on Rykodisc (RCD 10134) and in UK on EMI (CDP 79 4400 2); in 1990 as a limited-edition box set in US on Rykodisc (RCD 90134) and in UK on EMI (CDEMCX 3577) with bonus tracks (see above); in 1999 in UK on EMI (7243 5219000); in 2002 in UK as a 2CD 30th-anniversary edition on EMI (539 8262) with bonus tracks: 'Moonage Daydream (Arnold Corns)'/ 'Hang On To Yourself (Arnold Corns)'/ 'Lady Stardust (demo)'/ 'Ziggy Stardust (demo)'/ 'John, I'm Only Dancing'/ 'Velvet Goldmine'/ 'Holy Holy'/ 'Amsterdam'/ 'The Supermen'/ 'Round And Round'/ 'Sweet Head (take 4)'/ 'Moonage Daydream (new mix)'.

ALADDIN SANE 1973

Recorded at Trident Studios
17 St Anne's Court, Wardour Street, Soho, London, UK
RCA Studios
155 East 24th Street, Manhattan, New York, USA
RCA Studios
1611 Roy Acuff Place, Nashville, Tennessee, USA
Produced by Ken Scott and David Bowie

Personnel
David Bowie – Vocals, Guitar, Harmonica, Saxophone
Trevor Bolder – Bass
Mac Cormack (Geoff MacCormack) – Backing Vocals
Ken Fordham – Saxophone
Juanita 'Honey' Franklin – Backing Vocals
Mike Garson – Piano
Linda Lewis – Backing Vocals
Mick Ronson – Guitar, Piano, Vocals
Brian 'Bux' Wilshaw – Flute, Saxophone
Mick 'Woody' Woodmansey – Drums

Cover Art
Brian Duffy – Photography

Side One
'Watch That Man'/ 'Aladdin Sane (1913–1938–197?)'/ 'Drive-In Saturday'/ 'Panic In Detroit'/ 'Cracked Actor'

Side Two
'Time'/ 'The Prettiest Star'/ 'Let's Spend The Night Together'/ 'The Jean Genie'/ 'Lady Grinning Soul'

Release Date
13 April 1973

Label and Catalogue Number
RCA RS 1001

Highest Chart Position On Release
UK 1, US 17

Notes
All songs written by David Bowie except side two, track three: Mick Jagger/Keith Richards.
Reissued on vinyl in 1981 on RCA (INTS 5067); in 1984 on RCA (NL 83890); in 1984 as a picture disc on RCA (BOPIC 1); in 1990 in US on Rykodisc (RALP 0135-2) and in UK on EMI (EMC 3579); in 1999 in UK as Limited Millennium Edition on EMI (7243 4994631 6); in 2001 as part of the Virgin/EMI Simply Vinyl Series (SVLP 276). Reissued on CD in 1984 in Germany on RCA (PD 83890); in 1990 in US on Rykodisc (RCD 10135) and in UK on EMI (EMC 3579); in 1999 on EMI (7243 5219020); in 2003 as a 30th-anniversary 2CD edition on EMI (7243 5830122) with bonus tracks: 'John, I'm Only Dancing (sax version)'/ 'The Jean Genie (original single mix)'/ 'Time (single edit)'/ 'All The Young Dudes'/ 'Changes (live in Boston 1/10/72)'/ 'The Supermen (live in Boston 1/10/72)'/ 'Life On Mars? (live in Boston 1/10/72)'/ 'John, I'm Only Dancing (live in Boston 1/10/72)'/ 'The Jean Genie (live in Santa Monica 20/10/72)'/ 'Drive-In Saturday (live in Cleveland 25/11/72)'; and in 2013 as a 40th-anniversary remastered edition on EMI (DBAS40).

PIN UPS 1973

Recorded at Château d'Hérouville Studios
Pontoise, France
Produced by Ken Scott and David Bowie

Personnel
David Bowie – Vocals, Guitar, Saxophone
Trevor Bolder – Bass
Aynsley Dunbar – Drums
Ken Fordham – Saxophone
Mike Garson – Piano
G A MacCormack (Geoff MacCormack) – Backing Vocals
Mick Ronson – Guitar, Piano, Vocals

Cover Art
Justin de Villeneuve – Front cover photography
Mick Rock – Back cover photography

Side One
'Rosalyn'/ 'Here Comes The Night'/ 'I Wish You Would'/ 'See Emily Play'/ 'Everything's Alright'/ 'I Can't Explain'

Side Two
'Friday On My Mind'/ 'Sorrow'/ 'Don't Bring Me Down'/ 'Shapes Of Things'/ 'Anyway, Anyhow, Anywhere'/ 'Where Have All The Good Times Gone!'

Release Date
19 October 1973

Label and Catalogue Number
RCA RS 1003

Highest Chart Position on Release
UK 1, US 23

Notes

Tracks written by, in order: Jimmy Duncan/Bill Farley; Bert Berns; Billy Boy Arnold; Syd Barrett; Nicky Crouch/ John Konrad/Simon Stavely/Stuart James/Keith Karlson; Pete Townshend; George Young/Harry Vanda; Bob Feldman/ Jerry Goldstein/Richard Gotteher; Johnnie Dee; Paul Samwell-Smith/Jim McCarty/Keith Relf; Roger Daltrey/Pete Townshend; Ray Davies.
Reissued on vinyl in 1983 on RCA (INTS 5236); in 1984 as a limited-edition picture disc on RCA (BOPIC 4); in 1990 in US on Rykodisc (RALP 0136-2) and in UK on EMI (EMC 3580) with bonus tracks: 'Growin' Up'/ 'Amsterdam'; in 2001 as part of the Virgin/EMI Simply Vinyl Series (SVLP 277).
Reissued on CD in 1984 in Germany on RCA (PD 84653); in 1990 in US on Rykodisc (RCD 10146) and in UK on EMI (CDP 79 4767 2) with bonus tracks (see above); in 1999 on EMI (7243 5219030) remastered without the bonus tracks of the 1990 releases.

DIAMOND DOGS 1974

Recorded at Olympic Studios
117 Church Road, Barnes, London, UK
Island Studios
8–10 Basing Street, London, UK
Studio L. Ludolf
Machineweg 8–12, Hilversum, Netherlands
Produced by David Bowie

Personnel
David Bowie – Vocals, Guitar, Saxophones, Moog, Mellotron
Aynsley Dunbar – Drums
Herbie Flowers – Bass
Mike Garson – Keyboards
Tony Newman – Drums
Alan Parker – Guitar ('1984')
Tony Visconti – Strings

Cover Art
Guy Peellaert – Cover illustration
Terry O'Neill – Cover photography
Leee Black Childers – Gatefold collage

Side One
'Future Legend'/ 'Diamond Dogs'/ 'Sweet Thing'/ 'Candidate'/ 'Sweet Thing (reprise)'/ 'Rebel Rebel'

Side Two
'Rock 'n' Roll With Me'/ 'We Are The Dead'/ '1984'/ 'Big Brother'/ 'Chant Of The Ever Circling Skeletal Family'

Release Date
31 May 1974

Label and Catalogue Number
RCA APL1 0576

Highest Chart Position on Release
UK 1, US 5

Notes
All tracks written by David Bowie except side two, track one: David Bowie/Warren Peace (Geoff MacCormack).
In March 2004 an original uncensored sleeve sold for nearly £9,000.
The album was released in 2003 as a double-CD set with *Aladdin Sane*, and in 2004 as part of a 3CD set with *Aladdin Sane* and *Hunky Dory*.
Reissued on vinyl in 1983 on RCA (INTS 5068); in 1984 on RCA (NL 83889); in 1984 as a limited-edition picture disc on RCA (BOPIC 5); in 1990 in US on Rykodisc (RALP 0137-2) and in UK on EMI (EMC 3584) with uncensored cover and bonus tracks: 'Dodo'/ 'Candidate (demo)'.
Reissued on CD in 1985 in Germany on RCA (PD 83889); in 1990 in US on Rykodisc (RCD 10137) and in UK on EMI (CDP 79 5211 2) with bonus tracks (see above); in 1999 on EMI (7243 5219040) remastered; in 2004 on EMI (07243 57785754) as a 2CD 30th-anniversary edition with bonus tracks: '1984/ Dodo'/ 'Rebel Rebel (US single version)'/'Dodo'/ 'Growin' Up'/ 'Alternative Candidate'/ 'Diamond Dogs (K-Tel edit)'/ 'Candidate (*Intimacy* mix)'/ 'Rebel Rebel (2003)'.

YOUNG AMERICANS 1975

Recorded at Sigma Sound
212 North 12th Street, Philadelphia, USA
and Electric Lady
52 West 8th Street, New York, USA
Produced by Tony Visconti ('Across The Universe' and 'Fame' by David Bowie and Harry Maslin)

Personnel
David Bowie – Vocals, Guitar, Piano
Carlos Alomar – Guitar
Ava Cherry – Backing Vocals
Robin Clark – Backing Vocals
Mike Garson – Piano
Anthony Hinton – Backing Vocals
Warren Peace (Geoff MacCormack) – Backing Vocals
Andy Newmark – Drums
Pablo Rosario – Percussion

David Sanborn – Saxophone
Diane Sumler – Backing Vocals
Luther Vandross – Backing Vocals
Larry Washington – Conga
Willie Weeks – Bass
'Across The Universe' and 'Fame' only:
Dennis Davis – Drums
Jean Fineberg – Backing Vocals
Emir Kassan – Bass
John Lennon – Vocals, Guitar
Ralph McDonald – Percussion
Jean Millington – Backing vocals
Earl Slick – Guitar

Cover Art
Eric Stephen Jacobs – Photography

Side One
'Young Americans'/ 'Win'/ 'Fascination'/ 'Right'

Side Two
'Somebody Up There Likes Me'/ 'Across The Universe'/ 'Can You Hear Me'/ 'Fame'

Release Date
7 March 1975

Label and Catalogue Number
RCA RS 1006

Highest Chart Position on Release
UK 2, US 9

Notes
All tracks written by David Bowie except side one, track three: David Bowie/Luther Vandross; side two, track two: Lennon/ McCartney; side two, track four: David Bowie/Carlos Alomar/ John Lennon.
The album was released in 2004 as a 3CD set with *Let's Dance* and *Station To Station*.
Reissued on vinyl in 1984 on RCA (PL 80998); in 1991 on EMI (EMD 1021) with bonus tracks: 'Who Can I Be Now?'/ 'It's Gonna Be Me'/ 'John, I'm Only Dancing (Again)'. Reissued on CD in 1985 in Germany on RCA (PD 80998); in 1991 in US on Rykodisc (RCD 10140) and in UK on EMI (CDP 79 6436 2) with bonus tracks (see above); in 1999 on EMI (7243 5219050 8); in 2007 in US on EMI (0946 3 51260 2 0) and in UK (09463 51258 2 5) as two-disc CD/DVD with footage from *The Dick Cavett Show* including '1984', 'Young Americans' and an interview with Dick Cavett. Bonus tracks on CD: 'John, I'm Only Dancing (Again)'/ 'Who Can I Be Now?'/ 'It's Gonna Be Me (with strings)'.

STATION TO STATION 1976

Recorded at Cherokee Studios
751 North Fairfax Avenue, Los Angeles, USA
Record Plant Studios
8456 West Third Street, Los Angeles, USA
Produced by David Bowie and Harry Maslin

Personnel
David Bowie – Vocals, Guitar, Saxophone
Carlos Alomar – Guitar
Roy Bittan – Piano
Dennis Davis – Drums
George Murray – Bass
Warren Peace (Geoff MacCormack) – Vocals
Earl Slick – Guitar

Cover Art
Steve Schapiro – Photography

Side One
'Station To Station'/ 'Golden Years'/ 'Word On A Wing'

Side Two
'TVC15'/ 'Stay'/ 'Wild Is The Wind'

Release Date
23 January 1976

Label and Catalogue Number
RCA APLI 1327

Highest Chart Position on Release
UK 5, US 3

Notes
All tracks written by David Bowie except side two, track three: Ned Washington/ Dimitri Tiomkin.
The cover was initially designed unframed in full-colour until a last-minute change by Bowie. A few full-colour proof/promo copies do exist.
The album was released in 2004 as a 3CD set with *Let's Dance* and *Young Americans*.
Reissued on vinyl in 1984 on RCA (PL 81327); in 1991 on EMI (EMD 1020) with full-colour cover artwork and bonus tracks: 'Word On A Wing (live)'/ 'Stay (live)'.
Reissued on CD in 1985 in Germany on RCA (PD 8132); in 1991 in US on Rykodisc (RCD 10141) and in UK on EMI (CDP 79 6435

2) with full-colour cover art and bonus tracks (see above); in 1999 on EMI (7243 5219060 7) remastered with full-colour cover art; in 2010 on EMI (BOWSTSX2010) as a three-CD special edition with bonus tracks recorded live at Nassau Coliseum 1976: 'Station To Station'/ 'Suffragette City'/ 'Fame'/ 'Word On A Wing'/ 'Stay'/ 'Waiting For The Man'/ 'Queen Bitch'/ 'Life On Mars?'/ 'Five Years'/ 'Panic In Detroit'/ 'Changes'/ 'TVC15'/ 'Diamond Dogs'/ 'Rebel Rebel'/ 'The Jean Genie' and a download-only 'Panic In Detroit (unedited alternate mix)'; in 2010 on EMI (BOWSTSD2010) as a three-LP, five-CD, DVD deluxe edition with additional bonus tracks: 'Golden Years (single version)'/ 'TVC15 (single edit)'/ 'Stay (single edit)'/ 'Word On A Wing (single edit)'/ 'Station To Station (single edit)'.

LOW 1977

Recorded at Château d'Hérouville Studios
Pontoise, France
Hansa Studios
Köthener Strasse 38, Berlin, Germany
Produced by David Bowie and Tony Visconti

Personnel
David Bowie – Vocals, ARP, Tape Horn, Bass-Synthetic Strings, Saxophones, Cellos, Tape, Guitar, Pump Bass, Harmonica, Piano, Percussion, Chamberlain, Vibraphones, Xylophones, Ambient Sounds
Carlos Alomar – Guitar
Dennis Davis – Percussion
Brian Eno – Splinter Mini-Moog, Report ARP, Rimmer EMI, Guitar Treatments, Chamberlain, Vocals ('Sound And Vision')
Ricky Gardiner – Guitar
Eduard Meyer – Cellos ('Art Decade')
George Murray – Bass
Iggy Pop – Vocals ('What In The World')
Mary Visconti – Vocals ('Sound And Vision')
Roy Young – Piano, Farfisa Organ
Peter and Paul – Pianos, ARP ('Subterraneans')

Cover Art
Steve Schapiro – Photography

Side One
'Speed Of Life'/ 'Breaking Glass'/ 'What In The World'/ 'Sound And Vision'/ 'Always Crashing In The Same Car'/ 'Be My Wife'/ 'A New Career In A New Town'

Side Two
'Warszawa'/ 'Art Decade'/ 'Weeping Wall'/ 'Subterraneans'

Release Date
14 January 1977

Label and Catalogue Number
RCA PL 12030

Highest Chart Position on Release
UK 2, US 11

Notes
All tracks written by David Bowie except side one, track two: David Bowie/Dennis Davis/George Murray; side two, track one: David Bowie/Brian Eno.
A small number of original LPs were printed on red vinyl.
The album was released in 2004 as a double-CD set with *"Heroes"*.
Reissued on vinyl in 1983 on RCA (INTS 5065); in 1984 on RCA (NL 83856); in 1991 on EMI (EMD 1027) remastered with bonus tracks: 'Some Are'/ 'All Saints'/ 'Sound And Vision (remixed)'.
Reissued on CD in 1985 in Germany on RCA (PD 83856); in 1991 in USA on Rykodisc (RCD 10142) and in UK on EMI (CDP 79 7719 2) remastered with bonus tracks (see above); in 1999 on EMI (7243 521907 0 6).

"HEROES" 1977

Recorded at Hansa Studios
Köthener Strasse 38, Berlin, Germany
Produced by David Bowie and Tony Visconti

Personnel
David Bowie – Vocals, Keyboards, Guitar, Saxophone, Koto
Carlos Alomar – Guitar
Dennis Davis – Percussion
Brian Eno – Synthesizers, Keyboards, Guitar Treatments
Robert Fripp – Guitar
Antonia Maass – Backing Vocals
George Murray – Bass
Tony Visconti – Backing Vocals

Cover Art
Masayoshi Sukita – Photography

Side One
'Beauty and the Beast'/ 'Joe the Lion'/ "Heroes"/ 'Sons of the Silent Age'/ 'Blackout'

Side Two
'V-2 Schneider'/ 'Sense of Doubt'/ 'Moss Garden'/ 'Neuköln'/ 'The Secret Life of Arabia'

Release Date
14 October 1977

Label and Catalogue Number
RCA PL 12522

Highest Chart Position on Release
UK 3, US 35

Notes
All tracks written by David Bowie except side one, track three: David Bowie/Brian Eno; side two, tracks three and four: David Bowie/Brian Eno; side two, track five: David Bowie/Brian Eno/Carlos Alomar.
The album was released in 2003 as a double-CD set with *Scary Monsters... And Super Creeps*, and in 2004 as a double-CD set with *Low*.
Reissued on vinyl in 1983 on RCA (INTS 5066); in 1984 on RCA (NL 83857); in 1991 on EMI (EMD 1025) with a gatefold sleeve.
Reissued on CD in 1985 in Germany on RCA (PD 83857); in 1991 in USA on Rykodisc (RCD 10143) and in UK on EMI (CDP 79 7720 2) with bonus tracks: 'Abdulmajid'/'Joe The Lion (remixed)'; in 1999 on EMI (7243 5219080) remastered.

LODGER 1979

Recorded at Mountain Studios
Rue du Théâtre 9, Montreux, Switzerland
Record Plant Studios
321 West 44th Street, New York, USA
Produced by David Bowie and Tony Visconti

Personnel
David Bowie – Vocals, Piano, Synthesizer, Chamberlain, Guitar
Carlos Alomar – Guitar, Drums
Adrian Belew – Mandolin, Guitar
Dennis Davis – Percussion
Brian Eno – Ambient Drone, Prepared Piano and Cricket Menace, Synthesizer, Guitar Treatments, Horse Trumpets, Eroica Horn, Piano
Simon House – Mandolin, Violin
Sean Mayes – Piano
George Murray – Bass
Roger Powell – Synthesizer
Stan – Saxophone
Tony Visconti – Mandolin, Backing Voices, Guitar

Cover Art
Brian Duffy – Photography
Derek Boshier and David Bowie – Design

Side One
'Fantastic Voyage'/'African Night Flight'/'Move On'/'Yassassin'/'Red Sails'

Side Two
'D.J.'/'Look Back In Anger'/'Boys Keep Swinging'/'Repetition'/'Red Money'

Release Date
18 May 1979

Label and Catalogue Number
RCA BOWLP 1

Highest Chart Position on Release
UK 4, US 20

Notes
All tracks written by David Bowie/Brian Eno except side one, tracks three and four: David Bowie; side two, track one: David Bowie/Brian Eno/Carlos Alomar; side two, track four: David Bowie; side two, track five: David Bowie/Carlos Alomar.
The album was released in 2004 as a double-CD set with *Scary Monsters... And Super Creeps*.
Reissued on vinyl in 1982 on RCA (INTS 5212); in 1984 on RCA (NL 84234); in 1991 on EMI (064 7 97724 1) with bonus tracks: 'I Pray, Olé', 'Look Back In Anger (1988 version)'.
Reissued on CD in 1985 in Germany on RCA (PD 84234); in 1991 in USA on Rykodisc (RCD 10146) and in UK on EMI (EMD 1026) with bonus tracks (see above); in 1999 on EMI (7243 5219090) remastered.

SCARY MONSTERS... AND SUPER CREEPS 1980

Recorded at The Power Station
441 West 53rd Street, New York, USA
Good Earth Studios
59 Dean Street, London, UK
Produced by David Bowie and Tony Visconti

Personnel
David Bowie – Vocals, Keyboards
Carlos Alomar – Guitar
Roy Bittan – Piano
Andy Clark – Synthesizers
Dennis Davis – Percussion
Robert Fripp – Guitar
Chuck Hammer – Guitar ('Ashes To Ashes', 'Teenage Wildlife')
Michi Hirota – Voice ('It's No Game (No. 1)')

Lynn Maitland – Backing Vocals
George Murray – Bass
Chris Porter – Backing Vocals
Pete Townshend – Guitar ('Because You're Young')
Tony Visconti – Backing Vocals, Acoustic Guitar ('Up The Hill Backwards' and 'Scary Monsters')

Cover Art
Brian Duffy – Photography
Edward Bell – Illustration

Side One
'It's No Game (No. 1)'/ 'Up The Hill Backwards'/ 'Scary Monsters (And Super Creeps)'/ 'Ashes To Ashes'/ 'Fashion'

Side Two
'Teenage Wildlife'/ 'Scream Like A Baby'/ 'Kingdom Come'/ 'Because You're Young'/ 'It's No Game (No. 2)'

Release Date
12 September 1980

Label and Catalogue Number
RCA BOWLP 2

Highest Chart Position on Release
UK 1, US 12

Notes
All tracks written by David Bowie except side two, track three: Tom Verlaine.
The album was released in 2003 as a double-CD set with *"Heroes"* and in 2004 as a double-CD set with *Lodger*.
Reissued on vinyl in 1984 on RCA (PL 83647).
Reissued on CD in 1985 in Germany on RCA (PD 83647); in 1992 in US on Rykodisc (RCD 20147) and in UK on EMI (CDP 79 9331 2) with bonus tracks: 'Space Oddity (1979)'/ 'Panic In Detroit (1979)'/ 'Crystal Japan'/ 'Alabama Song'; in 1999 on EMI (7243 521 8950) remastered.

LET'S DANCE 1983

Recorded at The Power Station
441 West 53rd Street, New York, USA
Produced by David Bowie and Nile Rodgers

Personnel
David Bowie – Vocals
Robert Arron – Tenor Saxophone, Flute
Bernard Edwards – Bass ('Without You')
Steve Elson – Baritone Saxophone, Flute
Sammy Figueroa – Percussion
Mac Gollehon – Trumpet
Omar Hakim – Drums
Stan Harrison – Tenor Saxophone, Flute
Nile Rodgers – Guitar
Carmine Rojas – Bass
Rob Sabino – Keyboards
George and Frank Simms – Backing Vocals
David Spinner – Backing Vocals
Tony Thompson – Drums
Stevie Ray Vaughan – Lead Guitar

Cover Art
Greg Gorman – Photography
Derek Boshier – Illustration
Mick Haggerty – Design

Side One
'Modern Love'/ 'China Girl'/ 'Let's Dance'/ 'Without You'

Side Two
'Ricochet'/ 'Criminal World'/ 'Cat People (Putting Out Fire)'/ 'Shake It'

Release Date
14 April 1983

Label and Catalogue Number
EMI AML 3029

Highest Chart Position on Release
UK 1, US 4

Notes
All tracks written by David Bowie except side one, track two: David Bowie/Iggy Pop; side two, track two: Peter Godwin/ Duncan Browne/Sean Lyons; side two, track three: David Bowie/Giorgio Moroder.
The album was released in 2004 as a triple-CD set with *Station To Station* and *Young Americans*.
Reissued on vinyl as a picture disc in 1983 on EMI (AMLP 3029).
Reissued on CD in 1983 on EMI (EMI CDP 7 46002 2); in 1995 on Virgin (CDVUS96) with bonus track: 'Under Pressure'; in 1998 on EMI (7243 493094 2 5); in 1999 on EMI (7243 521896 0 1) remastered.

TONIGHT 1984

Recorded at Le Studio
Morin Heights, Canada
Produced by David Bowie, Derek Bramble
and Hugh Padgham

Personnel
David Bowie – Vocals
Carlos Alomar – Guitar
Derek Bramble – Bass, Synthesizer (Bass, Guitar, Synthesizer, Background)
Robin Clark – Backing Vocals
Steve Elson – Baritone Saxophone
Sammy Figueroa – Percussion
Omar Hakim – Drums
Stanley Harrison – Alto and Tenor Saxophone
Curtis King – Backing Vocals
Mark Pender – Trumpet, Flugelhorn
Lenny Pickett – Tenor Saxophone, Clarinet
Iggy Pop – Vocals ('Dancing With The Big Boys')
Carmine Rojas – Bass
George Simms – Backing vocals
Guy St Onge – Marimba
Tina Turner – Vocals ('Tonight')

Cover Art
Mick Haggerty – Illustration and design

Side One
'Loving The Alien'/'Don't Look Down'/
'God Only Knows'/'Tonight'

Side Two
'Neighborhood Threat'/'Blue Jean'/
'Tumble And Twirl'/'I Keep Forgettin''/
'Dancing With The Big Boys'

Release Date
24 September 1984

Label and Catalogue Number
EMI America DB 1

Highest Chart Position on Release
UK 1, US 11

Notes
Tracks written by, in order: David Bowie; Iggy Pop/James Williamson; Brian Wilson/Tony Asher; David Bowie/Iggy Pop; David Bowie/Iggy Pop/Ricky Gardiner; David Bowie; David Bowie/Iggy Pop; Jerry Leiber/Mike Stoller; David Bowie/Iggy Pop/Carlos Alomar.
The album was released in 2004 as a two-CD set with *Never Let Me Down*.
Reissued on CD in 1984 on EMI (CDP 7 46047 2); in 1995 on Virgin (CDVUS97) with bonus tracks: 'This Is Not America'/'Absolute Beginners'/'As The World Falls Down'; in 1998 on EMI (7243 493102 2 3); in 1999 on EMI (7243 521897 0 0) remastered.

LABYRINTH 1986

Recorded at Atlantic Studios
1841 Broadway, New York, USA
Abbey Road Studios
3 Abbey Road, St John's Wood, London, UK
Produced by David Bowie and Arif Mardin
('Chilly Down' by David Bowie; 'Opening Titles Including Underground' by Arif Mardin and Trevor Jones)

Personnel
David Bowie – Vocals
Garcia Alston – Backing Vocals
Robin Beck – Backing Vocals ('As The World Falls Down')
Robbie Buchanan – Keyboards, Synthesizers, Programming
Albert Collins – Guitar ('Underground')
Mary Davis Canty – Backing Vocals
Beverly Ferguson – Backing Vocals
Steve Ferrone – Drums, Drum Effects
A Marie Foster – Backing Vocals
Bob Gay – Alto Saxophone ('Underground')
James Glenn – Backing Vocals
Diva Gray – Backing Vocals
Cissy Houston – Backing Vocals
Dan Huff – Guitar ('Magic Dance')
Chaka Khan – Backing Vocals
Will Lee – Bass, Backing Vocals
Marcus Miller – Backing Vocals
Jeff Mironov – Guitar ('As The World Falls Down')
Nicky Moroch – Guitar ('Underground' and 'As The World Falls Down')
Eunice Peterson – Backing Vocals
Marc Stevens – Backing Vocals
Rennele Stafford – Backing Vocals
Richard Tee – Piano and Hammond B-3 Organ ('Underground')
Fonzi Thornton – Backing Vocals
Luther Vandross – Backing Vocals
Daphne Vega – Backing Vocals
'Chilly Down' only:
Kevin Armstrong – Guitar

Charles Augins – Vocals
Richard Bodkin – Vocals
Kevin Clash – Vocals
Neil Conti – Drums
Danny John-Jules – Vocals
Nick Plytas – Keyboards
Matthew Seligman – Bass
'Opening Titles Including Underground' only:
Harold Fisher – Drums
Brian Gascoigne – Keyboards
Trevor Jones – Keyboards
David Lawson – Keyboards
Ray Russell – Guitar
Paul Westwood – Bass

Side One
'Opening Titles Including Underground'/'Into The Labyrinth'/'Magic Dance'/'Sarah'/'Chilly Down'/'Hallucination'

Side Two
'As The World Falls Down'/'The Goblin Battle'/'Within You'/'Thirteen O'Clock'/ 'Home At Last'/'Underground'

Release Date
23 June 1986

Label and Catalogue Number
EMI America AML 3104

Highest Chart Position on Release
UK 38, US 68

Notes
All tracks written by David Bowie except side one, track one: Trevor Jones/David Bowie; side one, tracks two, four and six, and side two, tracks two, four and five: Trevor Jones.

NEVER LET ME DOWN 1987

Recorded at Mountain Studios
Rue du Théâtre 9, Montreux, Switzerland
The Power Station
441 West 53rd Street, New York, USA
Produced by David Bowie and David Richards

Personnel
David Bowie – Vocals, Guitar, Keyboards, Mellotron, Moog, Harmonica, Tambourine
Carlos Alomar – Guitar, Guitar Synthesizer, Tambourine, Backing Vocals
Crusher Bennett – Percussion
Robin Clark – Backing Vocals
Steve Elson – Baritone Saxophone
Peter Frampton – Guitar
Laurie Frink – Trumpet
Earl Gardner – Trumpet, Flugelhorn
Diva Gray – Backing Vocals
Gordon Grodie – Backing Vocals
Loni Groves – Backing Vocals
Stan Harrison – Alto Saxophone
Erdal Kizilcay – Keyboards, Drums, Bass, Trumpet, Backing Vocals, Guitar ('Time Will Crawl), Violins ('Bang Bang')
Sid McGinnis – Guitar ('Bang Bang', 'Time Will Crawl', 'Day-In Day-Out')
Lenny Pickett – Tenor Saxophone
Carmine Rojas – Bass
Mickey Rourke – Rap ('Shining Star (Makin' My Love)')
Philippe Saisse – Piano, Keyboards
'Zeroes' only:
Aglae – Backing Vocals
Joe Jones – Backing Vocals
Clement – Backing Vocals
Coco – Backing Vocals
John – Backing Vocals
Charuvan Suchi – Backing Vocals
Sandro Sursock – Backing Vocals

Cover Art
Greg Gorman – Photography
Mick Haggerty – Art direction and design

Side One
'Day-In Day-Out'/'Time Will Crawl'/'Beat Of Your Drum'/'Never Let Me Down'/'Zeroes'

Side Two
'Glass Spider'/'Shining Star (Makin' My Love)'/'New York's In Love'/''87 And Cry'/'Too Dizzy'/'Bang Bang'

Release Date
27 April 1987

Label and Catalogue Numbers
Vinyl: EMI America AMLS 3117
CD: EMI America CDP 7 46677 2

Highest Chart Position on Release
UK 6, US 34

Notes
All tracks written by David Bowie except side one, track four: David Bowie/Carlos Alomar; side two, track five: David Bowie/Erdal Kizilcay; side two, track six: Iggy Pop/Ivan Kral.
The original UK vinyl release contained edited versions of the tracks 'Day-In Day-Out'/'Beat Of Your Drum'/'Glass Spider'/'Shining Star (Makin' My Love)'/'New York's In Love'/'Bang Bang'.
The album was released in 2004 as a two-CD set with *Tonight*.
Reissued on CD in 1995 on Virgin (CDVUS98) without 'Too Dizzy' but with bonus tracks: 'Julie'/'Girls'/'When The Wind Blows'; in 1999 on EMI (7243 521894 0 3) remastered.

TIN MACHINE 1989

Recorded at Mountain Studios
Rue du Théâtre 9, Montreux, Switzerland
Compass Point Studios
West Bay Street, Nassau, Bahamas
Produced by Tin Machine and Tim Palmer

Personnel
David Bowie – Vocals, Guitar
Kevin Armstrong – Guitar, Hammond B3
Reeves Gabrels – Guitar
Hunt Sales – Drums, Vocals
Tony Sales – Bass, Vocals

Cover Art
Masayoshi Sukita – Photography

Side One
'Heaven's In Here'/'Tin Machine'/'Prisoner Of Love'/'Crack City'/'I Can't Read'/'Under The God'

Side Two
'Amazing'/'Working Class Hero'/'Bus Stop'/'Pretty Thing'/'Video Crime'/'Run' (not on vinyl)/'Sacrifice Yourself' (not on vinyl)/'Baby Can Dance'

Release Date
22 May 1989

Label and Catalogue Numbers
Vinyl: EMI USA MTLS 1044
CD: EMI USA CDP 7919902

Highest Chart Position on Release
UK 3, US 28

Notes
All tracks written by David Bowie except side one, tracks two and three: David Bowie/Reeves Gabrels/Hunt Sales/Tony Sales; side one, track five, and side two, tracks one and three: David Bowie/Reeves Gabrels; side two, track two: John Lennon; side two, tracks five and seven: David Bowie/Hunt Sales/Tony Sales; side two, track six: Kevin Armstrong/David Bowie.
The original vinyl, CD and cassette releases each feature different cover photos.
Reissued on CD in 1995 on Virgin (CDVUS99) with bonus track: 'Bus Stop (Live Country Version)'; in 1998 on EMI (493 1012); in 1999 on EMI (7243 521910 0 0) remastered.

TIN MACHINE II 1991

Recorded at Studios 301
18 Mitchell Road, Sydney, Australia
A&M Studios
1416 North La Brea Avenue, Hollywood, USA
Produced by Tin Machine and Tim Palmer
('One Shot' by Hugh Padgham)

Personnel
David Bowie – Vocals, Guitar, Piano, Saxophone
Kevin Armstrong – Piano ('Shopping For Girls'),
Guitar ('If There Is Something')
Reeves Gabrels – Guitar, Backing Vocals, Vibrators, Drano, Organ
Tim Palmer – Piano, Percussion
Hunt Sales – Drums, Percussion, Vocals
Tony Sales – Bass, Backing Vocals

Cover Art
Edward Bell – Illustration

Side One
'Baby Universal'/'One Shot'/'You Belong In Rock 'n' Roll'/'If There Is Something'/'Amlapura'/'Betty Wrong'

Side Two
'You Can't Talk'/'Stateside'/'Shopping For Girls'/'A Big Hurt'/'Sorry'/'Goodbye Mr. Ed'

Release Date
2 September 1991

Label and Catalogue Numbers
Vinyl: London 828 2721
CD: London 828 2722

Highest Chart Position on Release
UK 23, US DNC

Notes
All tracks written by David Bowie/Reeves Gabrels except side one, track two, and side two, track one: David Bowie/Reeves Gabrels/Hunt Sales/Tony Sales; side one, track four: Bryan Ferry; side two, track two: Hunt Sales/David Bowie; side two, track four: David Bowie; side two, track five: Hunt Sales; side two, track six: David Bowie/Hunt Sales/Tony Sales. Original US release featured censored sleeve; an uncensored digipack limited edition was available on Victory (314 511 575-2).

BLACK TIE WHITE NOISE 1993

Recorded at Mountain Studios
Rue du Théâtre 9, Montreux, Switzerland
38 Fresh Recording Studios
1119 North Las Palmas Avenue, Hollywood, USA
The Hit Factory
421 West 54th Street, New York, USA
Produced by David Bowie and Nile Rodgers

Personnel
David Bowie – Vocals, Guitar, Saxophone, Dog Alto
Tawatha Agee – Backing Vocals
Lamya Al-Mughiery – Backing Vocals
Pugi Bell – Drums
Lester Bowie – Trumpet
Barry Campbell – Bass
Sterling Campbell – Drums
Dennis Collins – Backing Vocals
Maryl Epps – Backing Vocals
Reeves Gabrels – Guitar ('You've Been Around')
Mike Garson – Piano ('Looking For Lester')
Richard Hilton – Keyboards
Curtis King Jr – Backing Vocals
Connie Petruk – Backing Vocals
John Regan – Bass
Michael Reisman – Harp, Tubular Bells
Dave Richards – Keyboards
Nile Rodgers – Guitar, Backing Vocals
Mick Ronson – Guitar ('I Feel Free')
Philippe Saisse – Keyboards
George and Frank Simms – Backing Vocals
David Spinner – Backing Vocals
Wild T Springer – Guitar ('I Know It's Gonna Happen Someday')
Al B Sure! – Vocals ('Black Tie White Noise')
Richard Tee – Keyboards
Fonzi Thornton – Backing Vocals
Gerardo Velez – Percussion
Brenda White-King – Backing Vocals

Cover Art
Peter Gabriel – Photography
Nick Knight – Photography

Side One
'The Wedding' (not on vinyl)/ 'You've Been Around'/ 'I Feel Free'/ 'Black Tie White Noise'/ 'Jump They Say'/ 'Nite Flights'/ 'Pallas Athena'

Side Two
'Miracle Goodnight'/ 'Don't Let Me Down & Down'/ 'Looking For Lester'/ 'I Know It's Gonna Happen Someday'/ 'The Wedding Song'/ 'Jump They Say (alternate mix)' (not on vinyl)/ 'Lucy Can't Dance' (CD only)

Release Date
5 April 1993

Label and Catalogue Numbers
Vinyl: BMG/Arista 74321 13697 1
CD: BMG/Arista 74321 13697 2

Highest Chart Position on Release
UK 1, US 39

Notes
All tracks written by David Bowie except side one, track two: David Bowie/Reeves Gabrels; side one, track three: Jack Bruce/Pete Brown; side one, track six: Noel Scott Engel; side two, track two: Tarha/Martine Valmont; side two, track three: David Bowie/Nile Rodgers; and side two, track four: Morrissey/Mark Nevin.
Reissued on CD in 2003 as a limited-edition double-CD and DVD set on EMI (7243 584814 0 2) with bonus tracks: 'Real Cool World'/ 'Lucy Can't Dance'/ 'Jump They Say (Rock Mix)'/ 'Black Tie White Noise (3rd Floor US Radio Mix)'/ 'Miracle Goodnight (Make Believe Mix)'/ 'Don't Let Me Down & Down (Indonesian Vocal Version)'/ 'You've Been Around (Dangers 12-inch Remix)'/ 'Jump They Say (Brothers In Rhythm 12-inch Remix)'/ 'Black Tie White Noise (Here Come Da Jazz)'/ 'Pallas Athena (Don't Stop Praying Remix No. 2)'/ 'Nite Flights (Moodswings Back To Basics Remix)'/ 'Jump They Say (Dub Oddity)'; the DVD featured the video of 'Black Tie White Noise'.

THE BUDDHA OF SUBURBIA 1993

Recorded at Mountain Studios
Rue du Théâtre 9, Montreux, Switzerland
O'Henry Sound Studios
4200 West Magnolia Blvd, Burbank, USA
Produced by David Bowie and David Richards

Personnel
David Bowie – Vocals, Keyboards, Synthesizers, Guitar, Saxophones, Keyboard Percussion
Mike Garson – Piano ('South Horizon' and 'Bleed Like A Craze, Dad')
Erdal Kizilcay – Keyboards, Trumpet, Bass, Guitar, Live Drums, Percussion
Lenny Kravitz – Guitar ('Buddha Of Suburbia' second version)
3D Echo – Drum, Bass, Guitar ('Bleed Like A Craze, Dad')

Cover Art
John Jefford/BBC – Photography (UK release)
Frank Ockenfels 3 – Photography (US release and reissue)

Side One
'Buddha Of Suburbia'/'Sex And The Church'/
'South Horizon'/'The Mysteries'/'Bleed Like A Craze, Dad'

Side Two
'Strangers When We Meet'/'Dead Against It'/'Untitled No. 1'/
'Ian Fish, U.K. Heir'/'Buddha Of Suburbia'

Release Dates
UK 8 November 1993, US 24 October 1995

Label and Catalogue Numbers
UK BMG/Arista 74321 170042, US Virgin 7243 8 40988 2 7

Highest Chart Position on Release
UK 87, US DNC

Notes
All tracks written by David Bowie.
Also available on Arista/BMG as a special edition with CD and Hanif Kureishi's book in a translucent plastic box as (BMG 4321178222).
Reissued on CD in 1995 on Virgin in US (7243 8 40988 2 7) with a different, monochrome sleeve; in 2007 on EMI (5004632) with US edition artwork in colour.

1.OUTSIDE 1995

Recorded at Mountain Studios
Rue du Théâtre 9, Montreux, Switzerland
The Hit Factory
421 West 54th Street, New York, USA
Produced by David Bowie, Brian Eno and David Richards

Personnel
David Bowie – Vocals, Guitar, Saxophones, Keyboards
Carlos Alomar – Guitar
Kevin Armstrong – Guitar ('Thru' These Architects Eyes')
Joey Barron – Drums
Sterling Campbell – Drums
Bryony, Lola, Josey and Ruby Edwards – Backing Vocals ('Hearts Filthy Lesson', 'I Am With Name')
Brian Eno – Synthesizers, Treatments, Strategies
Yossi Fine – Bass
Tom Frish – Guitar ('Strangers When We Meet')
Reeves Gabrels – Guitar
Mike Garson – Piano
Erdal Kizilcay – Bass, Keyboards

Cover Art
Denovo – Design
David Bowie – Illustration
John Scarisbrick – Photography

Track Listing
'Leon Takes Us Outside'/'Outside'/'Hearts Filthy Lesson'/
'A Small Plot Of Land'/'Segue – Baby Grace (A Horrid Cassette)'/
'Hallo Spaceboy'/'The Motel'/ 'I Have Not Been To Oxford Town'/
'No Control'/ 'Segue – Algeria Touchshriek'/'The Voyeur Of Utter Destruction (As Beauty)'/'Segue – Ramona A. Stone/
I Am With Name'/'Wishful Beginnings'/'We Prick You'/'Segue – Nathan Adler'/'I'm Deranged'/'Thru' These Architects Eyes'/
'Segue – Nathan Adler'/'Strangers When We Meet'

Release Date
25 September 1995

Label and Catalogue Number
RCA 74321 310662

Highest Chart Position on Release
UK 8, US 21

Notes
Tracks one, three, four, five, ten, twelve and fifteen by David Bowie/Reeves Gabrels/Mike Garson/Erdal Kizilcay/Sterling

Campbell; track two: Kevin Armstrong/David Bowie; tracks six, eight, nine, thirteen, fourteen, sixteen and eighteen by David Bowie/Brian Eno; tracks seven and nineteen: David Bowie; track eleven: David Bowie/Brian Eno/Reeves Gabrels; track seventeen: David Bowie/Reeves Gabrels. All lyrics by David Bowie.
Vinyl version available as *Excerpts From 1.Outside* in 1995 on Arista/RCA (74321307021) with edited versions of 'Leon Takes Us Outside'/ 'The Motel' and missing tracks: 'No Control'/ 'Segue – Algeria Touchshriek'/ 'Wishful Beginnings'/ 'Thru' These Architects Eyes'/ 'Segue – Nathan Adler (No.2)'/ 'Strangers When We Meet'.
Reissued on CD in 1999 on Arista/BMG (74321 36009 2) as *1.Outside Version 2* with bonus track: 'Hallo Spaceboy (Pet Shop Boys Remix)' and missing track: 'Wishful Beginnings'; in 2004 on ISO/Columbia in US (CK 92100) and in UK (511934 2) with bonus track: 'Get Real'; in 2004 on ISO/Columbia (511934 9) as a two-CD limited edition with bonus tracks: 'Hearts Filthy Lesson (Trent Reznor Alternative Mix)'/ 'Hearts Filthy Lesson (Rubber Mix)'/ 'Hearts Filthy Lesson (Simple Text Mix)'/ 'Hearts Filthy Lesson (Filthy Mix)'/ 'Hearts Filthy Lesson (Good Karma Mix By Tim Simenon)'/ 'A Small Plot Of Land (*Basquiat*)'/ 'Hallo Spaceboy (12-inch Remix)'/ 'Hallo Spaceboy (Double Click Mix)'/ 'Hallo Spaceboy (Instrumental)'/ 'Hallo Spaceboy (Lost In Space Mix)'/ 'I Am With Name (Album Version)'/ 'I'm Deranged (Jungle Mix)'/ 'Get Real'/ 'Nothing To Be Desired'.
The two-CD edition was also released in 2004 as a limited-edition box set with the two-CD remastered versions of *Earthling* and *'hours...'*.

EARTHLING 1997

Recorded at Looking Glass Studios
632 Broadway, New York, USA
Mountain Studios
Rue du Théâtre 9, Montreux, Switzerland
Produced by David Bowie

Personnel
David Bowie – Vocals, Guitar, Saxophones, Samples, Keyboards
Zachary Alford – Drum Loops, Acoustic Drums, Electronic Percussion
Gail Ann Dorsey – Bass, Vocals
Reeves Gabrels – Programming, Synthesizers, Guitar, Sampled Guitar, Vocals
Mike Garson – Piano
Mark Plati – Programming Loops, Samples, Keyboards

Cover Art
Davide De Angelis – Design
Frank Ockenfels – Photography

Track Listing
'Little Wonder'/ 'Looking For Satellites'/ 'Battle For Britain (The Letter)'/ 'Seven Years In Tibet'/ 'Dead Man Walking'/ 'Telling Lies'/ 'The Last Thing You Should Do'/ 'I'm Afraid Of Americans'/ 'Law (Earthlings On Fire)'

Release Date
3 February 1997

Label and Catalogue Numbers
UK RCA 74321 449442, US Virgin 7243 8 42627 23

Highest Chart Position on Release
UK 6, US 39

Notes
All tracks written by David Bowie/Reeves Gabrels/Mark Plati except tracks four, five and nine: David Bowie/Reeves Gabrels; track six: David Bowie; track eight: David Bowie/Brian Eno. All lyrics by David Bowie.
Available as limited-edition vinyl in UK on RCA (74321 449441) and in US on Arista (74321 43077 1).
Reissued on CD in 2003 in UK on ISO/Columbia (511935 2); in 2004 in US on ISO/Columbia (CK 92098) with bonus tracks: 'Little Wonder (Danny Saber Dance Mix)'/ 'I'm Afraid Of Americans (NIN V1 Mix)'/ 'Dead Man Walking (Moby Mix 2)'/ 'Telling Lies (Adam F Mix)'; in 2004 in UK as a two-CD limited edition on ISO/Columbia (COL 511935 9) with bonus tracks: 'Little Wonder (Censored Video Edit)'/ 'Little Wonder (Junior Vasquez Club Mix)'/ 'Little Wonder (Danny Saber Dance Mix)'/ 'Seven Years In Tibet (Mandarin Version)'/ 'Dead Man Walking (Moby Mix 1)'/ 'Dead Man Walking (Moby Mix 2)'/ 'Telling Lies (Feelgood Mix)'/ 'Telling Lies (Paradox Mix)'/ 'I'm Afraid Of Americans (*Showgirls* OST Version)'/ 'I'm Afraid Of Americans (Nine Inch Nails V1 Mix)'/ 'I'm Afraid Of Americans (Original Edit)'/ 'V-2 Schneider (Live in Amsterdam as Tao Jones Index)'/ 'Pallas Athena (Live in Amsterdam as Tao Jones Index)'.
The two-CD edition was also released in 2004 as a limited-edition box set with the two-CD remastered versions of *1. Outside* and *'hours...'*.

'HOURS...' 1999

Recorded at Seaview Studios,
Bermuda
Looking Glass Studios
632 Broadway, New York, USA
Chung King Studios
170 Varick Street, New York, USA
Produced by David Bowie and Reeves Gabrels

Personnel
David Bowie – Vocals, Keyboards, Acoustic Guitar, Roland 707 Drum Programming
Everett Bradley – Percussion ('Seven')
Sterling Campbell – Drums ('Seven', 'New Angels Of Promise', 'The Dreamers')
Reeves Gabrels – Guitar, Drum Loops, Synthesizer and Drum Programming
Chris Haskett – Guitar ('If I'm Dreaming My Life')
Mike Levesque – Drums
Holly Palmer – Backing Vocals ('Thursday's Child')
Mark Plati – Bass, Guitar, Synthesizer and Drum Programming, Mellotron ('Survive')
Marcus Salisbury – Bass ('New Angels Of Promise')

Cover Art
Rex Ray – Design
Tim Bret Day – Illustration and photography
Frank Ockenfels 3 – Photography

Track Listing
'Thursday's Child'/ 'Something In The Air'/ 'Survive'/ 'If I'm Dreaming My Life'/ 'Seven'/ 'What's Really Happening?'/ 'The Pretty Things Are Going To Hell'/ 'New Angels Of Promise'/ 'Brilliant Adventure'/ 'The Dreamers'

Release Dates
Download: 21 September 1999
CD: 4 October 1999

Label and Catalogue Number
Virgin CDVX 2900/7243 8 48158 20

Highest Chart Position on Release
UK 5, US 47

Notes
All tracks written by David Bowie/Reeves Gabrels except track six: David Bowie/Reeves Gabrels/Alex Grant.
The first 450,000 copies featured a lenticular cover.
Reissued on CD in 2003 in UK on ISO/Columbia (511936 2); in 2004 in US on ISO/Columbia (CK 92099) with bonus tracks: 'Something In The Air (*American Psycho* Remix)'/ 'Survive (Marius de Vries Mix)'/ 'Seven (Demo)'/ 'The Pretty Things Are Going To Hell (*Stigmata* Film Version)'/ 'We All Go Through'; in 2004 in UK on ISO/Columbia (511936 9) as two-CD limited edition with bonus tracks: 'Thursday's Child (Rock Mix)'/ 'Thursday's Child (*Omikron: The Nomad Soul* Slower Version)'/ 'Something In The Air (*American Psycho* Remix)'/ 'Survive (Marius de Vries Mix)'/ 'Seven (Demo Version)'/ 'Seven (Marius de Vries Mix)'/ 'Seven (Beck Mix No.1)'/ 'Seven (Beck Mix No.2)'/ 'The Pretty Things Are Going To Hell (Edit)'/ 'The Pretty Things Are Going To Hell (*Stigmata* Film Version)'/ 'The Pretty Things Are Going To Hell (*Stigmata* Film Only Version)'/ 'New Angels Of Promise (*Omikron: The Nomad Soul* Version)'/ 'The Dreamers (*Omikron: The Nomad Soul* Longer Version)'/ '1917'/ 'We Shall Go To Town'/ 'We All Go Through'/ 'No One Calls'; in 2012 on Friday Music/Columbia (48157) as a collector's edition with bonus tracks: 'Something In the Air (*American Psycho* Remix)'/ 'Survive (Marius de Vries Mix)'/ 'Seven (Demo)'/ 'The Pretty Things Are Going To Hell (*Stigmata* Film Version)'/ 'We All Go Through'.
The two-CD edition was also released in 2004 as a limited-edition boxed set with the two-CD remastered versions of *1.Outside* and *Earthling*.

HEATHEN 2002

Recorded at Allaire Studios,
486 Pitcairn Road, Shokan, New York, USA
Looking Glass Studios
632 Broadway, New York, USA
Produced by David Bowie and Tony Visconti ('Afraid' by Mark Plati and David Bowie; 'Everyone Says 'Hi'' by Brian Rawling and Gary Miller)

Personnel
David Bowie – Vocals, Keyboards, Guitar, Saxophone, Stylophone, Drums
Solá Ackingbolá – Percussion ('Everyone Says 'Hi'')
Carlos Alomar – Guitar
Matt Chamberlain – Drums, Loop Programming, Percussion
Sterling Campbell – Drums, Percussion
Dave Clayton – Keyboards ('Everyone Says 'Hi'')
Lisa Germano – Violin
Dave Grohl – Guitar ('I've Been Waiting For You')
Gerry Leonard – Guitar
Tony Levin – Bass
Gary Miller – Guitar ('Everyone Says 'Hi'')
Mark Plati – Guitar, Bass

John Read – Bass ('Everyone Says 'Hi'')
Jordan Ruddess – Keyboards
Philip Sheppard – Electric Cello ('Everyone Says 'Hi'')
David Torn – Guitar, Guitar Loops, Omnichord
Pete Townshend – Guitar ('Slow Burn')
Tony Visconti – Bass, Guitar, Recorders, String Arrangements, Backing Vocals
Kristeen Young – Backing Vocals, Piano
The Scorchio Quartet:
Greg Kitzis – First Violin
Martha Mooke – Viola
Meg Okura – Second Violin
Mary Wooten – Cello
The Borneo Horns:
Steve Elson – Tenor Saxophone
Stan Harrison – Alto Saxophone
Lenny Pickett – Baritone Saxophone

Cover Art
Indrani/Barnbrook Design – Design
Jonathan Barnbrook – Typography
Marcus Klinko – Photography

Track Listing
'Sunday'/'Cactus'/'Slip Away'/'Slow Burn'/'Afraid'/'I've Been Waiting For You'/'I Would Be Your Slave'/'I Took A Trip On A Gemini Spaceship'/'5.15 The Angels Have Gone'/'Everyone Says 'Hi''/'A Better Future'/'Heathen (The Rays)'

Release Date
10 June 2002

Label and Catalogue Numbers
UK ISO/Columbia 508222 2/9, US ISO/Columbia CK86630

Highest Chart Position on Release
UK 5, US 14

Notes
All tracks written by David Bowie except track two: Black Francis; track six: Neil Young; and track eight: Norman Carl Odam.
Originally available on vinyl in US on ISO/Columbia (C 86630) and in UK (508222 1).
Originally available on release on ISO/Columbia (508222 9) as a two-CD limited edition with bonus tracks: 'Sunday (Moby Remix)'/'A Better Future (Remix By Air)'/'Conversation Piece (re-recorded 2002)'/'Panic In Detroit (Outtake From A 1979 Recording)'; in US on ISO/Columbia (CK 86657) and in UK (508222 0) as special-edition CD in 12-inch sleeve.
Reissued on vinyl in 2011 on Music On Vinyl (MOVLP470).

REALITY 2003

Recorded at Looking Glass Studios
632 Broadway, New York, USA
Allaire Studios,
486 Pitcairn Road, Shokan, New York, USA
The Hitching Post Studio
Bell Canyon, USA
Produced by David Bowie and Tony Visconti

Personnel
David Bowie – Vocals, Keyboards, Guitar, Baritone Saxophone, Stylophone, Percussion, Synthesizers
Carlos Alomar – Guitar ('Fly' on limited-edition bonus disc)
Sterling Campbell – Drums
Matt Chamberlain – Drums ('Bring Me The Disco King', 'Fly' on limited-edition bonus disc)
Gail Ann Dorsey – Backing Vocals
Mike Garson – Piano
Bill Jenkins – Piano ('The Loneliest Guy')
Gerry Leonard – Guitar
Mario J McNulty – Additional Percussion, Additional Engineering, Drums ('Fall Dog Bombs The Moon')
Mark Plati – Guitar, Bass
Catherine Russell – Backing Vocals
Earl Slick – Guitar
David Torn – Guitar
Tony Visconti – Bass, Guitar, Keyboards, Backing Vocals

Cover Art
Rex Ray – Illustration
Jonathan Barnbrook – Typography
Frank Ockenfels 3 – Photography

Track Listing
'New Killer Star'/'Pablo Picasso'/'Never Get Old'/'The Loneliest Guy'/'Looking For Water'/'She'll Drive The Big Car'/'Days'/'Fall Dog Bombs The Moon'/'Try Some, Buy Some'/'Reality'/'Bring Me The Disco King'

Release Date
15 September 2003

Label and Catalogue Numbers
UK ISO/Columbia 512555 2/9,
US ISO/Columbia CK 90576/90660

Highest Chart Position on Release
UK 3, US 29

Notes
All tracks written by David Bowie except track two: Jonathan Richman; and track nine: George Harrison.
Originally available in US on ISO/Columbia (CK90660) and in UK (COL 512555 9) as a two-CD limited edition with bonus tracks: 'Fly'/ 'Queen Of All The Tarts (Overture)'/ 'Rebel Rebel (2002 Recording)'; on ISO/Columbia (512555 3) as a CD and DVD tour edition with bonus track: 'Waterloo Sunset', and live DVD from Hammersmith Riverside Studios, London, 8 September 2003 of: 'New Killer Star'/ 'Pablo Picasso'/ 'Never Get Old'/ 'The Loneliest Guy'/ 'Looking For Water'/ 'She'll Drive The Big Car'/ 'Days'/ 'Fall Dog Bombs The Moon'/ 'Try Some, Buy Some'/ 'Reality'/ 'Bring Me The Disco King'.
Reissued on CD in 2004 in US on ISO/Columbia (CN 90743) and in 2005 in UK (512555 7) as dual-disc edition featuring album CD and DVD mixed in 5.1 surround sound with bonus material including the film *Reality* with exclusive videos of: 'Never Get Old'/ 'The Loneliest Guy'/ 'Bring Me The Disco King'/ 'New Killer Star'.

THE NEXT DAY 2013

Recorded at The Magic Shop
49 Crosby Street, New York, USA
Human
New York, USA
Produced by David Bowie and Tony Visconti

Personnel
David Bowie – Vocals, Keyboards, Acoustic Guitar, String Arrangements
Alex Alexander – Percussion ('I'll Take You There' on deluxe edition)
Zachary Alford – Drums, Percussion
Sterling Campbell – Drums, Tambourine
Gail Ann Dorsey – Bass, Backing Vocals
Steve Elson – Baritone Saxophone, Contrabass Clarinet
Henry Hey – Piano
Gerry Leonard – Guitar, Keyboards
Tony Levin – Bass
Maxim Moston – Strings
Janice Pendarvis – Backing Vocals
Antoine Silverman – Strings
Earl Slick – Guitar
Hiroko Taguchi – Strings
David Torn – Guitar
Tony Visconti – Bass, Guitar, Recorder, Strings, String Arrangements
Anja Wood – Strings

Cover Art
Jonathan Barnbrook – Design
Masayoshi Sukita – Original *"Heroes"* Photography
Jimmy King – Interior Photography

Track Listing
'The Next Day'/ 'Dirty Boys'/ 'The Stars (Are Out Tonight)'/ 'Love Is Lost'/ 'Where Are We Now?'/ 'Valentine's Day'/ 'If You Can See Me'/ 'I'd Rather Be High'/ 'Boss Of Me'/ 'Dancing Out In Space'/ 'How Does The Grass Grow?'/ '(You Will) Set The World On Fire'/ 'You Feel So Lonely You Could Die'/ 'Heat'

Release Date
11 March 2013

Label and Catalogue Number
ISO/Columbia 88765 461862

Highest Chart Position on Release
UK 1, US 2

Notes
All tracks written by David Bowie except track nine and bonus track three (see below):
David Bowie/Gerry Leonard; and track eleven: David Bowie/ Jerry Lordan (interpolation of 'Apache').
Originally available on ISO/Columbia (88765 461922) as a deluxe-edition CD with bonus tracks: 'So She'/ 'Plan'/ 'I'll Take You There' and as a double LP on vinyl (88765 461861) featuring the same track listing as the deluxe CD.
Reissued in November 2013 as *The Next Day Extra* (ISO/ Columbia 88883 787812), with a bonus CD containing the three extra deluxe edition tracks as well as: 'Atomica'/ 'Love Is Lost (Hello Steve Reich Mix For The DFA)'/ 'The Informer'/ 'I'd Rather Be High (Venetian Mix)'/ 'Like A Rocket Man'/ 'Born In A UFO'/ 'God Bless The Girl'. The package also contained a DVD of the videos for the four singles released from the original album.

BLACKSTAR 2016

Recorded at The Magic Shop
49 Crosby Street, New York, USA
Human
New York, USA
Produced by David Bowie and Tony Visconti

Personnel
David Bowie – Vocals, Acoustic Guitar, Fender Guitar ('Lazarus'), String Arrangements ('Blackstar')
Mark Guiliana – Drums, Percussion
Tim Lefebvre – Bass
Jason Lindner – Piano, Wurlitzer Organ, Keyboards
Donny McCaslin – Saxophone, Flute, Woodwind
Ben Monder – Guitar
James Murphy – Percussion ('Sue (Or In A Season Of Crime)' and 'Girl Loves Me')
Erin Tonkon – Backing Vocals (''Tis A Pity She Was A Whore')
Tony Visconti – Strings ('Blackstar')

Cover Art
Jonathan Barnbrook – Design
Jimmy King – Interior Photography
Johan Renck – Interior Photography

Track Listing
'Blackstar'/ ''Tis A Pity She Was A Whore'/ 'Lazarus'/ 'Sue (Or In A Season Of Crime)'/ 'Girl Loves Me'/ 'Dollar Days'/ 'I Can't Give Everything Away'

Release Date
8 January 2016

Label and Catalogue Number
ISO/Columbia 88875 173862

Highest Chart Position on Release
UK 1, US 1

Notes
All tracks written by David Bowie except track four: David Bowie/Maria Schneider/Paul Bateman & Bob Bharma (as 'Plastic Soul'). The digital download contains the 'Blackstar' video as a bonus item. Also available on ISO/Columbia as a vinyl LP (88875 173871) featuring the same track listing as the CD.

LIVE ALBUMS

DAVID LIVE

Released October 1974
RCA/Victor APL 2 0771
UK 2, US 8
Recorded at Tower Theater, Philadelphia, 11–12 July, 1974
Track Listing '1984'/ 'Rebel Rebel'/ 'Moonage Daydream'/ 'Sweet Thing'/ 'Changes'/ 'Suffragette City'/ 'Aladdin Sane'/ 'All The Young Dudes'/ 'Cracked Actor'/ 'Rock 'n' Roll With Me'/ 'Watch That Man'/ 'Knock On Wood'/ 'Diamond Dogs'/ 'Big Brother'/ 'The Width Of A Circle'/ 'The Jean Genie'/ 'Rock 'n' Roll Suicide'

Notes
Reissued on vinyl in 1984 on RCA (PL80771); in 1990 on Rykodisc/EMI (164 79 5362 1).
Reissued on CD in 1990 in US on Rykodisc (RCD 10138/39) and in UK on EMI (CDP 79 5364 2) with bonus tracks: 'Here Today, Gone Tomorrow'/ 'Time'/ 'Band Intro'; in 2005 in US on Virgin, in UK on EMI (7243 8 74304 2 5) remastered with bonus tracks and original live running order: '1984'/ 'Rebel Rebel'/ 'Moonage Daydream'/ 'Sweet Thing'/ 'Candidate'/ 'Sweet Thing (Reprise)'/ 'Changes'/ 'Suffragette City'/ 'Aladdin Sane'/ 'All The Young Dudes'/ 'Cracked Actor'/ 'Rock 'n' Roll With Me'/ 'Watch That Man'/ 'Knock On Wood'/ 'Here Today, Gone Tomorrow'/ 'Space Oddity'/ 'Diamond Dogs'/ 'Panic In Detroit'/ 'Big Brother'/ 'Time'/ 'The Width Of A Circle'/ 'The Jean Genie'/ 'Rock 'n' Roll Suicide'.

STAGE

Released September 1978
RCA/Victor PL 02913
UK 5, US 44
Recorded at Spectrum Arena, Philadelphia, 28–29 April, 1978; Civic Centre, Providence, 5 May, 1978; New Boston Garden Arena, Boston, 6 May, 1978
Track Listing 'Hang On To Yourself'/ 'Ziggy Stardust'/ 'Five Years'/ 'Soul Love'/ 'Star'/ 'Station To Station'/ 'Fame'/ 'TVC15'/ 'Warszawa'/ 'Speed Of Life'/ 'Art Decade'/ 'Sense Of Doubt'/ 'Breaking Glass'/ "Heroes"/ 'What In The World'/ 'Blackout'/ 'Beauty And The Beast'

Notes
First reissued on CD in 1983 in Germany on RCA (PD 89002 2); in 1991 in US on Rykodisc (RCD 10144/45) and in UK on EMI (EMD1030) with bonus track: 'Alabama Song'; in 2005 in US on Virgin and in UK on EMI (7243 8 63436 2 8) remastered with bonus tracks and original live running order:

'Warszawa'/"Heroes"/'What In The World'/ 'Be My Wife'/ 'Blackout'/'Sense Of Doubt'/'Speed Of Life'/'Breaking Glass'/'Beauty And The Beast'/'Fame'/'Five Years'/ 'Soul Love'/'Star'/'Hang On To Yourself'/'Ziggy Stardust'/ 'Art Decade'/'Alabama Song'/'Station To Station'/'Stay'/'TVC15'.

ZIGGY STARDUST: THE MOTION PICTURE

Released October 1983
RCA PL 84862
UK 17, US 89
Recorded at Hammersmith Odeon, London, 3 July 1973
Track Listing 'Hang On To Yourself'/'Ziggy Stardust'/ 'Watch That Man'/'Wild Eyed Boy From Freecloud'/ 'All The Young Dudes'/'Oh! You Pretty Things'/ 'Moonage Daydream'/'Space Oddity'/'My Death'/ 'Cracked Actor'/'Time'/'The Width Of A Circle'/ 'Changes'/'Let's Spend The Night Together'/'Suffragette City'/'White Light/White Heat'/'Rock 'n' Roll Suicide'

Notes
Reissued on limited-edition red vinyl in 2003 on EMI (ZIGGYRIP 3773) as 30th-anniversary edition with bonus tracks and original live running order: 'Intro'/'Hang On To Yourself'/ 'Ziggy Stardust'/'Watch That Man'/'Wild Eyed Boy From Freecloud'/'All The Young Dudes'/'Oh! You Pretty Things'/ 'Moonage Daydream'/'Changes'/'Space Oddity'/'My Death'/ 'Intro'/'Cracked Actor'/'Time'/'The Width Of A Circle'/'Let's Spend The Night Together'/'Suffragette City'/'White Light/ White Heat'/'Farewell Speech'/'Rock 'n' Roll Suicide'
Reissued on CD in 1992 in US on Rykodisc (RCD 40148) and in UK on EMI (0777 7 80411 22); in 2003 on EMI (72435 41979 25) as 30th-anniversary edition with bonus tracks and original live running order (see above).

TIN MACHINE LIVE: OY VEY, BABY

Released July 1992
Vinyl: London 828 3281; CD: London 828 3282
UK and US: did not chart (DNC)
Recorded at Orpheum Theatre, Boston, 20 November 1991; Academy, New York, 27–29 November 1991; Riviera, Chicago, 7 December 1991; NHK Hall, Tokyo, 5–6 February 1992; Koseinenkin Kaikan, Sapporo, 10–11 February 1992
Track Listing 'If There Is Something'/'Amazing'/'I Can't Read'/'Stateside'/'Under The God'/'Goodbye Mr. Ed'/ 'Heaven's In Here'/'You Belong In Rock 'n' Roll'

SANTA MONICA '72

Released April 1994
Golden Years/Trident Music International GY002
Recorded at Civic Auditorium, Santa Monica, 20 October 1972
UK 74, US DNC
Track Listing 'Intro'/'Hang On To Yourself'/'Ziggy Stardust'/ 'Changes'/'The Supermen'/'Life On Mars?'/'Five Years'/ 'Space Oddity'/'Andy Warhol'/'My Death'/'The Width Of A Circle'/'Queen Bitch'/'Moonage Daydream'/'John, I'm Only Dancing'/'Waiting For The Man'/'The Jean Genie'/ 'Suffragette City'/'Rock 'n' Roll Suicide'

Notes
Reissued on vinyl in UK on Golden Years (GYLP 002). Reissued on CD in US in 1995 on Griffin Music Inc. (GCD 392 2); in 1995 on Griffin Music Inc. (GCD-357-1/2) as a limited-edition digipack with bonus 7-inch single; in 2008 on EMI (07243 583221) remastered and re-titled *Live Santa Monica '72*.

LIVEANDWELL.COM

Released September 2000
Virgin/Risky Folio
Available as a limited-edition double-CD to BowieNet subscribers only
Recorded at Paradiso, Amsterdam, 10 June 1997; Phoenix Festival, Stratford-upon-Avon, 19 July 1997; *GQ* Awards, Radio City Music Hall, New York, 15 October 1997; Metropolitan, Rio de Janeiro, 2 November 1997
Track Listing Disc 1: 'I'm Afraid Of Americans'/'Hearts Filthy Lesson'/'I'm Deranged'/'Hallo Spaceboy'/'Telling Lies'/ 'The Motel'/'The Voyeur Of Utter Destruction (As Beauty)'/ 'Battle For Britain (The Letter)'/'Seven Years In Tibet'/'Little Wonder'; Disc 2: 'Fun (Dillinja Mix)'/'Little Wonder (Danny Saber Dance Mix)'/'Dead Man Walking (Moby Mix 1)'/'Telling Lies (Paradox Mix)'

GLASS SPIDER

June 2007
UK EMI 09463 91002 24, US EMI 09463 90979 20
Recorded at Olympic Stadium, Montreal, 30 August, 1987
Released as accompanying double-CD with DVD concert video
Track Listing Disc 1: 'Intro/Up The Hill Backwards'/'Glass Spider'/'Day-In Day-Out'/'Up The Hill Backwards'/'Bang Bang'/'Absolute Beginners'/'Loving The Alien'/'China Girl'/ 'Rebel Rebel'/'Fashion'/'Scary Monsters (And Super Creeps)'/ 'All The Madmen'/'Never Let Me Down'; Disc 2: 'Big Brother'/' '87 And Cry'/"Heroes"/'Sons Of The Silent Age'/'Time Will Crawl/Band Intro'/'Young Americans'/'Beat Of Your Drum'/ 'The Jean Genie'/'Let's Dance'/'Fame'/'Time'/'Blue Jean'/ 'Modern Love'

VH1 STORYTELLERS

Released July 2009
EMI 509999 649 0921
Recorded at Manhattan Center Studios, New York, 23 August, 1999
Released as accompanying CD with DVD live video
Track Listing 'Life On Mars?'/ 'Rebel Rebel (truncated)'/ 'Thursday's Child'/ 'Can't Help Thinking About Me'/ 'China Girl'/ 'Seven'/ 'Drive-In Saturday'/ 'Word On A Wing'

Notes
Four tracks featured on the DVD were later available as downloads: 'Survive'/ 'I Can't Read'/ 'Always Crashing In The Same Car'/ 'If I'm Dreaming My Life'.

A REALITY TOUR

Released January 2010
ISO/Sony 8 8697 58827 24
UK 53, US DNC
Recorded at The Point, Dublin, 22–23 November 2003
Track Listing Disc 1: 'Rebel Rebel'/ 'New Killer Star'/ 'Reality'/ 'Fame'/ 'Cactus'/ 'Sister Midnight'/ 'Afraid'/ 'All The Young Dudes'/ 'Be My Wife'/ 'The Loneliest Guy'/ 'The Man Who Sold The World'/ 'Fantastic Voyage'/ 'Hallo Spaceboy'/ 'Sunday'/ 'Under Pressure'/ 'Life On Mars?'/ 'Battle For Britain (The Letter)'; Disc 2: 'Ashes To Ashes'/ 'The Motel'/ 'Loving The Alien'/ 'Never Get Old'/ 'Changes'/ 'I'm Afraid Of Americans'/ "Heroes"/ 'Bring Me The Disco King'/ 'Slip Away'/ 'Heathen (The Rays)'/ 'Five Years'/ 'Hang On To Yourself'/ 'Ziggy Stardust'/ 'Fall Dog Bombs The Moon'/ 'Breaking Glass'/ 'China Girl'

Notes
Available as a download with two bonus tracks: '5.15 The Angels Have Gone'/ 'Days'.

LIVE NASSAU COLISEUM '76

Released September 2010
Recorded at Nassau Coliseum, Uniondale, New York, 23 March 1976
Released as accompanying double-CD with 2010 re-issue of *Station To Station* (EMI BOWSTSX2010)
Track Listing Disc 1: 'Station To Station'/ 'Suffragette City'/ 'Fame'/ 'Word On A Wing'/ 'Stay'/ 'Waiting For The Man'/ 'Queen Bitch'; Disc 2: 'Life On Mars?'/ 'Five Years'/ 'Panic In Detroit'/ 'Changes'/ 'TVC15'/ 'Diamond Dogs'/ 'Rebel Rebel'/ 'The Jean Genie'

Notes
Available as a download with unedited version of 'Panic In Detroit'.

NOTABLE COMPILATIONS

There have been dozens of compilations of David Bowie's work. Such a varied career makes it very difficult for the compiler to create anything truly comprehensive. The following is a list of some of the best-selling, most enduring and most interesting collections.

THE WORLD OF DAVID BOWIE

Released March 1970
Decca SPA 58
Track Listing 'Uncle Arthur'/ 'Love You Till Tuesday'/ 'There Is A Happy Land'/ 'Little Bombardier'/ 'Sell Me A Coat'/ 'Silly Boy Blue'/ 'The London Boys'/ 'Karma Man'/ 'Rubber Band'/ 'Let Me Sleep Beside You'/ 'Come And Buy My Toys'/ 'She's Got Medals'/ 'In The Heat Of The Morning'/ 'When I Live My Dream'

Notes
Reissued in 1973 with a Ziggy cover photograph.

IMAGES 1966–1967

Released February 1973
US London BP 628/9
Track Listing 'Rubber Band'/ 'Maid Of Bond Street'/ 'Sell Me A Coat'/ 'Love You Till Tuesday'/ 'There Is A Happy Land'/ 'The Laughing Gnome'/ 'The Gospel According To Tony Day'/ 'Did You Ever Have A Dream'/ 'Uncle Arthur'/ 'We Are Hungry Men'/ 'When I Live My Dream'/ 'Join The Gang'/ 'Little Bombardier'/ 'Come And Buy My Toys'/ 'Silly Boy Blue'/ 'She's Got Medals'/ 'Please Mr Gravedigger'/ 'The London Boys'/ 'Karma Man'/ 'Let Me Sleep Beside You'/ 'In The Heat Of The Morning'

Notes
Reissued in 1975 in UK on Deram (DPA 3017/18).

CHANGESONEBOWIE

Released May 1976
UK RCA Victor RS 1055, US RCA APL1 1732
UK 2, US 10
Track Listing 'Space Oddity'/ 'John, I'm Only Dancing'/ 'Changes'/ 'Ziggy Stardust'/ 'Suffragette City'/ 'The Jean Genie'/ 'Diamond Dogs'/ 'Rebel Rebel'/ 'Young Americans'/ 'Fame'/ 'Golden Years'

Notes
Reissued on vinyl and CD in 1984 on RCA (PL/PD 81732).

THE BEST OF BOWIE

Released December 1980
K-Tel NE 1111
UK 3

Track Listing 'Space Oddity'/ 'Life On Mars?'/ 'Starman'/ 'Rock 'n' Roll Suicide'/ 'John, I'm Only Dancing'/ 'The Jean Genie'/ 'Breaking Glass (live)'/ 'Sorrow'/ 'Diamond Dogs'/ 'Young Americans'/ 'Fame'/ 'Golden Years'/ 'TVC15'/ 'Sound And Vision'/ "Heroes"/ 'Boys Keep Swinging'

CHANGESTWOBOWIE

Released November 1981
UK RCA BOWLP 3, US RCA AFL1 4202
UK 24, US 68
Track Listing 'Aladdin Sane'/ 'Oh! You Pretty Things'/ 'Starman'/ '1984'/ 'Ashes To Ashes'/ 'Sound And Vision'/ 'Fashion'/ 'Wild Is The Wind'/ 'John, I'm Only Dancing (Again)'/ 'D.J.'

Notes
Reissued on vinyl and CD in 1984 on RCA (PL84202/ PCD14202).

BOWIE RARE

Released December 1982
RCA PL45406
UK 34
Track Listing 'Ragazzo Solo, Ragazza Sola'/ 'Round And Round'/ 'Amsterdam'/ 'Holy Holy (1972)'/ 'Panic In Detroit (live)'/ 'Young Americans'/ 'Velvet Goldmine'/ "Helden"/ 'John, I'm Only Dancing (Again)'/ 'Alabama Song'/ 'Crystal Japan'

LOVE YOU TILL TUESDAY

Released April 1984
UK Deram BOWIE1, US Deram 820 083 1
UK 53, US DNC
Track Listing 'Love You Till Tuesday'/ 'The London Boys'/ 'Ching-A-Ling'/ 'The Laughing Gnome'/ 'Liza Jane'/ 'When I'm Five'/ 'Space Oddity'/ 'Sell Me A Coat'/ 'Rubber Band'/ 'Let Me Sleep Beside You'/ 'When I Live My Dream'

Notes
Reissued on CD in 1992 on Pickwick (PWKS 4131P).

SOUND+VISION

Released September 1989
Rykodisc RCD 90120/21/22/RCDV1018
US 97
Track Listing Disc 1: 'Space Oddity (Demo)'/ 'Wild Eyed Boy From Freecloud (Acoustic)'/ 'The Prettiest Star (1970)'/ 'London Bye Ta-Ta (1970)'/ 'Black Country Rock'/ 'The Man Who Sold The World'/ 'The Bewlay Brothers'/ 'Changes'/ 'Round And Round'/ 'Moonage Daydream'/ 'John, I'm Only Dancing (Sax Version)'/ 'Drive-In Saturday'/ 'Panic In Detroit'/ 'Ziggy Stardust (Live 1973)'/ 'White Light/White Heat (Live 1973)'/ 'Rock 'n' Roll Suicide (Live 1973)'; Disc 2: 'Anyway, Anyhow, Anywhere'/ 'Sorrow'/ 'Don't Bring Me Down'/ '1984/Dodo'/ 'Big Brother'/ 'Rebel Rebel (Rare Single Version)'/ 'Suffragette City (Live 1974)'/ 'Watch That Man (Live 1974)'/ 'Cracked Actor (Live 1974)'/ 'Young Americans'/ 'Fascination'/ 'After Today'/ 'It's Hard To Be A Saint In The City'/ 'TVC15'/ 'Wild Is The Wind'; Disc 3: 'Sound And Vision'/ 'Be My Wife'/ 'Speed Of Life'/ "Helden" (1989 Remix)'/ 'Joe The Lion'/ 'Sons Of The Silent Age'/ 'Station To Station (Live 1978)'/ 'Warszawa (Live 1978)'/ 'Breaking Glass (Live 1978)'/ 'Red Sails'/ 'Look Back In Anger'/ 'Boys Keep Swinging'/ 'Up The Hill Backwards'/ 'Kingdom Come'/ 'Ashes To Ashes'; Video CD: 'John, I'm Only Dancing (Live 1972)'/ 'Changes (Live 1972)'/ 'The Supermen (Live 1972)'/ 'Ashes To Ashes (CD Video Version)'

Notes
Reissued in 1995 on Rykodisc (RCD 90330/31/32); in 2003 on EMI (7243 9451121) with bonus tracks: 'Wild Eyed Boy From Freecloud (Rare B-Side Version)'/ 'London Bye Ta-Ta (Previously Unreleased Stereo Mix)'/ 'Round And Round (Alternate Vocal Take)'/ 'Baal's Hymn'/ 'The Drowned Girl'/ 'Cat People (Putting Out Fire)'/ 'China Girl'/ 'Ricochet'/ 'Modern Love (Live)'/ 'Loving The Alien'/ 'Dancing With The Big Boys'/ 'Blue Jean'/ 'Time Will Crawl'/ 'Baby Can Dance'/ 'Amazing'/ 'I Can't Read'/ 'Shopping For Girls'/ 'Goodbye Mr. Ed'/ 'Amlapura'/ 'You've Been Around'/ 'Nite Flights (Moodswings Back To Basics Remix Radio Edit)'/ 'Pallas Athena (Gone Midnight Mix)'/ 'Jump They Say'/ 'Buddha Of Suburbia'/ 'Dead Against It'/ 'South Horizon'/ 'Pallas Athena (Live)'.

CHANGESBOWIE

Released March 1990
UK EMI DBTV1, US Rykodisc RCD 20171
UK 1, US 39
Track Listing 'Space Oddity'/ 'John, I'm Only Dancing'/ 'Changes'/ 'Ziggy Stardust'/ 'Suffragette City'/ 'The Jean Genie'/ 'Diamond Dogs'/ 'Rebel Rebel'/ 'Young Americans'/ 'Fame 90'/ 'Golden Years'/ "Heroes"/ 'Ashes To Ashes'/ 'Fashion'/ 'Let's Dance'/ 'China Girl'/ 'Modern Love'/ 'Blue Jean'

EARLY ON (1964–1966)

Released August 1991
Rhino R2 70526
Track Listing 'Liza Jane'/ 'Louie Louie Go Home'/ 'I Pity The Fool'/ 'Take My Tip'/ 'That's Where My Heart Is'/ 'I Want My Baby Back'/ 'Bars Of The County Jail'/ 'You've Got A Habit Of Leaving'/ 'Baby Loves That Way'/ 'I'll Follow You'/ 'Glad I've Got Nobody'/ 'Can't Help Thinking About Me'/ 'And I Say To Myself'/ 'Do Anything You Say'/ 'Good Morning Girl'/ 'I Dig Everything'/ 'I'm Not Losing Sleep'

THE SINGLES COLLECTION

Released November 1993
UK EMI CDEM 1512
UK 9
Track Listing 'Space Oddity'/ 'Changes'/ 'Starman'/ 'Ziggy Stardust'/ 'Suffragette City'/ 'John, I'm Only Dancing'/ 'The Jean Genie'/ 'Drive-In Saturday'/ 'Life On Mars?'/ 'Sorrow'/ 'Rebel Rebel'/ 'Rock 'n' Roll Suicide'/ 'Diamond Dogs'/ 'Knock On Wood (Live)'/ 'Young Americans'/ 'Fame'/ 'Golden Years'/ 'TVC15'/ 'Sound And Vision'/"Heroes"/ 'Beauty And The Beast'/ 'Boys Keep Swinging'/ 'DJ'/ 'Alabama Song'/ 'Ashes To Ashes'/ 'Fashion'/ 'Scary Monsters (And Super Creeps)'/ 'Under Pressure'/ 'Wild Is The Wind'/ 'Let's Dance'/ 'China Girl'/ 'Modern Love'/ 'Blue Jean'/ 'This Is Not America'/ 'Dancing In The Street'/ 'Absolute Beginners'/ 'Day-In Day-Out'

THE SINGLES 1969 TO 1993

Released November 1993
US Rykodisc RCD 10218/19
Track Listing 'Space Oddity'/ 'Changes'/ 'Oh! You Pretty Things'/ 'Life On Mars?'/ 'Ziggy Stardust'/ 'Starman'/ 'John, I'm Only Dancing'/ 'Suffragette City'/ 'The Jean Genie'/ 'Sorrow'/ 'Drive-In Saturday'/ 'Diamond Dogs'/ 'Rebel Rebel'/ 'Young Americans'/ 'Fame'/ 'Golden Years'/ 'TVC15'/ 'Be My Wife'/ 'Sound And Vision'/ 'Beauty And The Beast'/ "Heroes"/ 'Boys Keep Swinging'/ 'DJ'/ 'Look Back In Anger'/ 'Ashes To Ashes'/ 'Fashion'/ 'Scary Monsters (And Super Creeps)'/ 'Under Pressure'/ 'Cat People'/ 'Let's Dance'/ 'China Girl'/ 'Modern Love'/ 'Blue Jean'/ 'Loving The Alien'/ 'Dancing In The Street'/ 'Absolute Beginners'/ 'Day-In Day-Out'/ 'Never Let Me Down'/ 'Jump They Say'

BOWIE AT THE BEEB

Released September 2000
EMI 7243 528958 24
UK 7, US DNC
Track Listing Disc 1: 'In The Heat Of The Morning'/ 'London Bye Ta-Ta'/ 'Karma Man'/ 'Silly Boy Blue'/ 'Let Me Sleep Beside You'/ 'Janine'/ 'Amsterdam'/ 'God Knows I'm Good'/ 'The Width Of A Circle'/ 'Unwashed And Somewhat Slightly Dazed'/ 'Cygnet Committee'/ 'Memory Of A Free Festival'/ 'Wild Eyed Boy From Freecloud'/ 'Bombers'/ 'Looking For A Friend'/ 'Almost Grown'/ 'Kooks'/ 'It Ain't Easy'; Disc 2: 'The Supermen'/ 'Eight Line Poem'/ 'Hang On To Yourself'/ 'Ziggy Stardust'/ 'Queen Bitch'/ 'Waiting For The Man'/ 'Five Years'/ 'White Light/White Heat'/ 'Moonage Daydream'/ 'Hang On To Yourself'/ 'Suffragette City'/ 'Ziggy Stardust'/ 'Starman'/ 'Space Oddity'/ 'Changes'/ 'Oh! You Pretty Things'/ 'Andy Warhol'/ 'Lady Stardust'/ 'Rock 'n' Roll Suicide'

Notes
Disc One, tracks one to four recorded for *Top Gear*, 13 May 1968; tracks five to six recorded for *The Dave Lee Travis Show*, 20 October 1969; tracks seven to twelve recorded for *The Sunday Show*, 5 February 1970; track thirteen from *Sounds Of The 70s*, 25 March 1970 (as Hype); tracks fourteen to eighteen recorded for *In Concert: John Peel*, 3 June 1971. Disc Two, tracks one to two recorded for *Sounds Of The 70s*, 21 September 1971; tracks three to seven recorded for *Sounds Of The 70s*, 18 January 1972; tracks eight to twelve recorded for *Sounds Of The 70s*, 16 May 1972; tracks thirteen to sixteen recorded for *The Johnnie Walker Lunchtime Show*, 22 May 1972; tracks seventeen to nineteen recorded for *Sounds Of The 70s*, 23 May 1972. Limited-edition three-CD set available with *BBC Radio Theatre, London, June 27, 2000* (7243 528958 23) with bonus tracks: 'Wild Is The Wind'/ 'Ashes To Ashes'/ 'Seven'/ 'This Is Not America'/ 'Absolute Beginners'/ 'Always Crashing In The Same Car'/ 'Survive'/ 'Little Wonder'/ 'The Man Who Sold The World'/ 'Fame'/ 'Stay'/ 'Hallo Spaceboy'/ 'Cracked Actor'/ 'I'm Afraid Of Americans'/ 'Let's Dance'

NOTHING HAS CHANGED

Released November 2014
UK Parlophone 825646205769, US Legacy/Columbia 88875030982 SC1
UK 9, US 57
Track Listing (3-CD Deluxe Edition) Disc 1: 'Sue (Or In A Season Of Crime)'/ 'Where Are We Now?'/ 'Love Is Lost'/ 'The Stars (Are Out Tonight)'/ 'New Killer Star'/ 'Everyone Says "Hi"'/ 'Slow Burn'/ 'Let Me Sleep Beside You'/ 'Your Turn To Drive'/ 'Shadow Man'/ 'Seven'/ 'Survive'/ 'Thursday's Child'/ 'I'm Afraid Of Americans'/ 'Little Wonder'/ 'Hallo Spaceboy'/ 'The Heart's Filthy Lesson'/ 'Strangers When We Meet'; Disc 2: 'The Buddha Of Suburbia'/ 'Jump They Say'/ 'Time Will Crawl'/ 'Absolute Beginners'/ 'Dancing In The Street'/ 'Loving The Alien'/ 'This Is Not America'/ 'Blue Jean'/ 'Modern Love'/ 'China Girl'/ 'Let's Dance'/ 'Fashion'/ 'Scary Monsters (And Super Creeps)'/ 'Ashes To Ashes'/ 'Under Pressure'/ 'Boys Keep Swinging'/"Heroes"/ 'Sound And Vision'/ 'Golden Years'/ 'Wild Is The Wind'; Disc 3: 'Fame'/ 'Young Americans'/ 'Diamond Dogs'/ 'Rebel Rebel'/ 'Sorrow'/ 'Drive-In Saturday'/ 'All The Young Dudes'/ 'The Jean Genie'/ 'Moonage Daydream'/ 'Ziggy Stardust'/ 'Starman'/ 'Life On Mars?'/ 'Oh! You Pretty Things'/ 'Changes'/ 'The Man Who Sold The World'/ 'Space Oddity'/ 'In The Heat Of The Morning'/ 'Silly Boy Blue'/ 'Can't Help Thinking About Me'/ 'You've Got A Habit Of Leaving'/ 'Liza Jane'

Notes
Also released as a 2-CD edition (UK Parlophone 825646205745, US Legacy/Columbia 888750309723).

SOUNDTRACKS

David Bowie's songs have graced over seventy soundtracks for film and television. The following list is of those on which he made a significant contribution or which contain songs unavailable elsewhere or notable remixes.

JUST A GIGOLO

Released June 1979
Jambo Records JAM 1
Tracks by David Bowie: 'Revolutionary Song'

CHRISTIANE F. WIR KINDER VOM BAHNHOF ZOO

Released April 1981
Germany RCA BL 43606
Reissued in July 2001 on EMI (7243 5 33093 29)
Tracks by David Bowie: 'V-2 Schneider'/ 'TVC15'/ "Helden"/ 'Boys Keep Swinging'/ 'Sense Of Doubt'/ 'Station To Station'/ 'Look Back In Anger'/ 'Stay'/ 'Warszawa'

DAVID BOWIE IN BERTOLT BRECHT'S BAAL

Released February 1982
UK RCA BOW11, US RCA CPL1-4346
UK 29
Reissued as a download in 2007
Tracks by David Bowie: 'Baal's Hymn'/ 'Remembering Marie A.'/ 'Ballad Of The Adventurers'/ 'The Drowned Girl'/ 'The Dirty Song'

CAT PEOPLE

Released April 1982
UK MCA MCF3138, US MCA 1498
Tracks by David Bowie: 'Cat People (Putting Out Fire)'/ 'The Myth'

THE FALCON AND THE SNOWMAN

Released April 1985
Vinyl: EMI America SV 17150
CD: EMI-Manhattan Records CDP 7 484112
Tracks by David Bowie (with Pat Metheny Group): 'This Is Not America'

ABSOLUTE BEGINNERS

Released April 1986
UK Vinyl: Virgin V2386
UK Double LP: Virgin VD2514
UK CD: Virgin CDV 2386
US Vinyl: EMI/Virgin SV-17182
UK 19, US 62
Reissued on CD in 1991 on Virgin (VVIPD112)
Tracks by David Bowie: 'Absolute Beginners'/ 'That's Motivation'/ 'Volare'
Single vinyl release omits 'Volare'

LABYRINTH

See main discography

WHEN THE WIND BLOWS

Released November 1986
UK Vinyl: Virgin V2406
UK CD: Virgin CDV 2406
US: Virgin 7 90599 4
Tracks by David Bowie: 'When The Wind Blows'

THE CROSSING

Released November 1990
Chrysalis CCD/CHR 1826
Tracks by David Bowie (Tin Machine): 'Betty Wrong'

SONGS FROM THE COOL WORLD

Released December 1992
Germany Warner Bros. 9 45009 2/9362 450782
Tracks by David Bowie: 'Real Cool World'

THE BUDDHA OF SUBURBIA

See main discography

BASQUIAT

Released July 1996
Island 314 524 260 2
Tracks by David Bowie: 'A Small Plot Of Land'

LOST HIGHWAY

Released February 1997
Interscope INTD 90090
Tracks by David Bowie: 'I'm Deranged (Edit)'/ 'I'm Deranged (Reprise)'

THE ICE STORM

Released October 1997
Velvel VEL 79713
Tracks by David Bowie (Tin Machine): 'I Can't Read'

STIGMATA

Released August 1999
UK Virgin CDVUS 161
US Virgin 7243 847753 22
Tracks by David Bowie: 'The Pretty Things Are Going To Hell'

AMERICAN PSYCHO

Released April 2000
Koch Records KOC-CD 8164
Tracks by David Bowie: 'Something In The Air (*American Psycho* Remix)'

INTIMITÉ

Released March 2001
France Virgin 7243 8100582 8
Tracks by David Bowie: 'Candidate'/ 'The Motel'

MOULIN ROUGE

Released May 2001
UK Twentieth Century Fox/Interscope 493 035 2
US Twentieth Century Fox/Interscope 490 507 2
Tracks by David Bowie: 'Nature Boy'/ 'Nature Boy (with Massive Attack)'
Also features Beck and Timbaland's cover of 'Diamond Dogs'

TRAINING DAY

Released September 2001
Priority 7243 8 11278 27
Tracks by David Bowie: 'American Dream'

MAYOR OF SUNSET STRIP

Released March 2004
Shout! Factory DK 34096
Tracks by David Bowie: 'All The Madmen (Live Intro/ Original LP Version)'

SHREK 2

Released May 2004
Dreamworks/Geffen 9862698
Tracks by David Bowie: 'Changes'
Duet with Butterfly Boucher

THE LIFE AQUATIC WITH STEVE ZISSOU

Released December 2004
Hollywood 2061 1624942
Tracks by David Bowie: 'Life On Mars?'/ 'Queen Bitch'
Also features Seu Jorge covers of 'Starman'/ 'Rebel Rebel'/ 'Rock 'n' Roll Suicide'/ 'Life On Mars?'/ 'Five Years'

STEALTH

Released July 2005
Epic/Sony 5204202
Tracks by David Bowie: '(She Can) Do That'

Overleaf: 'One magical moment'. Station To Station tour, Wembley Empire Pool, London, May 1976.

PICTURE CREDITS

Every effort has been made to trace and acknowledge the copyright holders. We apologise in advance for any unintentional omissions and would be pleased, if any such case should arise, to add appropriate acknowledgement in any future edition of the book. Please note below all sources for copyright associated where applicable with the images used.

T: top; B: bottom; R: right; L: left; C: centre

Getty Images: 10 TC, 11 T, 14, 24, 41, 42, 43 R, 78 T, 96, 115 B, 135 L (Michael Ochs Archives); 18 (Popperfoto); 30 T (Frank Barratt); 48, 49, 238 (Redferns); 52 (Michael Putland); 71 (Justin de Villeneuve); 76–77 (NBCU Photo Bank/NBC); 81, 89, 93, 94–95, 199 (Terry O'Neill); 82, 86 L (Redferns/Gijsbert Hanekroot); 84 L, 127 B (Redferns/Gab Archive); 97 T (Ron Galella); 116 (Redferns/Beth Gwinn); 120 L (*Evening Standard*); 154 –155, 165 (Denis O'Regan); 157 (Peter Still); 172–173, 174, 177 R (George DeKeerle); 178 TR (Time Life Pictures/DMI/Ann Clifford); 178 CR (Dave Hogan); 179 (Richard Young); 191 (Ebert Roberts); 214, 224–225, 234 (WireImage/KMazur); 218 (Evan Agostini); 219, 240–241 (Dave Benett); 226 B (Online USA, Inc/Miramax); 251 (WireImage/L Cohen); 261 (AFP/Justin Tallis); **Mick Rock 1973, 2012:** 1, 47 T, 51, 56–57, 59 BR, 69, 72; **Rex Features:** 10 BL, 178 BR, 203, 235 L (Rex Features); 13, 19, 20–21 (Dezo Hoffman); 26, 30 B, 31, 38 (Ray Stevenson); 39 T (Peter Sanders); 87 L (Roger Bamber); 97 BL (Stephen Morley); 117 (Les Lambert), 160 R (Everett Collection), 202 (Andre Csillag); 204–205, 217 (Richard Young); **London Features:** 10 BC (Pictorial Press); 29, 132–133 (London Features); 33 (Govert de Roos); 122–123 (Andy Kent); 245 (Scope); **Alamy:** 11 B, 23, 34, 35 T, 36–37, 85, 109 TL, 208 (Pictorial Press); 108 T (Mug Shot); 160 L (Pictorial Press/ UA/MGM); 170 (Alan Burles); **Photoshot:** 17 (Unfried/Good Times/Vanit); 148 (Starstock); 161 (London Features); **Barry Plummer:** 28, 131; **Mirrorpix:** 39 B (Dennis Stone); 45 (Ron Burton); 149 L (Albert Cooper); **Kevin Cann:** 43 L; **Sukita:** 55, 61, 65, 77 R, 79 TR, 125, 134, 152, 153, 188, 194, 197, 237, 242, 262; **Joe Stevens:** 57, 66, 75 T & B; **Photo Duffy/Duffy Archive:** 62, 110–111, 137, 142–143, 145, 146, 151; **Brian Ward/David Bowie:** 67 L; **Geoff MacCormack:** 67 R, 102, 103, 104; **Alpha Press:** 68, 90, 92, 105, 166; 254 (ISO/Columbia); **Allstar/Cinetext Collection:** 99 (British Lion Film Company); **Corbis:** 100, 114 (Steve Schapiro); 118–119, 128–129, 138 (Sygma/Christian Simonpietri); 140 (Lynn Goldsmith); 171, 193 (Neal Preston); 182 (Denis O'Regan); 187 (LGI Stock); 200, 207, 211 (Albert Sanchez); 213 (Gavin Evans); 221 (Michael Benabit); 222 (Reuters); 229, 230 (Jill Greenberg); 233 (Kipa/Fabrice Vallon); 246 (Sari Gustafsson); 248 (Ian Hodgson); 250 (David W. Cerny); 255 (Rune Hellestad); **Andrew Kent:** 106–107, 108 B, 288; **Phil King:** 15 R, 109 TR & CR; **Norman Parkinson Ltd./courtesy Norman Parkinson Archive:** 113; **Celebrity Pictures:** 126 (Clive Arrowsmith); 158 (Tony McGee); **Photograph by Snowdon, Camera Press, London:** 141; **Denis O'Regan:** 162–163, 168, 168–169, 180–181, 185, 216; **The Kobal Collection:** 176 (Jim Henson Productions); **Bauer Media:** 253 R.

Printed ephemera (sourced Simon Halfon): 6, 10 TL, 10 BR, 16 R, 53, 58 R, 73,83 B, 97 BR, 115 T, 120 R, 127 TR, 139 R, 149 R, 178 L, 183, 201 L, 201 R, 215 L, 223 L , 257 (various), 10 TR (Vocalion), 84 R (*Strange People* by Frank Edwards, Pan Books, 1966), 86 T (Guy Peellaert/RCA), 87 TR & BR, 121 (RCA), 109 BL (British Lion Film Company), 127 TL (*A Grave For A Dolphin* by Alberto Denti di Pirajno, Andre Deutsch, 1956), 209 (*The Buddha Of Suburbia* by Hanif Kureishi, Faber & Faber, 2009) 226 T (Miramax Films). **Other materials:** 259 (ISO/Columbia). **Album/single covers** (sourced Kevin Cann, with thanks to Tris Penna and Michael Setek/Art4Site for scanning; original label of release given in brackets): 12, 15 L (Deram); 16 L (Coral); 22 (Philips); 25 L, 32, 35 B (Mercury); 25 R (Decca); 40, 46 R, 50, 59 TR, 59 BL, 59 BC, 60, 63, 70, 78 BR, 79 TL, 80, 83 T, 88, 91, 98, 101, 109 BR, 112, 124, 135 TR& B, 136, 139 L, 143 R, 144, 147, 150, 215 R, 223 R (RCA); 6 L (CBS/Columbia); 47 B (Cotillion); 59 CL (Barclay); 78 BL, 195 (London); 156, 159, 164, 167, 172 L, 175, 180, 186, 189 (EMI); 172 R, 177 TL (Virgin/UK/EMI); 192 (Victory Music/ London); 198 (BMG/Arista); 206 (BMG/Arista/UK/Virgin); 212, 220 (RCA/UK/Virgin); 228, 235 R (Virgin); 236, 239, 243, 244, 252, 253 L, 256 (ISO/Columbia).
The art for *Diamond Dogs* on pages 80, 83, 86 and 87 is © The Estate of Guy Peellaert.

ACKNOWLEDGEMENTS

Timeline by James Hodgson.

Author's Acknowledgements:
Big thanks to Nick, Russ, Sox and Wahl – The Spiders From Salisbury – and to Kevin Cann for his great insights into the great man's work.